MAN IN NATURE
and BEHAVIOR

MAN IN NATURE
and BEHAVIOR

By
J. M. MARTINEZ

PHILOSOPHICAL LIBRARY
New York

Printed in the United States of America

To my mother, to all the mothers who for a time hold man and his destiny in their arms, and to all the wives who again receive man in their arms this book is dedicated in the hope that it will give them a greater understanding of man.

ACKNOWLEDGMENTS

To Doctor Felix Matti Ibañez who read the manuscript and gave valuable criticism and collaboration, my most heartfelt gratitude.

Table of Contents

Dear Reader:

Even if you are one of those pessimists who believe that mankind is forever condemned to suffer wars and to live, if that can be called living, in a form of jungle surrounded by actual and potential enemies and tormented by many fears, you must give me a hearing. You may be wrong. The fact that wars, hatred and destruction have been plaguing man for thousands of years does not necessarily mean that our children must put up with this irrational and insane procedure.

You, like the great majority of human beings, want peace and security for yourself and for your family; and if you have children you don't want them to grow up to be slaughtered or crippled to prove that capitalism is superior to communism. There are easier, peaceful and more profitable ways to settle this question. But perhaps you have become cynical and shrugging your shoulders you say: what is the use, the world is going to the dogs, it cannot be saved, each man for himself.

Or you may feel impotent to stop the evil monsters that man has loosed upon the world. I admit that heretofore man was completely impotent to change the world or rather to change himself. He was impotent because he was weaponless and defenseless, lost in the darkness of his ignorance. But this is no longer true. Science has not only charted the waters that surround that Harbor of Peace and Security with which mankind has dreamed for thousands of years; it has also given us the ship and the compass to get there.

I know that you probably have been warned not to pin your faith on Science. Science, you may have been told is a false Messiah who carries hidden under his cloak the most horrible weapons for destruction. Science is godless, immoral or amoral; I assure you that you have been grossly misinformed. Have you ever stopped to take inventory of the many good things that Science has done and does for you every day

[1]

and every moment? Paraphrasing a famous saying, we can say of the scientists, that never have so few done so much for so many. I do not believe it necessary to enumerate the many ways in which Science enriches your life, gives you more leisure, more and better food, guards your health and protects you from the destructive forces of Nature.

The charge that Science is amoral, and that it leaves man stranded and helpless without knowing what to do with his knowledge, is hurled against Science by many critics who have nothing better to offer than old and worn out superstitions. This criticism is unjustified because Science does tell man what the results will be if he misuses his knowledge and his gadgets. True, many men of science have proven to be cruel and evil, but many religious men have proven to be far more cruel and evil; yet you do not blame religion.

The trouble is that to most people Science merely means radio, planes, cars, refrigerators, atomic bombs, etc. Science is and means much more than all that. It means that for the first time we can to a great extent control the environment; and since man is the product of heredity and environment, the importance of this conquest can hardly be over-rated. This conquest of Science is not as dramatic and spectacular as the conquest of the atom and unfortunately has been sadly neglected. But it is far more important and essential for the welfare of mankind than all the gadgets and inventions we so proudly exhibit; because unless we cleanse and purge the mind of man from the deep rooted hatreds, prejudices and other destructive emotions, all our inventions and gadgets not only will fail to bring happiness, they will bring unparalleled destruction and suffering. Science also means that for the first time we can study man, understand his nature and put our finger on the forces that move him to action and motivate his behavior and misbehavior. This study of man is imperative and the most important task of scientists, equalled only by the necessity of its prompt and thorough application.

Our educational system must be revised and brought into

harmony with the newer knowledge. Human "nature" can and must be changed or at least conditioned into that image that has become the repository of his noblest ideals and aspirations.

This all sounds very nice and very interesting, you may say, but there is nothing I can do to bring about this millennium. Other people with more knowledge and power have tried and failed. True, but show me any invention or achievement that has not been preceded by many failures. Why? Because men lacked sufficient knowledge. When that knowledge was attained it was easy to build a successful flying machine or a steam boiler that really worked.

Man is not really different from a machine, only much more complex and difficult to study, but he is subject to the same physical and chemical laws that govern other machines. The trouble is that man, for all his intelligence, lags behind the animals in a few important things; he has not learned yet what the animals have been practicing for millions of years—co-operation. A grain of sand does not amount to much; any one can trample on it, but many grains of sand together can form a mountain.

Whether future historians will write about the atom, or perhaps I should say, coca-cola, century with a light hand and a happy heart as a glorious century in which man reached for his dreams, or with sorrow and cursing words, as a century in which man had a glimpse of a wonderful future but remained stuck to his muddy past depends upon what we do here today.

There have been other critical transitions in the history of mankind, but none has even approached the crisis of the twentieth century, because man did not possess the weapons for destruction he has today; thus he stands at the crossroads of Destiny.

Under the progressive impact of Science a brave new world is trying to be born. Will it be born in peace and with a minimum of pain and attended by men of good will? Or will it be born in violence, greeted with the explosion of bombs and baptized with blood? The complete answer is not yet writ-

ten on the Book of Time; but every day, consciously or unconsciously, willingly or unwillingly and whether we are an active
part in the drama or remain passive spectators, every human
being adds something to that answer, and when it is finally
written we shall be absolutely unable to erase a single letter.

Don't you hear the rumblings and the cries? The people
of the world are on the march demanding a bigger and better
share in the banquet of life, and no amount of violence nor
beautiful words and promises are going to satisfy them and
keep them quiet.

This book about man is not flattering to his ego. There is
much in it that probably will shock you and make you angry,
but it is all too true, unfortunately. I use criticism as a sharp
scalpel to cut through the thick layers of lies and hypocrisy of
our civilization and expose the festering sores and cancerous
growths that are threatening the social organism; for only by
exposing them to the sun can they be healed and man made
healthy.

What Is Truth?

All faith is false, all Faith is true:
Truth is the shattered mirror strown
In myriad bits; while each believes
His little bit the whole to own.
*The Kasidah of
Haji Abba El-Yezdi*

Unless we can measure and weigh a thing we know nothing about it. —*Lord Kelvin*

Believing one thing does not make it true.

Absolute Truth, like all other Absolutes, is an illusion.

Doubt, when fertilized by investigation, is the mother of knowledge and Truth.

Criticism is the crucible where Truth is cleansed and purified.

A Truth is not a Truth unless it can be verified by any one.

WHAT IS TRUTH? This classic question can be asked again today of countless men and women without obtaining a more correct and appropriate answer than was obtained by Pilate, for even in this scientific age few people have the slightest idea of what constitutes Truth nor how it can be reached.

Consequently, the great majority of people are completely unable to distinguish between Truth and myth, between fact and illusion. It is not surprising then, that the history of mankind is to a great extent the struggle for supremacy of subjective experiences and hallucinations, presented and often imposed as the Absolute and Ultimate Truth. Men have fought, killed, persecuted and hated one another in defense of truths, that were at best beautiful fantasies and at worst absurd and crude superstitions.

We should expect that with the great advances of science and with its marvelous discoveries and achievements for the benefit of humanity, men would stop their quarreling

[5]

and feuding over meaningless words and myths created by ignorance. That this is not the case is only too obvious. Perhaps we are asking too much; after all, science has entered the home and the life of people in the form of cars, radios and many other gadgets, but it has not entered their minds, and since scientific truths render useless the "truths" they have believed for so long, there is a natural resistance against those new Truths. Moreover, there are many and powerful organizations and individuals that have grown fat and strong under the shadow of superstitions from which they draw their sustenance; and since these people control most of the means of communication, such as the press, the radio, etc., Truth finds a very hard and rough going. We are plagued by a state of confusion and untruthfulness, that would be comic were it not pregnant with tragedy.

These lamentable conditions are another evidence of the failure of our schools and colleges to inculcate in the pupil the love for Truth and to provide him with a sure and reliable guide for its search. Thus, Truth-seeking is rather an arduous task and most people are satisfied with unverifiable and unnecessary hypotheses masquerading as truths.

There is great fear in many quarters that a bold and frontal attack against honored and holy hypotheses would weaken the foundations upon which our "Christian Civilization" so shakily rests. I am of the opinion that what is rotten and false will crumble regardless how much it is sheltered and protected from the cold winds of criticism and that the guardians of those "sacred truths" are only prolonging their agony and postponing a well deserved and inevitable end.

The question: What is Truth? is no longer a difficult and embarrassing question as it was when Pilate allegedly asked it, and for a long time afterwards. Now it can be answered easily and correctly: A Truth is a statement of a verifiable fact or facts obtained by investigation, observation and correlation of things and phenomena. Truth is dynamic, not static. There are truths that seem eternal, but we have no means of proving that. Therefore, every truth must be dated. We must say: this is the truth today, as we see it from the facts available. Discovery of new facts may force us to reject things we hold as true today. This has happened very often.

All these claims about Absolute and unchangeable truths are pure propaganda for selfish reasons. There are truths and approximations to truth and hypotheses used as working truths till greater knowledge makes it possible to dispense with them or to establish them upon solid foundations. Religious "truths" are, usually, unverifiable hypotheses that pass as truths just as counterfeit money passes as good coin when people are unable to recognize it. The difference between scientific and religious hypotheses is that the first are presented as such and are not imposed as Truth, while the second are given as revealed and ultimate truths, not to be questioned and doubted under severe punishments here or in the other "world."

When a man or a group of men claim they possess all the Truths and not only resent criticism but try to silence it, we can be sure that those people have only superstitions and myths. People who honestly and sincerely seek Truth are never afraid of criticism, even of the most destructive kind. In fact, the test of the Truth-seeker is that he invites criticism and receives it with a smile, for he knows that every critical word can be and should be a push toward greater perfection and progress. And he has complete confidence in the effectiveness of scientific methods in his search for Truth.

The Truth shall make men free when it no longer makes them angry.

Dedication

The animal is born.

Man is not born. Man is made; or, rather, he must be made. Woman has the first opportunity and the great privilege to make a MAN out of the child.

Unfortunately, the fact that there are so few MEN shows that she fails tragically in this supremely important labor.

T O YOU, Woman, Mother of Man, this book is lovingly and reverently dedicated.

You carry man in your womb for nine months and thus give to him that taste of paradise, of which he will dream the rest of his life. Only while in your womb does man enjoy complete physical and mental security. Having been born he is ever haunted by the unconscious memory of that short stay in a paradise where all his needs were satisfied, without any effort on his part, and where the dangers and adversities of this world were unknown. . . . What are the different heavens invented by man's mind but dreams born of that unconscious memory and desire to return to that state of perfect bliss and security!

You attend to his first needs: satisfy his hunger, quench his thirst, greet his first words with joy and praise and guide his first steps. You are the first woman to give him love and to be loved by him.

Your arms are a haven,—in them he feels secure and strong. He runs to your arms when he is in trouble or when some danger, real or imaginary, threatens his safety. He knows that your arms will defend him against everyone and everything.

Man never forgets his mother: whose arms first held him, whose lips first kissed him, whose hands first caressed him,—first dried his tears.

Man is ever looking for his mother in other women and,

often, because he does not find her in his wife, sorrow and unhappiness come to both of them. No matter how old, how strong and tough a man may appear, there is always the child in him, and the loving arms and the soft words of a woman will easily reawaken that quality in his being.

Man is never happier than when he is in the arms of a woman who is to him, at one and the same time, sweetheart, wife and mother. That is a rare attribute and relatively few women possess it.

Man, on emerging from your womb, is plastic material in your hands. You can make or unmake him. You can break his manhood, you can make him unfit to become a lover and husband, by turning him into a eunuch devoid of that strength of will and character which woman seeks in her mate.

No artist has the privilege, the opportunity, you have, as he works with clay, stone, or other dead material and, therefore, can create only static and lifeless objects of art.

You deal with living clay, out of which you may create the greatest work of art: There is no greater work of art than a healthy, honest and kind man, whose integrity and dignity cannot be bought in the market place.

Yet, you often leave this most vital and supremely important of all creative labors to other people and run to perform menial or much less important tasks.

Do you know, oh, Mother of Man! how to minister to and guide the dynamic forces that stir within that wee bundle of pink and white flesh you love so much?

The answer is written in blood, pain and sorrow in the pages of history and in the soul of woman, who is the greatest sufferer of her failure. To love a child and to smother it with kisses is not enough.

Mother love can wreak great damage, and it often does. The hand that rocks the cradle also wrecks the world.

Under the circumstances, however, mothers hardly can be expected to do a better job. They never have had the chance to learn the art and science of making men out of their boys.

That is why most boys, while having physically developed into manhood, mentally and emotionally they have never passed beyond the adolescent stage. They never have and they never do reach mental and emotional maturity.

That is the great tragedy of mankind!

But, now, science has provided us with new knowledge of the real nature and of the biological and psychological needs of man, and with improved methods and means to produce a creature worthy of the name MAN.

To you, Woman,—Sweetheart and Wife of Man, I offer reverently, this critical study of man. You cannot really live without him. In his company you find your sweetest happiness and your most bitter grief.

When a boy I sensed that man without woman and woman without man are just dislocated halves wandering in search of each other.

Yet a cold war has existed for centuries between man and woman. Man has been afraid of woman ever since he evolved from the ape-man state into that of so-called man and acquired the powers of reason and imagination.

Because man identified woman with the fertility of the earth, he placed her on the pedestal of the Olympus and worshipped her. The first gods were the Goddess of Rice and the Goddess of Corn.

At the same time he developed a pathological fear of woman: Menstruation, pregnancy and childbirth and nursing were phenomena he did not understand and which caused him to regard woman as a creature endowed with supernatural powers. This superstition and fear, born of ignorance, led him to invent and to apply all kinds of tabus concerning woman: to reduce her to economic and sexual slavery and to degrade her from the Olympus to the lowest depths.

Woman became the personification of evil, the temptress, whose beauty and charms lured poor trusting Adam, that is, Man, into partaking of the forbidden fruit. Woman became the witch whose magic, supernatural powers and mystery made it possible for her to fly through the air on a broomstick and curse and cast evil spells wherever she chose.

Man was so frightened by those imagined powers that he burned countless women to protect and defend himself. Could there be anything more fiendishly stupid, cruel and tragic? . . . Yet, in the whole Christian world scarcely a voice was raised in protest.

In his ignorance, and his misguidance by fanatics and disappointed and embittered ascetics, man exalted virginity above all other virtues, forgetting that virginity is sterility,—death, suicide of the race,—and that he never would have been born had his mother listened to those eunuchs and remained a virgin.

Man and Woman. Here we have two creatures who have evolved as a complement to each other, regarding each other with suspicion and even with hatred. To man, woman is still sexual prey: Half of the time he is afraid of not being able to conquer and possess her, and the other half of the time he is afraid of losing her.

To woman, man is still the conqueror, the hunter setting traps to snare her; while she also tries to ensnare him, for her economic security.

There is no doubt that the biological advantages and disadvantages, which make a woman, brought about the patriarchal society in which we live and gave to man the power and opportunity to deprive woman of her economic independence and to reduce her to sexual slavery.

Thus man was able to satisfy his polygamous instincts and to become lord and master of the home and of the community. Woman had no rights, only duties; she was supposed to have little or no intelligence. She was bought and sold on the market place like an animal, or sold in marriage to the highest bidder.

She was the bearer and giver of pleasure, but she herself must have none, lest she be branded as a lascivious harlot. Yet, with an inconsistency and a chivalry worthy of a better cause, man made woman the repository of his honor, which he was ready to defend and avenge by killing or being killed. (Strange how blood could wash a blot from his honor. Soap and water would have done much better.)

Today woman, at least in some countries, has regained much of her power, economic independence, and many political and civil rights.

But her relations with man, with some exceptions, still are tinged with suspicion and fear. The man and woman of today are not much happier together than their more primitive sisters and brothers. Is woman becoming the "lost sex," as some writers claim? The growing number of divorces seems to testify to this. The picture is still more alarming and tragic if we take into consideration that divorce alone is not an index to the failure of marriage, because there are many husbands and wives who, for reasons discussed elsewhere, cannot or do not want to obtain a divorce, although living together long since has ceased being the happy experience they had anticipated.

The reason is that after living and sleeping together for thousands of years, man and woman still are complete strangers. They simply do not know each other. The erroneous and mistaken notions they have formed about each other are a barrier to understanding and friendly relations, because true and lasting friendship cannot be built on lies, good intentions, ignorance and hypocrisy. Wishful thinking and pollyanna talk are like aspirin: They alleviate the pain for a little while, but they do not touch the causes of the disease which grows steadily worse.

It is the duty of the State to help its citizens in the pursuit of happiness, as enunciated in our Declaration of Independence. The State can do this by making sure that the people receive the right kind of education.

People now marry without any knowledge of each other's anatomical and psychological makeup; without knowing how to live with each other; without knowing the first principle of rearing their children.

Living together is not easy, as most people find out. It requires understanding of each other's personality and character; it requires tact, tolerance and patience.

In many States the Law is beginning to take cognizance of its duty toward the protection of the health of its citizens, and it has enacted legislation compelling the prospective husband and wife to pass a serological test to make sure they are free from syphilis. That is very commendable, but it is not enough.

The State should pass a law compelling every prospective husband and wife to take something like a six-months' course in the art of living together and bringing children into the world. The man should be instructed in the anatomy and psychology of woman, and the woman should be instructed in the anatomy and psychology of man.

In my professional experience hundreds of women have confided to me the fact that they were being deprived of most of the sexual pleasure because their husbands were selfish and ignorant of the most elementary knowledge of woman's physical structure. Woman after woman has told me that she seldom or never had an orgasm; but she never dared complain. The subject is so delicate that usually only the doctor hears about it. Yet the woman and the man are supposed to share equally the pleasure and satisfaction of the sex act.

Love was adumbrated in the first mother, and thus she became the repository of the real and highest values. Man has power, energy, ambition, intellect, and aggressiveness, but all those things cannot achieve the fulfillment of his being, nor can they alone build the human society of which he dreams. Only in the love of the mother, in the devotion of friendship of man and woman, can man find peace and happiness and build a better world.

The Romans made the Vestals the guardians of the Sacred Fire. In common with ancient people they realized that woman is the guardian of Life. The icy winds of asceticism did put out the Sacred Fire, thereby forcing woman into the chains of slavery and degradation.

Woman again must become the Vestal Mother, the Guardian of the Sacred Fire of Life. Merely to bring a child into the world is not sufficient. You must make a MAN out of the child. You must sculpture an object of art, outwardly and inwardly, which will command respect and admiration and which will serve to inspire everyone beholding it. Then the words of Shakespeare:

> What a piece of work is man!
> How noble in reason! How infinite in faculties!
> In form and moving how express and admirable! In action
> how like an angel! In apprehension how like a god!

shall become a reality and you shall be able to feel proud of your creation. Love in one hand and the Torch of Knowledge in the other are all you need to fulfil your destiny and to help man to fulfil his.

To give you this indispensable knowledge of man and thus enable you to carry out to its fullness the function of motherhood, is the purpose of this book and my dream.

May it accomplish its purpose and help to make my dream a reality!

What Is Wrong With Man?

Life is the art of drawing sufficient conclusions from insufficient reasons. —*Samuel Butler*

Learn to make glorious the ordinary of the day's work. Artists paint sunlight with emetics, the juices of fruit pests, and camel's dung.

It is not hard to learn more. What is hard is to unlearn when you discover yourself wrong. —*Dr. Martin H. Fischer*

Life is hardly respectable if it has no generous task, no duties or affections that constitute a necessity of existence. Every man's task is which is to come—a wish. —*G. A. Sala*

Life according to an Arabic proverb, is composed of two parts: that which is past—a dream; (more often a nightmare) and that his life preserve. —*Emerson*

He that embarks in the voyage of life will always wish to advance rather by impulse of the wind than the stroke of the oar; and many founder in their passage while they lie waiting for the gale. —*Johnson*

The life of every man is a diary in which he means to write one story and writes another; and his humblest hour is when he compares the volume as it is with what he hoped to make it. —*James M. Barrie*

Let your life lightly dance on the edges of time like dew on the tip of a leaf. —*Rabindranath Tagore*

The poorest way to face life is with a sneer. —*Theodore Roosevelt*

It is impossible to live pleasurably without living prudently, and honorably, and justly; or to live prudently, and honorably and justly without living pleasurably. —*Epicurus*

Who would venture upon the journey of life, if compelled to begin it at the end? —*Madame de Maintenon*

Our grand business in life is not to see what lies dimly at a distance, but to do what lies clearly at hand. —*Carlyle*

Life is thick with thorns, and I know no other remedy than to pass quickly through them. The longer we dwell in our misfortunes, the greater is their power to harm us. —*Voltaire*

The trouble with life is that people keep on trying to get out as much as they can while putting in as little as they can.

He who knows not the differences between living and existing does not live at all; he merely exists.

There is nothing wrong in being selfish. Being unwisely selfish, that is the great tragedy of life.

Once upon a time life was the survival of the strongest; later it was the survival of the fittest; today it has degenerated into the survival of the crookedest.

Most human beings spend their lives brooding about the past; wasting and misusing the present, and worrying about a future they may never see.

L IFE may be viewed as a continuous series of problems. From the moment we are born till we give out our last breath we are confronted with situations and conditions more or less difficult which require adjustment and are beset by biological needs that demand satisfaction. To the basic problems of obtaining food, shelter and mate, common practically to all animals, human beings have added other various problems resulting from the development of the brain, from the complexity of our civilization and from the formulation of tabus and moral codes not in harmony with our biological urges. While animals are equipped with instincts good enough to solve quite satisfactorily the basic problems of their existence, man is not so equipped. That animals can cope instinctively with natural and normal conditions is proven by the absence of crimes, immorality, perversions, cruelty, prostitution and religionists, moralists and ascetics to plague and confuse them with absurd counsel and to threaten them with eternal punishment. Consequently they are free from neuroses and frustrations. The libido of the female acts as a check upon the sexual urge of the male, and no female can be raped nor forced into sexual slavery.

Human beings have left behind these saving instincts, but have failed to develop new techniques and methods to solve the problems of life in a manner harmonious with their ideals of peace and brotherhood which they rightly claim as the basis of our civilization.

WHAT IS WRONG WITH MAN?

The enormous amount of violence, cruelty and hatred, individual and collective, that has existed and exists in the world are tragic witness to his failure to solve satisfactorily his problems. If to this we add the numerous mental disorders, diseases, perversions, wars with their enormous destruction of life and property and the inner conflicts that make life miserable for the afflicted and for those who live with them, and the preparations for another world war more destructive than anything yet suffered, we will realize the immense tragedy that confronts us and the imperative necessity to attack this situation promptly and with all the energies and resources at our command.

When I say that man has failed to develop new techniques and methods to cope with the problems of life I must qualify this statement by adding that he has not learned the correct methods to deal with his new environment and his newly acquired mental and emotional qualities. During his long evolution man has developed many ways and means to deal with all kinds of situations and to "solve" all his problems. He has also invented and opened roads to escape from the numerous dangers, real or imaginary, that continuously threaten his life and security. But for all this intelligence man fails to be aware that those roads of escape, some beautiful, others ugly and bloody, all lead to destruction, individually or collectively.

The air rings day and night with praises for our Christian (?) civilization and its superiority over all other civilizations and cultures. Yet there is ample and irrefutable evidence that man has deteriorated morally and even physically and that human relations instead of improving with the growth of intelligence and knowledge, have worsened and probably will reach a new low under the shadow of the greatest achievement of science: the atomic bomb.

An inquiry into the whys and wherefores of the failure of the old and accepted methods and techniques to deal with life and into the causes of this moral and physical deterioration is essential. We cannot treat the patient successfully unless we have an accurate case history and a correct diagnosis.

Firstly we must take a good look at the past and follow man from his emergence from forests into the plains up to the present.

Anthropologists and other investigators who have studied primitive man tell us that he was humble before Nature. He was awed and frightened by the mighty forces of Nature that so often endangered and even destroyed his life and his food supply and also by his own powers of speech and imagination. Therefore he attempted to control those forces with the same methods and things he used in appeasing and influencing other men. His knowledge of Nature and its phenomena was zero; he had to start his journey without a map, therefore his conception of things had to be necessarily egocentric, egoistic and anthropomorphic. Consequently he fashioned a universe in his own image and believed that every object was animated by a being like himself but invisible and that every phenomenon was the result of the activity of those invisible beings.

His exclusive power to speak amazed him no end and gave him a sense of superiority and power over other creatures, and naturally enough he came to believe that words had magic powers. Thus he spoke to the sun, to the moon, to every object large or small and to the animals, now commanding and demanding obedience or favors, now pleadingly, promising, begging for something. The fact that his magic words and incantations failed again and again did not discourage him nor did it change his attitude toward Nature. So enormously great and so deeply rooted is man's faith in the power of words and so strong his hope that even in this scientific age man still mumbles meaningless words he calls prayers expecting, with the ignorance and naiveté of primitive man, to obtain special favors from his God and to change the course of events.

Offerings and ceremonies, sometimes beautiful but most times grotesque and humiliating, and sacrifices of animals and even human beings, were gradually added to the words. These beliefs made inevitable the appearance of the medicine man, the magician or the witch who pretended to possess supernatural powers and took over the task of protecting the tribe and the crops from evil spirits, and to bring rain when needed. The witch also made inevitable the priestly class who before long became powerful and arrogant, claiming to be the only oracles of the gods. The priesthood demanded and obtained complete obedience from king, master and slave. Through their mouths the gods spoke, commanding, threatening and demanding more and better offerings, more sacrifices with which they grew wealthy and lived in luxury.

As man became more God-intoxicated and more conscious of his superiority and of his alleged divinity, he grew more conceited, more egoist and cruel. The progressive divinization of man reached its zenith with the advent of Christianity. But ironically enough the dehumanization of man also reached its peak at the same time. One moment man was exalted and elevated to heaven as the special creation of God, superior even to the angels, and next moment he was taunted and denounced as a wicked sinner; thus his songs of joy were mixed with lamentations and self-accusations of being the most sinful and unworthy creature on the face of the earth.

Before Christianity cast its shadow upon the world, the idea of original sin was unknown. True, man had notions of sin and often felt guilty of having broken some tabu, but he was quickly cleansed of all his sins by some ceremony or by transferring them to an animal which became the scapegoat. Men lived fairly well integrated lives, and psychiatrists would have starved in those pre-Christian civilizations. Polygamy was a matter of economics and sex potency, not of morals and law. Any man who could afford more than one wife was free to do so; sex had not been degraded and blackened with sin.

Rivers of ink have leaked into acres of paper in an attempt to explain the appearance of Christianity, mostly as a supernatural event. God becomes man to atone for a sin that according to the theory of evolution man could never have committed. And why, as I have pointed out elsewhere, should God send his Son into a corner of the earth where only a handful of people could listen to him? Surely God must have known there were other lands besides Galilee and other peoples besides the Jews. And what kind of God is this that he could not even save his own people? Any politician can do a better job at convincing people than Jesus did. The whole thing is so incredible, so absurd that the only explanation is that one given by Tertulian when he said: "Credo quian absurdum."

Long before the alleged coming of Jesus, Christianity had already made its appearance with the mystics and ascetics in India, in the deserts of Judea, with the Essenes and in Greece with the stoics and the philosophers like Plato. The decadence and breaking down of the Egyptian, Greek and Roman civilizations left the pagan world in confusion and despair. Pagan people had seen the gods of the Persians, of the Egyptians and of the Romans impotent and unable to help their believers and to crumble into the dust before the attacks of mere mortals. Thus the pagan world was ready to discard its gods and to accept the one God, whom his believers claimed was more powerful and better than all the gods ever worshipped by man, in the hope He would do for the people more good and better things. The real founders of Christianity were not Jesus and his disciples, but St. Paul, the mystics and ascetics, the Fathers of the Church and the writers of the most successful piece of fiction ever written: the Four Gospels.

Neither Jesus nor his disciples left anything written, as far as we know, therefore we have no reliable historical account of them. The earliest Gospel was written about seventy years after the supposed death of Jesus. Those who take the Gospels as the Truth should, if they really seek the Truth, read: *The Case of the Nazarene Reopened,* by Hyman Goldin, where they will find ample and irrefutable evidence that the Gospels are brimful with contradictions and falsehoods and could not have been written by anyone familiar with the Jewish and Roman laws and customs, because the events they describe would be practically impossible to happen under the Jewish and Roman jurisprudence and tabus in force at the time of Jesus. Thus the saying, "the Gospel Truth" loses its meaning because there is no Truth in the Gospels.

Christianity was a revolutionary movement; this cannot be denied. It was the revolt of the humble, of the hungry and enslaved. Christianity elevated these people to the level of the master and the emperor. But practically like all revolutions, it soon created worse and more evils than it had destroyed. Every man has an immortal soul created by God, therefore all men are equal before God. All human beings are brothers and must love one another. Beautiful and inspiring words. But in practice the emperor, the master and the wealthy continue to live in luxury and to enjoy more freedom than the serfs. True, a few of them gave up their wealth and went with the poor, but the majority took their place with the rich.

Moreover, Christianity at the same time degraded both the emperor and the slave as miserable and unworthy sinners and brought them down to the lower depths, mentally and physically. Mentally because it taught that joy and pleasure were evil and surrounded people with fear of the devil, of witches, of temptation and of eternal punishment. Physically because it branded the body as impure, filthy and evil and its biological needs as sinful. There are three enemies of the Soul, says the Church: the World, the Devil and the Flesh. The Flesh is the worse enemy because we cannot run away from it. Therefore Christianity declared war against these enemies of man's salvation only to suffer total and ignominious defeat; the Flesh and the World have triumphed completely. Man was caught in the middle of this titanic struggle between illusion and reality and suffered and still suffers incredible misery and slavery. Because although the Christian leaders promised freedom from the master and from the king, this freedom was only for the soul, not for the body, and the tyranny imposed by the Christian leaders made the tyranny of the pagan masters look like freedom.

The dualism of body and soul, opposed to each other, brought the splitting of the personality with painful tensions, destructive inner conflicts and greater insecurity than ever. The Flesh demanded satisfaction while the Soul refused or at least tried to refuse that satisfaction. Self-denial and mortification were considered the only remedy. The degradation of man was surpassed by the degradation of woman. The condemnation of sex and its pleasures as filthy, evil and sinful reacted upon woman with terrific impact. Woman became the temptress, "the gate of hell" who with her beauty and charms leads men into perdition. Many pages could be filled with the castigations that the Fathers of the Church heaped upon woman. The weakness and evil nature of woman is symbolized in Eve. Poor Adam is pictured as a trusting and innocent fellow who could not resist charming Eve when she tempted him with the forbidden fruit (theologians are not sure it was an apple). What a convenient but silly and absurd scapegoat! What a childish way to evade responsibility. Thus man threw all the blame for his sexual lust and for his troubles upon the fragile shoulders of woman. But it did not take the Christian leaders very long to realize their colossal blunder and to begin making amends by idealizing woman in the Virgin Mary. This divinization of woman was only theoretical because in real life she remained enslaved and treated like cattle.

The Christian leaders attempted to eliminate temptation by ordering woman to cover her body and hide her charms with unattractive and often filthy garments, but all in vain. Woman proved to be more than a match for the poor naive Fathers and the very dresses they forced upon her to hide what men wanted to see, were turned into means to accentuate those charms and tempt man.

Thousands upon thousands of men and women took vows of chastity and many clothed in rags went to the desert to torture themselves in the hope to suppress the urgent demands of the Flesh and to expiate real or imaginary sins. Some men like Origines sought a sure victory over the Flesh by emasculating themselves. The immense majority of men and women, however, refused to follow Origines into castration and self-destruction.

The corruption and debauchery brought forth by this betrayal of life made the orgies of the Roman emperors and the polygamous behavior of the pagans look like Sunday-school picnics. Let us hear what a historian says about this: "Concubinage, as a substitute for the interdicted marriage, continued to be practiced down to the sixteenth century, nor was this form of illicit living the worst vice of the clergy. Debauchery spread throughout the country (England) until in the sixteenth century it is said that as many as one hundred thousand women fell under the seduction of the priests, for whose particular pleasures houses of ill fame were kept. . . . From the laity, complaints became general that their wives and daughters were not safe from advances from the priests. . . . All the literature of the Middle Ages leads to but one conclusion—that the clergy were the greatest corrupters of domestic virtue among the burgher and agricultural classes."[1]

"The century that witnessed the outbreak of the Reformation is commonly regarded as exceptional for the laxity of religious principle and perversion of the institutional ideals of the Church; but from the eighth century, the ecclesiastical morality was of such low order as seriously to affect the moral tone of the people and to invalidate the efficacy of the Church as a teacher of religion. The celibacy that was enjoined upon the clergy was largely responsible for this state of affairs. It is unfortunately not true that the ages of faith, so called, were ages of great moral purity."[2]

This is what Christianity, the religion that came to save mankind from sin, has done to man. This is what the priest-

[1] Barlett Burleigh James, Ph.D., *Woman in All Ages and in All Countries,* Volume "Women of England", pages 110, 111.

[2] *Woman in All Ages and in All Countries*, page 155.

hood, who worshipped Virgin Mary and sang daily hymns to virginity, have done to woman. And if anyone believes that the priesthood of today keeps its vows of chastity better than in the Middle Ages, he is more naive than he has the right to be.

If from sexuality we pass to examine the health and hygienic record of Christianity, the conclusions are just as tragic and devastating. Pagan man was fairly clean and observed certain hygienic rules. The Greeks glorified the human body as no other people had ever done before. They went in for athletics, massages, baths, cleansing and therapeutic and sunshine. The Romans did not equal the Greeks in the care and glorification of the body, but bathed often and wherever they went as conquerors they built thermas, or baths. The Arabs carried the torch of the Greeks into Spain and their cities were noted by their cleanliness, baths and libraries.

The Christian leaders denounced with fanatical fury these hygienic and health-giving practices of the infidels as instruments of the devil to lead man and woman into sin and eternal damnation. The only thing that matters is the soul, said the Christian leaders; and since the body with its passions and desires endangers the salvation of the soul, let the body suffer and rot in filth, pain and disease. Consequently, the beautiful baths of the Romans and of the Arabs were destroyed, athletic and sun baths substituted by duelling and jousting knights leaving the body to wallow in filth, ugliness and disease. St Mary the Egyptiac boasted of not having taken a bath in sixty years . . . no wonder she and other saints died in "odor" of sanctity (?)

As it was to be expected, disease increased by leaps and bounds through Europe; the Black Plague is said to have killed 20,000,000 people. It is still within our memory when people hardly bathed at all, neither at home nor at the beach and when they began to go bathing they did not dare to expose any more anatomy than when they walked on the streets. Think of the millions of human beings who never enjoyed

[24]

the freedom from clothes, the caresses of the sun and the refreshing and cleansing touch of the sea. We are lucky indeed to have freed ourselves from some tabus. But there are other tabus no less harmful that rob us of peace and happiness.

From the moment that man is born he knows suppression, guilt, frustration, lies and hypocrisy. As soon as he opens his eyes he sees people violating the principles and teachings they pretend to cherish as the only way to salvation. Is it any wonder that man becomes cynical, cruel, egotistic, mistrustful, dishonest and lascivious? He soon loses respect for the Christian teachings and for the ministers but plays the game, going to church and paying lip service to God and to brotherhood. But many of those Christians are ready to lynch a Negro or to come to blows with another Christian at the slightest provocation. Violence, hatred and cruelty reside in them like water in a reservoir and only need a small crack to pour out like a mighty torrent.

There was plenty of violence and wars before Christianity; but these wars lacked the fury and fanatical hatred of the Christian wars. Men went to conquer territory, to obtain food and slaves or made war in self-defense, but men did not go to war to conquer souls nor to impose religious dogmas; they did not murder, torture and persecute people in the name of God even though their gods were not gods of love and justice. The Romans conquered most of the known world, but wherever they arrived as conquerors they usually respected the local gods and religious beliefs, so long as they were not used against the emperor. There were no Torquemadas burning witches, hunting heretics, setting brother against brother and children against father because of religious differences. True, the Romans threw a few Christians to the lions, but this was done rather reluctantly and under great provocation; they hardly could remain indifferent while their emperor and their gods were insulted and ridiculed.

It remained for the Christians, who claimed to profess a religion of love and compassion, to invent the most refined instruments of torture, to devise the most diabolical methods of inflicting pain and to burn men, women and children at the stake just for a mere suspicion of heresy.

Only recently we saw a nation, a Christian nation high on the roster of cultured and civilized nations, go berserk and unleash upon the world the bloodiest and most destructive of all wars. Germany became the theatre of sadistic orgies incredible and unparalleled in the history of mankind. Yet, the German people were religious people, Catholics and Protestants; practically all the German leaders had received religious education. And only four years after the guns were silenced, we are priming them and sharpening the bayonets for a greater and more destructive war.

We live in a jungle where man is a wolf to man; where most everybody regards everybody with suspicion. Yet we have the nerve to boast of our Christian civilization. If by civilization we mean wearing nice clothes, riding in cars, using telephones and other gadgets and going to church, then we are civilized. A savage could very well put on an evening suit and use all our gadgets on short notice, but he still would remain a savage and we would only need to scratch lightly to find that civilization is more than those trappings. The fact is that there has not been a real civilization; what we call civilizations were only more or less cultured groups, small islands of knowledge amid a sea of ignorance which carried in themselves the seed of their own destruction.

A civilized man is one who uses his intelligence and his reasoning power, not his fists or his gun, to solve and settle all the problems and differences arising from his relations with other human beings. The most important business today is to civilize man.

Why have all the religious methods and techniques failed to civilize man, to bring peace and freedom and self-control? Here is a $64 question that must be answered today not tomorrow. Too long already has this question been evaded. We cannot longer accept the usual pious lies that it is man who has failed because he is born in sin, because he is weak and must suffer in this world to gain happiness in the other. We must honestly and courageously search for the causes of this failure and bring these causes before the sun, no matter whom it hurts. There is too much at stake to pussyfoot and whitewash the guilty: the welfare and the future of man are in the balance. Man must be saved, but there is no Messiah to save him. Too long has man waited for a saviour, in vain. Man must save himself by applying all the knowledge he has acquired for the welfare not of the few, but of all mankind. Man has become the Faustian man, divided in his loyalties, schizophrenic, neurotic, frustrated, at war with himself and with his fellow humans. Our growing insane asylums and mental disorders are tragic witness to this. Man seeks escape from his problems in illusion, delusions and wishful thinking more or less destructive but equally ineffective.

There must be a reintegration of man; this age old duality of body and soul is the most colossal fraud and the most tragic delusion ever spawned by ignorance and imagination. No one can measure the suffering and the bloodshed it has caused. Man is one: his mind and his "soul" are the product of his body. No one ever has seen a mind without a body, but one often encounters a body without a mind.

Let us do away once and for all with the pernicious and defeatist superstition that man is born evil and in sin. Man is not born good nor evil; he is born with enormous capacities for both, but destructive emotions, for reasons explained in this book, constitute the line of least resistance. The same forces that produced a Torquemada, a Hitler and a Franco also produced a Socrates and a Francis of Assisi. This is why I have faith in man and his future.

I am fully aware that religious institutions and churches are the stoutest pillars of the "status quo" and will resist any serious attempt to reform; but man must be reformed or perish. Human nature can be changed or at least conditioned in the image of that symbol that has become the repository of all that is best and noblest in man. Never in its long history has he had the knowledge and the tools to control the environment. We could change the world in a couple of generations; we could bring abundant living to every human being, abolish war and most diseases before long if we applied to this glorious task only a part of the energies and money used for wholesale murder and for destruction—but man is laboring under a compulsive neurosis that leads him to commit suicide.

The destiny of the world is not in the hands of the wise or the good, nor in the hands of men of science, but in the hands of menopausal or old men who move under the heavy burden of frustration, oozing bitterness and hatred and whose brain has become ankylosed and closed to the very virtues they claim to defend. Their greed for power and for money has become to a great extent a substitute for the loss of their virility. Everything is bought and sold, including the "soul." Practically every man has a price tag; nobody, to my knowledge, has expressed this more poetically and truthfully than Shelley in the following words:

> Commerce has set the mark of selfishness,
> The signet of its all enslaving power
> Upon a shining ore, and called it gold:
> Before whose image bow the vulgar great,
> The vainly rich, the miserable proud,
> The mob of peasants, nobles, priests and kings,
> And with blind feelings reverence the power
> That grinds them to the dust of misery.
> But in the temple of their hireling hearts
> Gold is a living god, and rules in scorn
> All earthly things but virtue.[3]

Man fears anonymity, sometimes worse than death, and often writes his name in the pages of history with blood and tears of his fellow men and of his own, while in other cases it leads man to invent, to explore and blaze new trails for the welfare of mankind. Adrift in a sea of confusion, without a compass or star to guide him, man anxiously scans the dark horizon for a harbor where he can find complete security. The

[3] Percy Bysshe Shelley, *Queen Mab.*

beacons and navigation charts set up by supernaturalists, always misleading, have completely broken down. Rugged and ruthless individualism, like the walking aids of a child, has had its time; but today it is more than a hindrance: it is harmful to the utmost. Man has misread Nature and drawn wrong conclusions from the struggle for life; he has yet to learn that co-operation, in the higher forms of life, is just as essential as individualism. Loyalties? Yes, man must be loyal, but not to the secular and religious powers that demand his loyalty in conflicting ways; he must be loyal to humanity, loyal to Life, to himself.

Lack of printing gadgets and other elements made possible the monopoly of knowledge by few men; mass illiteracy, which in many countries is still very high, has been an unsurmountable obstacle to the progress and betterment of mankind. But there are two kinds of illiteracy: those who cannot read, and those who can read but cannot distinguish between fact and illusion. This illiteracy of the literate is just as dangerous and harmful as the first.

In the last century, man has built great numbers of schools, colleges and universities that are turning out educated men and women like an assembly line. Once upon a time there was the belief that educated men was the answer to our problems; but educated men, we have found to our sorrow, are no better ethically and morally than the uneducated. Education is not enough; it must be the right kind of education in a favorable environment. Our educational system is not geared to produce well integrated and clear thinking men. Success, and this means financial success, is the goal of our centers of learning and what the student seeks in his diploma; it is also the yard-stick with which we measure man. Thus we witness the pitiful spectacle of very clever and smart men who are mentally and emotionally immature and do not know how to arrange their lives to obtain a maximum of health and happiness.

Language was once used to express thoughts, but now it

is largely used to hide thoughts, to confuse and mislead people. Truth is something to be praised and placed on a pedestal, where it is usually left for fear it will hurt people and our chances of success. This indictment is not new or exhaustive; man has been indicted and accused before, but few of the accusers have given the proper remedy because it is only lately that we have acquired sufficient knowledge about man to make a correct diagnosis of his ills, and to formulate an effective prescription. Man is the product of heredity and environment; we cannot control heredity yet, but we can control environment to a great extent. Here is our hope.

What Is Man?

And God said, Let us make man in our image, after our own likeness: and let Him have dominion over the fish of the sea, and over the fowl of the air, and over the cattle, and over all the earth, and over every creeping thing that creepeth upon the earth.

So God created man in his own image, in the image of God created him; male and female created he them. *—Genesis 1:26:27*

Man is an animal; but he is an animal plus something else. He is a mythic earth-tree whose roots are in the ground, but whose topmost branches may blossom in the heavens. *—Henry George*

Men are the Universe become conscious; the simplest man should consider himself too great to be called after any name.
—John Davidson

The more I see of human beings the more I like my dog.
—Anonymous

Man is to man all kinds of beasts; a fawning dog, a roaring lion, a thieving fox, a robbing wolf, a dissembling crocodile, a treacherous decoy, a rapacious vulture. *—Carlyle*

Every man is a divinity in disguise, a god playing the fool. It seems as if heaven send the insane angels into the world as to an asylum. And here they will break into their native music, and utter at intervals the words they have heard in heaven, then the mad fit returns, and they mope and wallow like dogs. *—Emerson*

When man is a brute, (and he is very often a brute) he is the most sensual and loathsome of all brutes. *—Hawthorne*

Rounded in his nature, infinite in his desires, man is a fallen god who has recollections of heaven. *—Lamartine*

Man is an animal that makes bargains; no other animal does this —one dog does not change a bone with another. *—Adam Smith*

What a chimera is man! what a confused chaos! what a subject of contradiction! a professor of all things, and yet a feeble worm in the earth, the great depository and guardian of truth, and yet a mere huddle of uncertainty, the glory and the scandal of the universe.
—Pascal

Now thyself, presume not God to scan
The proper study of mankind is man. *—Alexander Pope*

[31]

MAN IN NATURE AND BEHAVIOR

Young Man: You have arrived at man, now?

Old Man: Yes. Man the machine. Man the impersonal engine. Whatever man is, it owes to *his* make, and to the *influence* brought to bear upon it by his heredities, his habitat, his associations. He is moved, directed, COMMANDED, by exterior influences—*solely.* He originates nothing, not even thought.   —*Mark Twain*

Man is the meeting ground of all the contradictions and opposites in the Universe and of some not found there; product of his exclusive brain and nervous system. This makes man the Supreme Contradiction of the Cosmos.

What a piece of work is man! How complex and how imperfect. Yet how marvelous! How limited in his capacity to love! How boundless in his capacity to hate! How infinite in his faculties for good and evil! And how finite in the application of his intelligence and his reason to the solution of the problems arising with other human beings!

He charters the stars on their course but he cannot fathom his own.

He explores the depths of the sea and of the sky, yet he has unexplored continents within himself.

He braves all kinds of dangers but cringes with fear before monsters created by his own mind and kneels in awe before his own shadow!   —*With apologies to Shakespeare*

MANY, diverse and contradictory are, as we can see, the answers given by man to this self-asked question: What is Man? But practically all the answers are incomplete, totally or partially wrong. It could hardly be otherwise because it is only recently that man has acquired the knowledge, the necessary instruments, scientific techniques and freedom to undertake a rational inquiry of himself.

Before the development of modern biology and psychology, man looked around and saw his own reflection everywhere: in the stars, in the mountains, in the clouds and the rivers, in the vast and restless sea, in the radiant sun and in the changing moon. But just as concave mirror gives a distorted image, thus his mind, unchecked by experience, gave man an egocentric image of the universe and a misleading portrait of himself. This picture can be compared to the picture of Dorian Grey which the evil deeds of the original turned into an ugly and horrible thing. Gradually, while man was on the one hand creating more beautiful and powerful images of himself, gods, he became more conscious of his weakness, of his contradictions and of his sins real and imaginary, and his evil deeds increased with alarming rapidity.

As the child grows, there comes a time when he wants to know where he comes from. There is no doubt that mankind has gone through the same process. And just as the parents, ashamed of our humble and "shameful" origin have invented the stork and other mythical but beautiful ways of coming into the world, man identified himself with the gods he had created to fit into the universe as the most important part of it, and wove childish and complicated stories about his origin, his ancestors, his nature and his destiny.

But all these stories were fantastic tales to cover up his ignorance, fortify his ego, allay his fears, and give him security in what he felt was a hostile universe. This supernatural explanation of man never really and fully has satisfied him. True, great numbers of people have accepted those stories, but for lack of better ones and because they inflate their ego and give them hope in a hopeless world. But even the unlearned and ignorant felt their contradictions and irrationality, only to be silenced by fear and wishful thinking.

The Greeks, who were first in so many things, also were first to search for a natural explanation of man and things, and got a glimpse of evolution. "Know thyself", they wrote over the door of their temples, thus giving advice and incitement to study and investigate. But the Greeks did not have reference books and no fund of knowledge, nor instruments to study the brain and the cells; therefore they did not go very far. In fact, some Greek philosophers did not get anywhere at all; they merely held to the supernaturalism and dualism of man and clothed these superstitions in such beautiful and complicated robes that myth became more attractive and resistant to science.

With the collapse of Greek civilization the scientific study of man came to an unfortunate end hardly before it had begun. Soon Christianity would throw an immense shadow over the earth and in this dark night of the mind, shackled to dogmas and superstitions, man would be unable to continue the search for truth started by the Greek philosophers.

The Reformation made a big breach in the walls of dogmatism and the scientific study of man and his nature, which religious and intolerant men had stopped, was taken up again by knowledge-hungry students. The Adam and Eve story, so beautiful, so simple and easy to understand, appeared like a pretty cake made of sawdust which did not satisfy the truth-seekers, and after many skirmishes between the proponents of the theory of evolution and the supernaturalists, a peaceful Englishman, Charles Darwin, gave the Adam and Eve story the fatal blow from which it can never recover, and pushed man from the throne, to which as king of creation he had elevated himself.

Darwin gathered facts for many years, and then showed that man has a common ancestry with animals. There was rage in heaven and on earth, but strangely enough, God did not come to the help of his defenders. The facts marshalled by Darwin could not be exorcised, nor silenced by the torrent of abuse and threats that poured out of enraged theologians and priests. Scientists could no longer be stopped by force, nor convinced by sophisms and went ahead widening the breach made by Darwin and adding more and more facts to the support of evolution. Today, even religionists are beginning to search ways and means to accept evolution without losing much face and with a minimum of damage to their religious dogmas, to their power and economic privileges.

Their strongest argument is that even if the body comes from lower organisms and is animal, in origin and nature, man has a soul, created by God, and this soul is the real man, the body being only a perishable instrument or garment. Without this soul, the body is nothing—a mass of matter incapable of thinking and even living.

Even after Darwin had taken the body out of the mythical creation, psychology, also initiated by the Greeks, remained a branch of philosophy, a speculative pastime for theologians and philosophers who wasted precious time trying to explain how the soul, or the *élan vital*, managed and directed the body with its complicated physiological functions.

Again, those men tormented by doubt and hungry for knowledge were searching, experimenting and accumulating ammunition, and one day Sigmund Freud fired a mighty broadside against this darling of religionists: the divine and supernatural man. When the smoke had cleared, the soul had vanished with it, and the most intense and fruitful study of man and his nature had begun. Thus in the study of man it can be said: B. F., and A. F., before and after Freud. But Freud has filled many gaps with clever and brilliant hypotheses not supported by facts. Many psychologists and psychiatrists are following in the foot-steps of Freud and attempting to explain much of behavior and misbehavior of man by postulating causes, factors and events of which they have no proof or of whose relationship there is not satisfactory evidence. They maintain, for instance, that slips of the tongue and even accidents are the result of unconscious wishes. This may or may not be true in some cases, but very often they could be traced to physiological and chemical processes taking place within the body.

The partial failure of Freud and other psychoanalysts to give us a rational explanation of some phases of the behavior of man is due to their negligence to take into consideration the peculiar and special qualities of protoplasm, both in the most simple and most complex organisms, and the ever-changing, yet basically stable chemistry of the human body. This failure has begotten a neo-metaphysical system in which psychiatrists get lost and wrangle with each other, generating more heat than light and more confusion than order.

With more precise and careful analysis of the fluids of the body, of the cells and nerves, we are finding explanations for aspects of behavior which previously were wholly attributed to mental conditions and to manifestations of the unconscious. Deficiency in iron, calcium, iodine and other minerals and vitamins often influence behavior in manners heretofore unknown and ascribed to external factors acting through the unconscious.

Man begins his life as a human being when the two cells, male and female, meet and embrace each other like long lost brothers in the dark and slimy caverns of the Fallopian tubes or the uterus. Each cell alone was nothing, weak and defenseless and condemned to an early death. Together they become active with something like atomic energy. No sooner have the sperm and the egg merged into one, than they begin to enact, hastily and sketchily, the long drama of evolution culminating in the formation of the human being in the short period of seven months. Here is mystery and wonder that taxes our imagination. In comparison to this phenomenon the seven wonders of the ancients seem trivial and insignificant. The formation of the human being in the womb is the most marvelous, the most mysterious, the most magnificent and thrilling phenomenon in the universe. The nebulae, the galaxies and the stars are immensely larger and awe inspiring, but they cannot match that tiny and delicate mass of protoplasm, nor do they present us with more complicated problems.

Some day, I believe and hope, science will enable us to take moving pictures to follow the egg and the sperm to their rendezvous with Destiny and observe the real birth of a human being, and thus perhaps solve many riddles of evolution and of the behavior of man.

At times I have sympathy for vitalists and metaphysicians who cling to the soul and refuse to accept the rational and materialistic explanation of man. They move under the heavy burden of that old superstition that matter is inert and incapable of action. There must be something, they say, that animates matter, directs the universe and evolution in general and the formation of man in particular. The animism of primitive man had to retreat before the march of physiology and biology, but supernaturalists did not concede defeat; they brought into play another supernatural force: the *élan vital* postulated by the French philosopher Bergson. This vitalist hypothesis has not contributed anything at all to the understanding of the human body nor explained anything; consequently it has been discarded by scientists.

Some people, unwilling to accept the emergence of life from matter in our planet, have proposed that life came to our earth from another planet in the distant past. But if another planet was able to produce life, why not ours? Nothing can be gained, nor explained, by pushing the problem away into the cosmic space. We may as well face the fact that life has emerged from lifeless matter as a result of a long chemical evolution; just the higher forms of life have emerged from a single cell. This, of course, means the spontaneous appearance of life, a very unpleasant hypothesis that has been pushed around. Up to the Middle Ages and later, people believed that flies and other animals were spontaneously formed in the mud or dirt. Spallanzani made the first experiments to disprove this belief, but the debate continued up to the nineteenth century when Pasteur attempted and claimed to have given a fatal blow to the theory of spontaneous generation. His experiment consisted in filling several sterilized flasks with sterile water and then to wait for some time for life to appear in those sealed and oxygenless containers. It is most amazing that a scientist like Pasteur and his contemporaries did not notice the enormous flaw that completely invalidated their experiment; for who would expect life to appear in such a short notice or even in millions of years in an artificial environment from which the very substance essential for the formation and maintenance of life had been excluded? The only thing Pasteur proved when he opened his bottles at the Sorbonne, amid great pomp and ceremony, before the emperor and the most important men and women of his day, was that life cannot appear in those artificial conditions.

Whether the formation of life or protoplasm was an episode that took place only once many millions of years ago when the earth was young and overflowing with vitality, or whether life is being created now in that vast and mysterious laboratory which is the sea, we do not know. It is possible that the earth has become sterile like an old woman and that her fertility was limited to a certain period of time.

Biologists have discovered viruses which seem to fill the gap between inorganic and organic matter. The fact that man has been unable to form life in his laboratories does not prove anything against the formation of life from non-living matter because we cannot duplicate the conditions and materials present in Nature when that event took place. All the substances found in living creatures are also found in lifeless matter; nothing really new is added, only the arrangement and structure of atoms and molecules.

There are four important events in the history of Life and Man: 1—The formation of our planet. 2—The appearance of the cell. 3—The agroupation of cells into colonies. 4—The appearance of man.

From amoeba to man is a long way, so long it over-taxes the eyes and the imagination of most people; but it is from the study of this and other lowly creatures that scientists have wrested an answer to that vital and long-asked question: What is Man? Never before has this question been answered fully and satisfactorily because even the wisest and most learned men did not have the knowledge and the powerful aids to our senses that we possess today.

Biologically, man is a series of protoplasms of different qualities, in different stages of evolution and of different rate of metabolism, but all united into one organism by the common purpose of maintaining their chemical and physical equilibrium; that is, to keep alive. This organism is the result of chance because the male germ cells are of two kinds: one kind has the full complement of forty-eight chromosomes and the other kind has forty-seven X chromosomes and one Y chromosome. If the egg is fertilized by a male cell with XX chromosomes, it will be a woman; if it is fertilized by a sperm with X and the smaller chromosome Y it will be a man. Since man seems to produce about half of each kind, the chances of producing man or woman are about fifty-fifty.

The fact that man is composed of different protoplasms, and what is just as important or more, that each man is composed of protoplasms different from the protoplasms of other men, has not received the attention it deserves. In the innumerable variations of which protoplasm is capable are the basis for the enormous variety of living things and for maximum individualization found in human beings, each being completely different from the other, yet alike in certain basic things. Only in true twins, which have been formed from the same protoplasm, do we find complete likeness between two human beings.

Animals, of course, are also composed of a series of protoplasms, but in them the highest and most specialized cells have reached only group differentiation and individualization; consequently, all the members of that particular group react alike to the same stimulus and to less stimulus than man. That is why when we know how a rat or a bird reacts to a situation, we know how all the other members will behave under identical conditions. Not so with man, because he is an individual whose reactions and behavior cannot be predicted by observing another individual.

This wide variation of protoplasm also explains the enormous differences, both physical and mental, exhibited by human beings and absent in animals; it also helps us to explain exceptional men. What does really make a man a genius but his capacity to learn more and quicker than the average individual, and to create new forms and combinations from the material received? Exceptional men are more efficient machines, with a higher metabolism and with greater energy which must be expended either in constructive or destructive activities.

There was never a Beethoven or a Shakespeare before because the environment was lacking; the group had not reached the cultural level nor acquired the tools necessary to produce these geniuses. It is true that a genius often transcends the culture of the group and raises himself above the level in which he is born, and for that he is often penalized by his short sighted fellow men. But this capacity to create something from the material received and to see farther than others is due to his hypersensitive nervous system and brain, to his powerful imagination, which activated by glandular secretions, is able to distill future sequences and to form synthesis from the past and from the present.

From the savage to modern man we can trace the genealogy of our culture with advancing and retreating steps, but each group raising itself to a higher level because it is able to draw upon the conquests and improvements of preceding cultures. This is what Korzibski calls time-binding, and man is the only animal capable to make Father Kronos prisoner, to a certain extent, with just a few signs or letters traced upon clay, stone, leather or paper. Without this time-binding device progress would be completely impossible and man would never have progressed beyond the lowest stage.

An analysis of the complex stages of evolution and of the elements that have brought forth the innumerable and divergent forms of living creatures is irrelevant to our study. Whether new species are the result of slow evolution or mutations, the question is that living matter responds to the environment with changes and adaptations that when not purposive put an end to the individual and to the species. Therefore, only purposive adaptations and changes are made permanent record of the genes and chromosomes and thus pass on to form part of coming generations.

The grey matter is without doubt the aristocrat of protoplasms, the neuron the king of the cells and the brain the most marvelous organ, and the most complex structure in the universe. In the grey matter we find the highest metabolism and consequently the highest sensibility and irritability, and of course, the greatest capacity to respond to the environment and for adaptation to it. Some day in the more or less distant future, man will be able to observe the brain alive, while in action with its billions of neurons flashing signals and making connections; then I am sure the answer to many of the problems and questions that seem insoluble today and for which religionists have formulated supernatural "explanations", will be forthcoming. Already the study of the brain waves and surgery are giving us a narrow but revealing glimpse of the activities and qualities of the grey matter. Perhaps then, man will be able to see the difference between the brain of a genius and the brain of an average man and a moron, and find confirmation to the theory that it is not the quantity of grey matter but its quality, and also the structure and connections of the neurons, that count. What a marvelous and enlightening spectacle that will be!

Biologically, man is also an animal with imagination and with reasoning faculties; an animal that has succeeded in walking erect thus freeing his hands for good and evil, more evil than good, unfortunately. His erect posture enabled him to lift his head upward and to interrogate the stars, which by the way, has caused him no end of trouble. Some doctors claim that walking erect has also brought all our digestive disorders; they are too modest in their claims: walking erect is responsible practically for all the ills and troubles that beset man, which could be easily cured by going back to all fours. But man's backbone has become too stiff to bend down again; therefore we must look for other solutions to our digestive and non-digestive disorders.

In terms of physics and mechanics, man is a machine that has taken millions of years to assemble; a self-made and self-regulating machine. "Man is *An Adaptive Mechanism*", says Dr. George W. Crile in his book of that title. "If the reactions of the human organism," continues Dr. Crile, "be reduced to their simple terms, probably none will be found more intricate than this food-catching reaction of the Venus' fly-trap and the frog. The principal differences between these three living mechanisms is rather a difference in range of activation and environment, resulting in the frog and in man in a larger number of reactions which in turn involve more complex effector mechanisms than are possessed by the fly-trap. Each reaction of man doubtless has more component parts than each reaction of Venus' fly-trap, just as a large home contains more bricks than a small house. The most complex machine ever invented by man looks like a grotesque monster to the savage; yet its complex movements are compounded of the two simple movements of translation and rotation."

Like other machines, man needs fuel and oxygen for its work, and whatever energy it produces it can be traced and accounted for to what he takes from the external world.

True, man is a purposive machine, but its mechanism often goes wrong, and what in some circumstances may be a beneficial process, may in others prove very harmful. For instance, the clotting of the blood is a defensive and purposive process, but when a contusion does not produce an open wound the blood clots just the same, although clotting in that case is often very harmful. The same thing happens with fever, which usually is a defensive mechanism; but in the case of malarial infection, fever does not do any good to the patient, and it is injurious. Moreover, the body can easily develop habits and cravings that are destructive, like smoking, alcohol, opium, etc.

To the chemist, man is a chemical formula whose whole equation still is unknown; a combination of thirteen major and few minor chemical elements whose atomic structure, while in the body, is unknown. None of the chemical substances can, when analyzed and studied, by itself give us the slightest idea of life and much less of man. No more than the analysis of hydrogen and oxygen can give us the most remote idea of the marvelous properties and behavior of water. If a chemist is given a small amount of thyroxine or testosterone and told to analyze those substances with the object of finding a clue to their role in man's intelligence and virility, he will find nothing in their atomic structure to show how or why they play such a vital role in the functioning of the mind and the nervous system. Yet a human being, lacking the secretion of the thyroid gland, is a cretin and without the male hormone he is not a man physically nor mentally. Experiments have shown that even the maternal instinct is dependent upon certain chemical elements.

If from the microcosmos we pass to the macrocosmos, we find ourselves in a similar blind alley, for no one by looking at the sun and analyzing his light would be able to find a clue to the earth with its innumerable aspects and qualities, nor to the enormous varieties of life. Yet the earth came out of the sun many millions of years ago, a flaming globe hurtling through space. The whole behavior of man is chemical in its ultimate analysis. A castrated man or woman is entirely different from a normal individual; yet we have removed only a very small amount of chemical substance. Man's dominance over woman and his aggressiveness are the result of his peculiar chemistry. Experiments with hens have proved that by injections of testosterone propionate a hen becomes aggressive and pecks all other hens.

Hormones, secretions of the pituitary, thyroid, adrenals, ovaries, testicles, pancreas, thymus, parathyroids and other substances, together with vitamins, food and minerals: this is man; an unfinished product of that vast laboratory that is Nature. His many flaws and defects are irrefutable testimony to his chaotic origin and haphazard evolution. Just as the nature and behavior of a chemical compound can be changed radically by the subtraction, addition or alteration of one single atom, thus can the nature and behavior of man be changed and altered by small chemical or physical changes. Too little or too much oxygen, too little or too much heat, etc., will cause alterations in the delicate and stable, yet unstable equilibrium and will alter his personality and his mind because these are the result of his body chemistry.

Sociologically, man is a community, a colony of cells all alike in certain basic features and needs, and yet very much unlike in their responses to the environment. In the human body we find the highest form of communism, as I have shown elsewhere. Communism works in the body of even the most rugged individualist; in fact, when the cells become individualistic and start growing at the expense of other cells, the most bitter enemy of communism would give anything to stop that ruthless individualism he proclaims as the best thing for society, for cancer inspires terror upon everyone.

This sociological biology has been studied and pointed out by sociologists like Comte, Spencer and Schaffle who have interpreted society in biological terms. It would take too long and it is outside the scope of this book to analyze the arguments pro and con this interpretation of society as a form of biological organism. In my opinion, the analogy is correct in its main points, and sociologists and politicians would do well to study the human body and to use it as a model for society. According to Childs, the human body is the result of a progressive evolution from autocracy to representative government, the cerebral cortex being the seat of government, the council where the most specialized cells receive all communications from the external and the internal world and decide what is to be done. Their decisions are transmitted to other cells through the nerves which can be compared to the telegraph. True, there are many functions that are not under the direction and command of the cortex; many of our actions being reflexes, instincts and trophisms acquired during our long evolution. The basic functions and processes of life like the heart and its beating, digestion and secretions, are independent of the thinking brain, and we become conscious of them only when there is something wrong.

But though the brain cells are of higher status and perform highly specialized or skilled labor than humble connective cells, they do not take more than they need. There is hoarding of food in the body for a rainy day, but when the reserved food is needed it is justly distributed; from each cell according to its capacity and to each cell according to its needs, is the law that governs the human body. We know only too well what happens to the body when some cells begin to grow at the expense of other cells; these gangster cells are a cancer that destroy the body and commit suicide if they are not killed before they do too much damage. Society has such greedy gangster "cells" too. The harmony and the efficiency with which the cells of our body perform their function should be a lesson and an inspiration to everyone and specially to those individuals who in the social organism play the role of brain cells. It is interesting to note that just as the cell had to associate itself with other cells to obtain its highest development, so does man associate himself with other human beings and surrender some of his individual qualities or rights to develop his faculties to the fullest and satisfy many of his essential needs.

Psychologically, man is the sum of his own experience and knowledge of the group in which he is born and grows. His conscious and unconscious behavior is the manifestation of his biological urges, usually and almost necessarily modified and conditioned by culture. Thus culture, which is the result of association of human beings for the satisfaction of their needs, becomes a cause and determines to a great extent the behavior of man and woman.

Biology and sociology have marched along separate paths because sociologists seldom have taken the trouble to study biology and thus become acquainted with the fundamental forces that motivate social and anti-social behavior, and because biologists have not dared to present the human body as a working model for society, which would be too revolutionary. Historians and sociologists have wasted precious time and much paper debating superficialities and ignoring that in the last resort, history is the history of exceptional men with greater vitality and more powerful biological urges than other men, and that society is the result of the dynamic efforts of protoplasm to maintain its chemical, physical, psychological and physiological equilibriums. It is also from these dynamic efforts of protoplasm to maintain its stability that have emerged the four fundamental biological urges or drives that form the basic nature of man and woman and from which flows every human activity. These biological urges are: 1—The will to live, or self-preservation. 2—Hunger. 3—Fear or the search for security. 4—Sex. It can be stated without fear of refutation that whatever human beings do, be it the most altruistic or the most selfish deed, the noblest or the most criminal act, it can be traced directly or indirectly to those biological urges. The same forces that make a saint make another a criminal. An understanding of their mechanism is essential if we want to produce better human beings.

The Biological Man

THE WILL to Live, or Self-Preservation: This is the most fundamental and powerful of all urges; all other biological urges and needs, all the complicated and defensive mechanisms and chemical processes in animals and man have but one purpose: to maintain the stability of protoplasm, that is, to keep living. We eat, not because we like food or because we want to, but because the cells need food from which to obtain chemical substances and energy lost in the process of metabolism. We drink water for the same reason.

The various processes of elimination constantly going on have for object to free the organism from waste and toxic products always being produced. Sex is also subordinated to the same purpose.

Fear or the search for security are equally protective manifestations of the will to live.

Since this is not a book on physiology, I shall not describe the complicated, unnecessarily complex mechanisms by which the human body keeps the stability and equilibrium of the blood and other fluids against the many enemies, internal and external, that continuously are trying to break it down. Death in the last analysis means the breaking down of this equilibrium. It is not surprising then that every living creature, whether existing as a single cell or in an organism, tends to live and to struggle for its life, usually at the cost of other living organisms. Life preys upon life, is a biological fact that has found in man its most senseless, destructive and cruel expression. This will to live is so strong that human beings even existing under most hopeless and adverse circumstances still want to go on living. Of the millions of human beings who suffered incredible tortures and degradation and lived in constant fear of death in the Nazi concentration camps, few committed suicide. They, like millions of other human beings, now and since the beginning of mankind, did cling to life in the faintest hope of deliverance. This fact alone constitutes conclusive and irrefutable proof that Freud was wrong in stating that there are two fundamental instincts in man: Eros and Thanatos. There is no death instinct in man, nor is there a love instinct. True, the wish to die is sometimes felt by human beings and in relatively few cases it becomes strong enough to overcome the will to live; but violence against the self is not instinctive, as it is shown in another chapter.

There is nothing supernatural about the will to live; this instinct of self-preservation is found in all matter, living and non-living, and its law can be stated as follows: every aggregation of matter, organic or inorganic, tends to maintain its physical and chemical equilibrium. A stone, a drop of water, a tree, a crystal and a cell, all try to maintain the stability and structure acquired through millions of years of evolution. If we chip a stone, it will not grow another piece; but a crystal already will grow and repair the damage. A tree manifests the same tendency of the crystal, but with more vigor and ingenuity; it grows new branches if we prune it. A Hydroid, if cut into small pieces, will grow a new animal from each piece.

The basic difference between non-living matter and protoplasm is that the second has achieved an atomic organization characterized by a high metabolism or exchange of products with the environment, which manifests itself in the dynamic and aggressive qualities of living things. Life is a form of fire and is constantly burning up fuel, and like a flame, is both stable and unstable. The stimulus or elements necessary to break down the integrity and stability of an aggregation of matter, be it organic or inorganic, will depend upon several factors, such as: the quality and quantity of the disturbing element and the peculiar characteristics of the object. The marvelous healing power of animals and human beings is but an effort of protoplasm to maintain its chemical and physical equilibrium.

THE BIOLOGICAL MAN

In plants, the will to live is rather simple and manifests itself in a passive and uneventful manner. Rooted to the ground, the plant must get its food from the soil and from the air, or perish. In animals, the will to live becomes already more complex, more dynamic and aggressive, but still lacks the complications and painful situations that obtain in man. The will to live and the fear of losing his life very often sink man into the lower depths, lead him to murder and destruction, and condemn him to slavery and to a most unhappy and miserable existence.

Out of this will to live have emerged the belief. and desire for immortality and the beautiful illusion of an eternal life free from the vicissitudes and suffering of this world. This instinct of self-preservation seems to be the most universal and stable of all instincts because it is not influenced by climate, nor by culture, environment, age or sex. Every human being wants to live and struggles for life with all his energies. Nobody, whether young or old and approaching the end of the journey, wants to leave this "valley of tears". The death instinct of Freud is hardly found anywhere, because it is a myth.

Protoplasm is selfish and aggressive because these qualities are necessary for its survival; consequently, man has also these qualities. It is for this reason that religious reformers have had such a meager success in their fight against selfishness and aggressiveness. The law of self-preservation is the first law of Nature. To the urge for self-preservation and to the search for security in a hostile world can also be traced all the rituals, religious ceremonies, magic, sacrifices, prayers and offerings to the gods, developed by primitive man, which form the basis of our religions. Protoplasm tends to increase and to fill the world; were it not for the many enemies and adverse environment and because, as stated before, life preys upon life, animals would have overfilled the earth long ago. Human beings, having to a great extent eliminated most of their enemies, and having learned to control their environment, are now in possession of favorable conditions for almost unlimited reproduction, and are growing at an alarming rate. Since 1936 the population of the world has increased by 176 millions, while food has not increased in the same proportions.

It has been said that man is a gregarious animal; this gregariousness is the source of much unhappiness and little happiness. Man is gregarious because only in the company of his fellow humans can he carry out the struggle for life with some degree of success; alone he is afraid and deprived of the means to satisfy some of his essential biological needs and his psychological requirements. But in all these thousand of years of gregarious life, man has not yet learned, like the animals, the art of living together without war and with a minimum of friction and discord. Only in the full and friendly co-operation with other human beings can man find full expression to his Will to Live.

Hunger

A well governed appetite is a great part of liberty.

—*Seneca*

People often dig their graves with their teeth.

—*Proverb*

Let good digestion wait on appetite and health on both.

—*Shakespeare*

Many dishes, many diseases.

—*Pliny*

An army marches on its belly.

—*Napoleon*

Eat to live, do not live to eat.

—*Proverb*

Animals feed, man eats. Only the man of intellectual judgment knows how to eat.

—*Savarin*

A full belly makes a happy heart.

—*Spanish Proverb*

Hunger is the great tyrant; so long as man has to fill his stomach he cannot be really free.

Many people think not with their heads, but with their bellies.

Hunger is very often the result of fear.

Hunger in the right proportion clears the brain and sharpens the mind. But in the wrong proportion confuses the brain and dulls the mind.

HUNGER is one of the four biological urges whose satisfaction is essential to life. Every living creature must eat, but only animals and man feel the pangs of hunger, and only man makes a ritual, both religious and gastronomic, of eating. The biology of hunger is simple and fundamentally identical in every organism; every form of life requires fuel and oxygen. In animals hunger acts only in the biological level; the animal eats when hungry, if food is at hand or can be found. There are no tabus, no social or psychological consequences attached to the seeking and eating of food. True, we find in some ani-

mals group-operation in the search for food from which we
can learn much; but animals, with the exception of some species of ants, do not plant nor cultivate food. Man, in his most
primitive stage, was hardly different from animals; he did not
plant and ate when hungry, if he had a meal.

Vegetarians and meat eaters have been debating for some
time about the "natural" diet of man; vegetarians maintaining
that he is frugivorous like his close relatives, the monkeys.
From the observation of the life and habits of primitive and
less primitive people we can state with certainty that the diet
of primitive man consisted of fruits, roots, vegetables and
nuts, supplemented with grubs, bird's eggs, fledglings, grass-
hoppers and lizards.

We do not know when man discovered the use of fire,
nor when he became a hunter, and the name of the man who
made the bow and shot the first arrow was not recorded for
posterity. It is very likely that during the glacial age food became very scarce, and hunger not only forced man to seek new
food supplies but also sharpened his mind; necessity is the
mother of invention. The fact that man was a hunter for many
thousands of years, much longer than he has been an agricul-
turist, and that he throve on a meat diet and that even today
the immense majority of people crave for meat, are too powerful arguments to be brushed aside by mere theories and anatomical technicalities. We have reasons to believe that if man
had had enough game he would never have bent his back to
till the land. Scarcity made food so precious, and ignorance so
difficult to increase its quantity, that man developed magic
ceremonies with which he thought he could increase the fertility of the earth and of animals, and the first fruits were
offered to the gods and the choicest lambs sacrificed upon the
altar. Practically all tribes have one animal whose qualities are
admired and envied; this animal is tabu. It can only be killed
on certain occasions to be eaten ceremoniously by all the members of the tribe. In many cases the king himself is killed and
eaten, believing that with the meat they acquire the strength

and other qualities of the animal and of the king. Out of these primitive banquets evolved the communion of our present religions. So deeply rooted is this superstition that even in this scientific age millions of human beings still believe that by eating a wafer or a crumb of bread they can obtain some of the qualities of their god.

The knights of the Middle Ages painted animals on their shields to symbolize their valor, strength or ability. We find still vestiges of that superstition in the animals adopted as emblems by the nations: the United States of America, the eagle; England, the lion, and so on.

There is no doubt that hunger and the search for food account for much of man's gregariousness and have played a most important part in the development of society. Civilizations have been born, have grown and fallen in the struggle for food. The Egyptian civilization, for instance, centered around the river Nile and the sun because both were essential to fertilize the soil and bring forth an abundant harvest. The great scarcity of food suffered by mankind is also reflected in the classic prayer: "Give us our daily bread", still mumbled by millions of people, who by now ought to be fully aware that no god ever gives bread or anything else to man. To tell millions of hungry and starving people that Jesus did once feed a great multitude by multiplying a few loaves of bread and a few fishes, is a tragic mockery of their hunger and a colossal abuse of their credulity, which does not enhance the reputation of God; if He could work that miracle once, there is no reason why He should not have repeated it, and saved millions of human beings, many of them innocent children, from the tortures and death by starvation. Prayers have never increased food by one grain, nor have they appeased the pangs of hunger, or stopped the destruction of crops by floods, droughts, insects and other adverse elements of Nature.

Many wars have been fought and people have been conquered and enslaved in the struggle for more food, and no doubt, more will be fought. Hunger is the best ally of the tyrant, of the war-maker, of the revolutionary and of the myth-makers. From time immemorial, some people have suffered hunger voluntarily for different reasons; to punish the body for sins, to weaken its passions and biological demands, and to sharpen the mind and the senses. The Prophets of the Bible fasted to get visions of God. Buddha, Jesus and other religious leaders also fasted to purify themselves and to establish communication with God. The discovery that hunger sharpens the mind and stimulates the senses, probably occurred accidentally, perhaps while men were hunting they got lost in the woods, without food. Amazed and pleased by their experience, which they considered supernatural, they repeated it and passed it to other people. Fasting also increases the number of dreams.

It is interesting to note that women never have taken up religious fasting seriously and with the zeal of men. There are biological and physiological reasons for this. Woman is the bearer of children, the guardian of life; we may say, therefore, she must eat regularly because privation of food would not only harm her but also her unborn children and the nursing infant. I have had extensive experience with men and women fasting for health, under my close supervision, and have found that men can fast much longer and with less discomfort than women. I have seen many men fast from one to thirty-five days, and one man up to sixty days in water and lemon juice, and then ten days on fruit juices without any harmful consequences; in fact, their health was greatly improved. Women seldom fasted more than ten or twelve days. Fasting, if properly done, can be a short cut to health and cure many diseases where orthodox medicine has failed. A couple days of hunger once or twice a month will be found beneficial in those cases where there are no contraindications. Religious fasting today does not seem to produce the same mystical experiences of other times. Perhaps the mind is too preoccupied with other problems and science has made some inroads into religious beliefs.

HUNGER

Hunger, as it is to be expected, influences greatly the behavior of men and women, both on the biological and the psychological levels; a well fed man who does not worry about tomorrow's meal behaves very differently than a hungry one. Hunger and the fear of hunger still cast a dark shadow over the world, and millions of hungry people ask themselves: shall I have my daily bread tomorrow? Will my children have anything to eat?

Up to now, hunger has been a common denominator for evil. Let us change that and make hunger a common denominator for good, for peace, for co-operation and prove that this monster that tyrannizes and terrorizes humanity can be slain and buried forever. I believe that Communists are as anxious as Christians to eliminate hunger, because an empty stomach is just as painful to both and equally dangerous to any kind of government.

The importance of good and sufficient food in the maintenance of health has been fully recognized in the last few years and knowledge of nutrition is progressing rapidly. Yet not long ago the importance of diet was a concept alien to orthodox medicine; it was only held by "faddists" and "quacks".

Heretofore, hunger has remained the champion. All magic, prayers, religious ceremonies and wishes for more food have utterly and completely failed. We, of the atomic age, have far stronger magic against hunger than all the medicine and so-called men of God ever had: we have *science*. The application of scientific discoveries on a global scale can transform much of the land into a garden blooming with food and it can neutralize most, if not all, of the enemies of our crops, thus materializing that dream of millions of human beings: to have enough food for today and tomorrow.

Fear, or the Search for Security

Thou shalt fear Jehovah (the Lord) thy God.

—*Deut. 6:13*

The fear of Jehovah (the Lord) is the beginning of wisdom . . .

—*Prov. 9:10*

Fear God, and keep His commandments, for this is the whole duty of man.

—*Ecl. 12:15*

Good men have the fewest fears. He who fears to do wrong has but one great fear; he has a thousand who has overcome it.

—*Bowes*

In morals, what begins in fear usually ends in wickedness; in religion what begins in fear usually ends in fanaticism. Fear, either as a principle or as a motive, is the beginning of all evil.

—*Mrs. Jameson*

No one loves the man whom he fears.

—*Aristotle*

He who fears being conquered is sure of defeat.

—*Napoleon*

Fear nothing but what thine industry may prevent, and be confident of nothing but what fortune cannot defeat; it is no less folly to fear what cannot be avoided than to be secure when there is possibility of preventing.

—*Quarless*

There is great beauty in going through life without anxiety or fear. Half our fears are baseless, and the other half discreditable.

—*Bowee*

Fear is the best ally of the tyrant, of the war-maker and of the high priest.

The right amount of fear at the right time is conducive to health and security. The wrong amount of fear at the wrong time is conducive to illness of body and mind, to insecurity, to slavery and poverty.

Wisdom is the greatest antidote to fear. The wise man is never afraid of anything, not even of death.

Anxiety is fear of having lost or losing psychological security.

Hate is the destructive manifestation of fear and it is found only in human beings.

Worry is chronic fear, very often unfounded, also exclusive of man.

FEAR, OR THE SEARCH FOR SECURITY

F EAR is, without doubt, the oldest and most primitive of all the emotions, being already present in the amoeba. Fear causes the animal to be cautious, to explore its environment, to avoid dangers and obtain security. Consequently, fear had great survival value and still has for the animals, but not for man. Science and civilization have made unnecessary many of the animal fears; but they in turn have created many new fears that not only lack survival value, but are highly destructive and harmful to health and happiness. Like all other emotions, fear is a reaction to external or internal stimulus, characterized by discharges of energy that normally lead the animal to escape danger or to fight it.

The amoeba swimming in the sea, although it has no eyes and no ears, senses danger, shows fear and moves away from danger seeking security. Animals, however, have only one kind of fear: physical fear, and therefore seek only physical security. Lacking imagination, animals cannot create mythical monsters, devils, spirits, gods and other imaginary dangers that frighten man and constantly threaten his security.

Primitive man feared some of the animals that roamed in the forests, but he feared most the unknown and supernatural beings by which he believed was always surrounded. To deal with those supernatural dangers and enemies that lurked everywhere and to allay his fears he evolved a system of magic as impressive as it was ineffective. This magic, with its many and diverse rituals, gave man a certain amount of security, but he never felt completely secure. There was always the feared possibility that the gods would become angry and refuse offerings, sacrifices and prayers and would destroy him of his food supply.

The child is born with two fears only: fear of loud noises, which no doubt suggest some danger besides jarring his sensitive nervous system, unaccustomed as yet to a noisy world, and fear of losing support. All the numerous fears that rob man of health and happiness are acquired. As soon as the child is born his education in fear begins, and he soon learns to be afraid of many things.

Fear is conditioned and influenced by several factors such as: age, sex, climate, disease, health, culture and experience. Infancy, as a rule, has few and unimportant fears. The child may be afraid of his father, afraid of being alone and of animals. Adolescence brings new fears. The boy begins to fear public opinion, and the traditions and tabus of the community, especially the opinion of other boys. The mere thought of being called a coward, yellow and a sissy, frightens him no end, and he is ready to fight at the slightest provocation and even to provoke a fight to prove to himself and to others that he has plenty of courage. Strange as it may seem, it is fear that very often leads men to perform heroic deeds and to risk their lives. Fear of losing face and the esteem of his fellow men is a powerful drive toward valiant acts. Were it not for fear, relatively few men would go to war. The great majority of soldiers when going into battle would throw away their guns and run in the opposite direction of the enemy. But every soldier, on both sides of the battlefield, is afraid that his comrades instead of following his example, will keep on fighting, and is frightened by the consequences of his cowardice. He knows that he will bring disgrace not only upon himself but also upon his family, that he may die an ignominious death, despised by his fellow soldiers and friends.

There is, of course, a limited number of men for whom danger is stimulating and in whom the love of adventure, glory, admiration and economic security are so strong that overweigh all fears and the instinct of self-preservation.

Adulthood and middle age bring again other fears unknown to the child and the boy; worry and anxiety appear in full bloom and with their poisonous emanations kill the beauty and happiness of life. At this point it should be pointed out that there are two main kinds of fear: acute and chronic. Acute fear is a sudden reaction to danger; this reaction, usually defensive, is characterized by certain physiological and psychological processes. There is a greater secretion of adrenalin, a quickening of the metabolism, with greater and faster combustion of fuel and a great increase in the output of energy. These changes produce greater strength and speedier movements; that is why both animals and man can perform feats they are unable to accomplish in ordinary circumstances. The heart is geared to pump the blood faster and oxygenation takes place rapidly. Sometimes, however, these changes go wrong and defeat their own purpose; the animal gets paralyzed with fear and is unable to fight or to run away. Man also suffers similar disabilities in body and mind. The effects of acute fear usually disappear with the elimination of danger. In some cases, however, the shock produced by acute fear may linger for a long time. An acute fear may cause a deep trauma in the unconscious from which a person may suffer for a long time or never recover.

Worry is chronic fear and its effects are destructive to body and mind; worry inhibits the circulation of the blood and the secretions of the endocrine glands; slows and may stop digestion; may cause colitis, gastric ulcers and many other diseases. Worry beclouds the mind and prevents clear thinking just when it is more necessary, thus impeding and even making impossible the solutions of the worrying problems. Worry acts like a microscope, magnifying evils and dangers; creating imaginary monsters that take away the joy of living and make life a sad and miserable burden.

Fear of want leads human beings to hoard food and money to insure economic security; under normal conditions there is nothing wrong with this, but this fear often becomes abnormal and destructive. The pathological symptoms of this fear are extreme selfishness, greed, envy and jealousy that usually grow instead of diminishing with the accumulation of wealth. We often read in the newspapers about men and women dying in poverty and hunger after a life of privations, and leaving great sums of money. We also see many people around us who have great wealth, yet they are stingy to the point of denying themselves many things, and worrying about tomorrow. These miserable rich shall always be poor; they do not have money—money has them. They do not possess things; they are possessed by things. Diogenes living in a barrel was richer than Alexander, and felt more secure than the conqueror.

The reasons for these contradictions and tragic paradoxes of human nature are not hard to find. Such people have never attained psychological security, nor have they achieved mental maturity; usually they lack love and are unable to love because they are burdened with frustrations. These people also crave for power and money, and even if it is hidden it represents a power they are afraid to lose.

There is also the fear of death. Man has not reconciled himself with death, though its inevitability is one of the few sure things in life. Fear of the hereafter also throws a dark shadow upon man's enjoyment of life; the cure for these fears can be found only in science and in a philosophical attitude towards life.

Disease and pain also bring much fear, but much of this fear would vanish or would never appear if man knew more about his body and how to take proper care of it. The art of living has been sadly neglected to the great detriment of our health, and pain and disease are the consequences of our negligence. When disease appears, fear and worry are bad company and will aggravate the ailments. There is the story that death, in the form of Plague, was going to a city and met a man in the road who asked her where she was going. "To kill ten thousand people," answered Death. Some time later, the same person met Death again and said to her: "You told me that you were going to kill only ten thousand people in the city, but you have killed fifty thousand." "Yes," answered Death, "I only killed ten thousand people; the others died from fear."

Fear is one of the strongest pillars of the "status quo" this and the other side of the Iron Curtain; it is the most important ingredient of religion. Without fear man would not kneel and crawl like a worm, either before a mythical God or before other men. He would walk erect, proud of his dignity and of his integrity, happy in his freedom from fear and with a feeling of security only felt so far by a few stoic philosophers, and he would extend his open hand instead of his fist to his fellow men. Fear is part and parcel of governments and dictators; our whole legal system and the administration of justice is based upon fear. For hundreds of years so-called civilized people have used the most cruel, sadistic and painful methods to punish even trivial violations of the laws of the community, even when those laws were unjust and contrary to the real welfare of the individual and of humanity. The failure of those methods is written with blood in the pages of history, and the cries of pain of the victims should haunt the conscience of men and women even today; but understanding and compassion are rare flowers in the human garden.

Goodness and morality induced by fear are of doubtful value, if not useless; the person who is held in restraint by fear of punishment alone, often gets the notion that he can get away with it, and rationalize fear out of his mind. Moreover, the brutal and barbaric methods used in punishing criminals or violators of the laws are degrading and brutalizing, not only to those who suffer the punishment, but also to those who apply it and to the society that condones it.

Hate is derived from fear; we hate what we fear. Hate is absent in animals because they lack reason and imagination. Fear and hate are symptoms of weakness and inferiority; under the influence of hate man plots revenge and destruction of the things he fears. Evil, no matter where it is found, must be combated without hatred, or if we must hate something, let us hate evil itself and not the people who do it. The administration of justice and the protection of the community from anti-social elements make necessary the removal of those elements, but this should be done like the surgeon who cuts a tumor or a diseased organ to save the body, without hating the diseased part. The religious leader usually fears criticism of his beliefs and dogmas and hates those who dare to attack his religion; this fear has caused wars, persecutions and sadistic punishments. It is obviously inconsistent and paradoxically tragic that men who claim to have the truth and God on their side should fear criticism. The fact is that these people feel insecure in the imposing castle of dogmas and beliefs in which they have taken shelter, and have found precarious security; they are afraid that their castle may come tumbling down like the walls of Jericho, but this time at the sound of the critic's trumpet.

Political parties often behave like religious organizations, and frighten and persecute their opponents; there is plenty of political persecution going on in the world; in fact, political persecution has practically replaced religious persecution on both sides of the "Iron Curtain." Dictators, whether political or religious, can rule only by fear, and they seem to have learned nothing from history, whose pages teach that empires and religions based upon fear bring bloodshed and destruction upon slaves and masters.

Where there is fear there cannot be friendship, no love, no peace; suspicion, mistrust and hatred are the poisonous flowers of fear. The destruction of those evil flowers and the conquest of fear are far more important than the conquest of the atom and the invention of gadgets, for those weapons, in the hands of men full of fear and hatred, are more dangerous than a loaded gun in the hand of a child.

Let all men of good will work incessantly and with all their energies for the elimination of fear, for as our late President Roosevelt said: "We have nothing to fear but fear itself."

The Sex Life of Man

Sex is like fire. People who do not know how to handle it usually get burned.

Sex can be beautiful or ugly; beneficial or harmful. It can bring happiness or pain and sorrow.

Many people confuse ignorance with innocence.

Sex is hunger in reverse.

True morality can never be the product of ignorance and hypocrisy.

EVERY human being is an act of sex; this obvious fact was not always so obvious. There was a time when the relation of sex to procreation was not clear and pleasurable, and romantic love did not form part of it: the biological act was merely a physiological function and its performance was not very different from the animal level. As human life grew more complex and complicated the sexual act became surrounded by tabus and superstitions so strong and so deeply rooted that they prevented, until recently, the scientific study of sex and its relation to human behavior.

It is within the memory of this generation that scientists and other investigators have been able to study the problems and phenomena of sex without risking their freedom or/and their lives. But despite the enormous amount of literature about sex, there is still a great deal of confusion and misunderstanding not only among laymen, which would be reasonable, but among so-called experts as well. In order to understand clearly the nature of sex and its normal and abnormal manifestations and to find a satisfactory solution to the many and pressing problems created by this biological urge that conflicts with our concept of morality, we must discard all preconceived notions and beliefs and cast overboard all the theological and religious explanations of sex and useless ballast.

We have been taught—and it is still a part of our education
—that sex was created for the exclusive purpose of procreation, and that its use for pleasure alone is a most wicked viola-
tion of the "Natural law" and a sinful practice punished by
God. We are also taught, and we have laws to enforce the
teaching, that sexual relations outside of the connubial cham-
ber are immoral. To the biologist all these dogmas, religious
tabus and morality are superstitions produced by ignorance and
imagination.

Sex in human beings can be defined as a powerful attraction between two members of the opposite sex, the urge to
get together in a coital embrace. It can be said that sex is hunger in reverse, because it is satisfied by elimination instead of
assimilation. This sex urge is the result of the specific function
and activity of the gonads; no gonads, no sex problems and no
immorality. But who wants this easy solution?

No clear and adequate understanding of sex can be obtained without at least a brief and elementary review of its
genesis and evolution, both biological and social. Human beings are colonies of cells, billions of them, living together,
working together harmoniously for the good of each and for
the good of the community. Here is communism at its best;
each cell performs its function, no matter how important or
unimportant, and takes from the blood stream the necessary
nourishment to live and do its work, and no more. But there
was a time when there were no such multicellular organisms;
each cell wandered alone in the primeval seas, as many still do.

A single living cell living by itself grows until it attains
a critical size and divides into two; now we have two completely new cells. This division goes on forever: here we
have immortality. Disease and old age and natural death are
unknown to the single cell; each new division brings youth and
rejuvenation. This division of the cell is procreation and reproduction in its most simple terms by which human beings
grow and reproduce themselves. Can anyone seriously affirm
that the cell divides in two because it wants to procreate more

cells, to perpetuate the race? Or that the "will of the species" drives the cell to reproduction? There are still many people who believe this, but they should not be taken seriously. Modern biology has shown the complete fallacy of their claims.

The growth, division and functions of the cell, whether swimming alone in the sea or bathed by the blood and lymph in the human body, are determined by physical and chemical laws. Sir D'Arcy Wentworth Thompson in his masterly work: *On Growth and Form,* and C. M. Childs in his no less important book: *Physiological Foundations of Behavior* give us a scientific explanation of the physical, physiological and chemical processes of the cell and of the organism, and have laid down for good the ghosts of vitalism and teleology.

Just as the cell divides in two, so do animals grow and procreate. When cats, dogs or any other animals get together sexually, we can be sure that they do not copulate because they want puppies or kittens to prevent the extinction of their respective race. Neither do they cohabit for pleasure because throughout the animal world coitus is rather a painful and uncomfortable affair, to judge by the reactions of the animals and the manner in which it is done. Animals get together sexually because they are attracted to each other by a powerful force they cannot resist. Man is not an exception. Few women, and less men, give any thought to procreation and to the continuation and perpetuation of the race when the sex urge is most pressing and strong, in that period that follows the onset of puberty. To understand the nature and origin of this mighty sexual attraction we must examine the evolution of man and woman.

When did the cells get together in colonies? Many millions of years ago. Why did the cells become gregarious and form colonies that eventually would lead to the appearance of human beings? Although there are still a few pieces missing to complete this jig-saw puzzle, we can assume with certainty that the cells did not get together at the command of a supernatural power ordering them to "Grow and multiply yourselves." There is no doubt that physical and chemical factors in a favorable environment must have brought to life the first community of living things; at first the relations between cells were weak and rather disjointed. We can still study such primitive relations in cellular colonies like the Volvox. Evolution has left sign-posts along its path, and this enables us to trace its march, sometimes backward, its mistakes and its triumphs. Gradually, in some cellular colonies, the cells became more independent of each other, and their relations grew more intimate. Some cells, cut off from the external environment, developed new functions, thus initiating specialization and division of labor; others took up digestion, others the transmission of sensation, others motion, and so on. But when the cells got together and formed higher organisms, they surrendered their immortality: the organism as a whole could no longer divide in two like each of the cells was able to do before.

Many lower organisms still possess such strong powers of regeneration that if cut in pieces, each piece will grow into a new animal; others will grow only a new tail. In human beings most of the tissues have lost their capacity for regeneration or have it in a very limited range. The more specialized the cell, the less its power of regeneration and growth if injured, or in normal conditions. The grey matter is the most highly specialized tissue in the human body, and it never regenerates itself nor does it grow like the skin if it is damaged. The same thing happens with other specialized tissues, like the heart, the lungs, etc.

There is one type of cell, however, that has retained the original quality of its primeval ancestors. More than that; it seems that this cell has become the repository of the conquests and acquired characteristics of the organism. The germ cell is still immortal and can reproduce the whole organism if given a chance. Weismann has called this the continuity of the germ plasm in which the individual is a link in the long chain of life.

There is no sex in the amoeba or single cell, but with the association of cells into colonies, sex came into existence. Thus from asexual cells, the two sexes, male and female, were born. There is evidence that this division of the cells into male and female was the result of nutritional and anatomical differences within the cellular colony. Thompson and Geddes in *The Evolution of Sex* make a very interesting analysis of these differences and show how the two sexes emerged from asexual cells. In some animals and plants, male and female cells have remained together; consequently these fortunate (?) animals or plants have no sex troubles, no difficulty in finding the right mate, no marriage and divorce laws to contend with. The male cell lives right next door to the female cell, and does not have to wander around chasing her, struggling and fighting to conquer and to keep her. It seems like an ideal arrangement, and I do not see why Nature did not stick to this simple and so very convenient "love" matching, and had to complicate matters by separating them so far apart. When the germ cells mature, they get together, thus closing one life cycle and starting another. In the higher animals the sex cells became separated into two different organisms, and ever since this separation they have been longing and looking for each other. Herein lies the cause and the reason for the powerful sex attraction that like a magnet attracts the male and the female together.

There are two fundamental processes in protoplasm: Anabolism and Catabolism. Anabolism means assimilation, building up and conservation of energy. This is the passive principle. Catabolism means breaking down, expending energy. This is the destructive process, the aggressive and active principle. The male cell has retained the catabolic qualities and therefore is aggressive and active. The female cell has retained the anabolic qualities of protoplasm; therefore it is conservative and passive. The egg stays in one place, the Fallopian tubes or the uterus waiting patiently for a visitor that may never come: the sperm. The variations exhibited by individuals do not alter this principle, and are the result of biological confusion during the formation of the fetus which produce a mix-up in the secondary sexual characteristics.

The gonads produce two kinds of secretions; one goes into the blood: it gives man and woman their masculine or feminine characteristics. This secretion of the testicles makes man more muscular, more hairy; gives hardness to his bones and muscles, a heavier voice; makes him more aggressive and also gives him certain mental qualities, like creative imagination and greater critical and analytical faculties. To woman the ovaries give wider hips, larger breasts, softer muscles and flesh, hairless body, softer voice, maternal instinct and mental and emotional qualities different from man. In woman the ovaries act as brakes and prevent the appearance of masculine characteristics. Many women develop some masculine qualities after the menopause, or when some glandular disturbance interferes with ovarian secretion. Physically and mentally woman retains most of the qualities of childhood, like small hands and feet, baby-like face, smooth and soft flesh and round arms and shoulders. These qualities are sought and admired by men.

The other function of the ovaries is the production of the eggs, and of the testicles the production of the sperm; and of course they partake of the anabolic and catabolic qualities already described. If the egg is not fertilized, it is eliminated without fuss or disturbance. The sperms, however, are not so easily satisfied with this uneventful dismissal; they are highly disturbing to the organism, and for this reason the body tries to get rid of them quickly. It can be said that sperms are quite toxic and sometimes produce a kind of madness that leads men to commit all sort of brutal acts, from rape to murder. After heavy petting, for instance, if man does not discharge the sperm, he feels very nervous and irritable, and his testicles are swollen and painful. For this reason men possess a specific desire for coitus from the onset of puberty, while women usually do not. The young girl wants to be caressed, kissed and embraced, but the specific desire for coitus is absent. This

[68]

great difference in the sexual needs causes much misunderstanding and trouble between man and woman. Sometimes no
petting is necessary; a touch, the scent, the sight of a woman's
clothing, specially underclothing, or even the shoes, can become a fetish with powerful stimulating qualities that will
fire the imagination and speed up the activity of the gonads.
Under these circumstances man looks, often frantically, for an
outlet for his sperms.

Woman may not even produce an egg, no matter how
much she pets, so she withstands the sexual pressure much
better, while man is tormented by millions of sperms fighting,
struggling to get out of the body, like convicts trying to get
out of prison. A woman is naturally and usually a desired
outlet and inlet for the sperms, but if pressed hard, man is not
too particular; masturbation, pederasty coitus with any female
at hand, old or young, pretty or ugly, black or white and even
with animals will do. It is a well known fact that when women
are absent, men indulge easily in any of those abnormal and
vicarious satisfactions of the sex hunger. The facility with
which men will indulge in those abnormal practices will depend primarily upon the strength of sexual urge, and secon-
darily upon the power of the moral brakes and self control of
the individual. These facts are evidence that the primary function of the sex urge is not procreation nor pleasure, but the
elimination of a disturbing and irritating element.

This picture of man is not pretty and probably will shock
and disappoint women; but it should help to understand the
promiscuous and "immoral" behavior of men and to deal with
it in more effective ways than just closing the eyes ostrich-like
or exorcising it as the moralists do. Nothing is to be gained by
becoming cynical nor by passing laws; the only remedy that
will prove effective is scientific education as discussed in another chapter.

The sexual behavior of man is determined by several factors. One is heredity. By this I mean that man is born with
a vital and sexual quantity which is the result of the genes

which in turn determines the glandular potency. Herein is the reason for the great differences that exist in the strength of the sex urge in man and woman, ranging from the very weak and practically absent to the very powerful and irresistible that often leads men to risk life, freedom and position in the community. The Kinsey report illustrates this point with two typical cases. One man was capable of having sexual intercourse thirty times a week for thirty years, while another man had only one coitus in the same period of time. There are men who at eighty or ninety years of age are potent and able to procreate children, while others are finished at fifty. Other factors that to some extent modify sex urge are: education, climate, disease, profession or work and early training or environment.

Although sexual hunger is usually called love, both stand at opposite poles. Basically, sex is aggressive, selfish, possessive and even cruel; coitus itself is primarily an act of aggression and of violence, not of love. Man likes to rape woman and he does just that, in his imagination at least, even when the woman yields willingly and lovingly. Resistance on the part of the woman acts upon man as a stimulant, as an excitant. The sperms move in solid phalanges like millions of soldiers storming a citadel, and charge toward the entrance of the uterus with as much courage and fury as the famous charge of the Light Brigade and with just the same fatal results, for most of them die in the charge.

Man acts in a similar way, charging against the sanctuary of Venus, phallus in hand. If the door is closed or narrow, so much the better; he will attack with greater fury and strength. Man and woman repeat in the macrocosmic scale the drama and the struggle of the microscopic world. Virginity is sought and valued by man because it gives him primacy of possession, and also because it means a narrow vagina and the promise of greater resistance to the entrance of the phallus and also a test to his manhood.

"Omni homo post coitus est triste." This Latin aphorism

that all men feel sad after coitus has gained wide acceptance
and it has some truth in it. Men feel sad and disappointed
after coitus, in some cases, but others feel exhilarated and
supremely happy. What are the reasons for this contradictory
and varied emotional feelings? Since sex is a form of hunger,
and coitus is the food that satisfies it, man may feel after
coitus like after having eaten a heavy meal or having eaten
food he should not have touched. In these conditions, food
becomes repulsive and a sense of guilt preys upon the mind.

Religion in general and Christianity in particular have
hammered this sense of sin and guilt upon man and woman to
such an extent that both have lost much capacity for the coital
pleasure and the enjoyment of life. Woman has suffered more
extensively than man; up to the nineteenth century woman was
forced to hide sexual pleasure because if she did not she was
branded as a lascivious, perverted and immoral creature: a
harlot. This stupid attitude toward sex has made woman more
frigid and irresponsive to sexual stimulation. When man no-
tices this frigidity, it detracts more or less from his pleasure.
"Civilized" man wants and needs to feel that his partner in
pleasure is all his and her thrill of joy and the orgasm will
make coitus a more pleasurable experience. Moreover, coitus
with its seminal discharge, eases the tension and brings a state
of relaxation and emptiness bordering on sadness.

There is also a philosophical aspect of coitus; coitus
means life and death at the same time. The union of man and
woman is to a great extent like the merging of the sperm and
the egg into one being: both cells die to create a new individual. Here are the biological reasons for that anxiety, longing
and deep desire that man and woman feel to become one, to
grasp each other in an eternal and unbreakable embrace, to
cease being one individual separate from the rest, to vanish
into nothingness, to die in each other's arms. And here, too, is
the biological spring from which flow all the songs, all the
music and all those beautiful and endearing words of "love".
And from this spring flow also the bitter waters of sorrow

and frustration, the tears that often water the weeds of cynicism and hate, of neurosis and escape into the world of unreality.

In animals, coitus is only a physical experience to get it over with, and in many men it is no more than that. But with the appearance of consciousness and imagination, coitus has acquired a new meaning; it is more than two bodies embracing each other in a spasm of physical pleasure; it is, at least for those whose senses are capable of receiving higher and finer vibrations, the embracing and merging into one of two "souls", of two persons. In this complete union of man and woman, there is a physical and a "spiritual" orgasm, brilliant and powerful like lightning, for which there is no substitute. Let the mystics rave and rant about their union with God; they have only an ersatz orgasm in their mystical coitus. Although coitus primarily has nothing to do with love nor with pleasure, and it is the opposite of both, it can, every time that it is performed, be like a link in a growing chain of love and the supreme pleasure.

So powerful is this hunger for coitus, that men often abandon family, throw away honor and position and risk even death to experience just one orgasm in the arms of the woman desired; for in the arms of the wanted woman, men can dream the most beautiful dreams and forget all the troubles of life; in those arms every function of the body seems to be in a state of suspended animation, and man is afraid to wake up, to find himself again alone against the world, to lose those soft and warm arms that hold him like steel chains. Time seems both to stand still, and to speed with the velocity of light, for in those few moments one lives an eternity.

Coitus has greater biological and psychological importance and meaning for woman than for man. To man, coitus is in many cases the elimination of a disturbing substance, with some pleasure thrown in, or the satisfaction of a passing fancy, or a conquest and a feather in his hat. In man, the libido is specifically located in the genital organs, while in woman it is more diffused throughout the body; consequently, man feels the specific urge to perform the coitus as soon as his phallus becomes capable of doing that.

Tumescence in man is under the control of the autonomous nervous system and cannot have an erection at will. With age comes a decrease of the glandular secretions, and with this a partial or a total loss of the power that hardens the phallus and thus makes coitus impossible. This fact gives a complete rebuttal to the popular notion that man can abuse his sexual power and pay heavily for such abuse. Man cannot really abuse his sexual power because, as I have pointed out, tumescence of the phallus is not under his will; therefore, he either has the power and substance to perform coitus or he does not have it. In the first place, it means that the body can afford to expend that energy; in the second place, it means that the body cannot afford that luxury, and all the wishing and trying will not change the situation. This mechanism is a great mistake of Nature. Think of the many hours and years of pleasure and happiness that are lost to man and woman because of this inefficient and wasteful mechanism. A better planned and more efficient organism would have conscious control of the production and expenditure of the germinal substance and would be able to perform coitus at will without wasting that substance. Thus man and woman would be able to enjoy coitus without that fear of pregnancy that often steals much pleasure from it, especially from the woman. All over Nature the germinal substance is squandered and wasted in a most reckless manner.

This brings up the problem of birth control. Every human being should be properly instructed on the art of preventing procreation while enjoying sexual intercourse. Every child ought to be a wanted child; there are too many unwanted children in the world. Those who oppose birth control in the name of God and of "Natural law" are inconsistent impostors and dispensers of metaphysical humbug. What proofs have they that God condemns birth control? Absolutely none. And why should God punish man for killing just one more sperm and egg when man throws away from two to five hundred millions of sperms in just one ejaculation? Man is capable of several ejaculations a week and often has them involuntarily while sleeping. Woman has a potentiality of from fifty to seventy thousand eggs and from puberty to menopause lays one egg every month, except when pregnant. It is obvious that God could not have punished Onan for refusing to procreate and wasting his seed—it has been done for thousands of years.

Faced with a growing rebellion against unsound and anti-biological morals and with the increasing demand for birth control, some religionists have grasped a physiological phenomenon as a convenient escape from their blind alley: the rhythm theory. Since woman only lays one egg a month, and this egg does not tarry long in the Fallopian tubes or the uterus, it follows that there must be a period in which there is no egg to be fertilized and consequently woman is sterile. Thus man and woman have only to consult the calendar and cohabit during the sterile period, about one week or ten days before and after menstruation. This method is not contrary to "Natural" or divine law, the moralists affirm. Firstly, there is ample evidence that this safe period is not as safe as they want us to believe; I have seen many a young woman pay very dearly for trusting the "safe" period. Moreover, I see no difference in destroying the sperms by placing them in a vagina we know is sterile and where they will die or to kill them with some chemical or mechanical device. I am sure it makes no difference to the sperms, and in both cases it is deliberate "murder". Men and women have the unalienable right to control the size of their family, and neither the state nor the church have authority to interfere in their procreative activities.

There is also the popular belief, fathered by early ignorant explorers and evil-minded missionaries, that the savage is very sensual, and possesses a very strong sex urge. A more careful investigation of the nature and behavior of the savage has shown the fallacy of this belief; the fact is that the savage has a rather weak sexuality and his sex urge is more periodic than in modern man. His religious dances and sexual orgies gave a wrong impression to white men and have different purposes than were thought at first. These purposes are: (a) to promote the fertility of the soil; (b) to express joy and thanks for some beneficial event and also to discharge pent-up tensions and energy; (c) to produce the necessary tumescence for the performance of the sexual act. "Civilized" man can attain tumescence with the greatest of ease; a woman's touch, scent, a picture of the stimulus of his own imagination are enough to produce the necessary anatomical and physiological conditions for coitus, but primitive man requires stronger stimulus.

This hypersensitivity and power of imagination of "civilized" man is without doubt the result of the ever-growing struggle for life that places enormous stress and strain upon our nervous system, and also of the blocking of the normal manifestations of the sex urge by tabus, laws and moral commands. This speedy tumescence is not always an asset; in fact, sometimes it is a liability. There are many men who have a quick erection and a quicker ejaculation, with consequent shortening of pleasure. This is more distressing, disappointing and harmful to man because a woman takes much longer to reach tumescence and achieve orgasm. Thus when a man obtains a rapid ejaculation, the woman is left unsatisfied; this condition often causes much unhappiness and trouble to married people, and a man should do everything possible to correct it, for his own and for his wife's sake. The causes of this impotence are physiological and/or psychological; it is prevalent around middle age when man is approaching or going through the climacteric as the glands, after having reached the peak of their activity, begin to decline.

Living together for many years is usually fatal to romance and to sex stimulation; nagging, quarrels and irritations, frustrations and disappointments take their toll, and throw water upon the fire. Man no longer gets excited by her touch; no longer thrilled by her kisses, by her voice and even by her scent, as he was in the days of courtship and honeymoon. No doubt women go through the same conditions, but they suffer with more resignation because of their nature. Man and woman behave somewhat like a battery that becomes neutral or dead; this polarization may never happen, or it may come slowly or fast, but it is like a wall of ice that grows between the two once passionate lovers until they sleep in the same bed without feeling the slightest thrill, but rather, experiencing a feeling of disgust and repulsion.

Man is frightened by this creeping impotence and feels lonely and deserted; he wants to prove to himself that he has not lost his virility, and hungers for the sexual thrill of his youth, so he goes out after other women, if he possibly can. Many men have confided to me that while they may have a quick ejaculation with their wives or are completely impotent, they are potent with another woman, and can hold off their ejaculation for a longer period. There are also physiological factors. Some women possess a chemical reaction much stronger and exciting than others that stimulate the weakening gonads and vigorize the waning libido. Woman must, if she loves her husband and wants to keep him, try very hard to prevent this condition, by remaining alluring, attractive and exciting, and by avoiding nagging and quarreling. For the physiological impotence of the middle aged man much can be done today; cold and hot sitz-baths are stimulating and tonifying. Testosterone, either orally or intramuscularly, is about the most effective treatment; sine wave may also prove beneficial in holding up the sagging foundations of virility.

Let us now inquire into the moral and ethical aspects of sex. It is only too obvious that religious morality is a colossal fraud and that secular laws have failed to make man and woman monogamous, to prevent adultery and to keep human beings chaste. The law can prevent man from having two legal wives, it can deprive him of divorce, but it cannot prevent him from having a mistress or from committing adultery with a prostitute. Wherever divorce is available, both man and woman will use it in growing numbers.

Sexual relations between man and woman are a private affair, and neither the state nor the church have the right to interfere, unless such relations bring children into the world, or do in any way or manner harm the community or some other person. If a man wishes to have more than one wife and can afford this luxury, and finds women willing to share his affections and his home, that is his business. The same thing goes for women, theoretically, because in practice it is far more difficult on account of child-bearing. It is the duty of the state to see that children do not suffer on account of the sexual relations of the parents and that nobody's freedom and welfare is injured. To deny that polygamy exists today is to close the eyes to reality. There is a great need for the formulation of a new ethical code in harmony with the biological needs of man and woman, and not with the arbitrary whims of some ascetics who had an abnormal and perverted idea of sex; mankind has too long suffered under these religious fanatics.

The ethics of the sexual act are simple and relatively easy to keep and their observation would avoid much suffering and bring undreamed happiness. These are the ethics of the sexual act: 1—The sexual act must never infringe upon the freedom and integrity of the individual; 2—It must be freely and consciously desired by both partners; 3—The sexual act must bring pleasure to both parties; 4—The sexual act must not be harmful nor bring injurious consequences; 5—The sexual act must never bring unwanted children into the world.

There is nothing shameful, nothing dirty, nothing immoral in the methods of preparation and consummation of the sexual act, if these methods are pleasurable to man and woman. Whether the act has been preceded or not by legal or religious sanctions should not make the least difference, for there is only one sanction that makes it "holy"—love, or its next substitute—a mutual desire for one another. Man and woman have the right to use the sexual act merely as a temporary pleasure to which no strings are attached, no emotional entanglements; or they can make it a sacrament, a love offering that merges them physically and "spiritually", not only for the moment, but for a long time. Sexual relations must cease being a source of sorrow, hatred, tears, and unwanted children. Animals are doing a better job of sex than intelligent human beings because the female dictates the when and how of the sexual act, and since it cannot be raped or bought or talked into submission, they have no sex problems to contend with, outside of finding and winning a mate. Since man and woman, for good or bad, have lost their protecting instincts, they must fill the vacuum with knowledge of the best ways and techniques to get the maximum of pleasure and happiness from sex. Let man and woman be guided by wisdom and rejoice in their freedom.

The Psychological Man

Psychology is physiology above the collar button.
—Dr. Martin H. Fischer

The human mind cannot create anything. It produces nothing until after having been fertilized by experience and meditation; its acquisitions are the germs of its productions.
—Buffon

The more accurately we search into the human mind, the stronger traces we find everywhere of the wisdom of Him who made it.
—Seneca

A weak mind is like a microscope, which magnifies trifling things, but cannot receive great ones.
—Hood

What is mind? No matter. What is matter? Never mind. What is the soul? It is immaterial.
—Burke

There is no mind. There are minds, that is, reactions and responses to external and internal stimulus.

Nobody has ever seen a mind without a body. But anyone can see many a body without a mind.

The mind may be immaterial, but it certainly is the product of a material organism.

Man is born without mind. Here is the hope and the task of education.

The soul may cover our ignorance and please our vanity, but it does not explain the mystery of life nor its purpose; it merely complicates things.

As the soil, however rich it may be, cannot be productive without cultivation, so the mind without culture can never produce good fruit.

The mind is the sum of knowledge and experience of the individual at a particular time, influenced and conditioned by several factors such as age, sex, health and disease.

There is nothing in the mind that has not entered through the senses.

Mind over matter? Or is it matter over mind? One thing is sure: there is matter without mind but not mind without matter.

[79]

W E ARE slowly and laboriously emerging from the dark ages when the mind was considered an activity of the soul and therefore apart and superior to the body. Animals were deprived of souls by the growing egotism and vanity of man, who claimed the soul and the mind as the exclusive gifts of God. Mental disorders were believed to be the work of the devil or evil spirits, or witches' spells, and the treatment of mental diseases was as barbarous as it was ineffective. Exorcisms, witchcraft, prayers, amulets, beatings, tortures, imprisonment in filthy dungeons and burning at the stake were applied with much zeal and little or no success. Theoretically, we have progressed beyond that barbarian stage, but in practice our mentally sick do not receive much better treatment.

Modern psychology and biology have administered a fatal blow to those superstitions and have shown that the mind is the product of the body in general and of the brain and the nervous system in particular. The new word, psychosomatic, from Psyche, mind, and soma, the body, expresses the intimate relation and unity of body and mind. There is no longer doubt that the mind is the product of heredity and environment; which is the most important is the subject of a dispute that has been raging for some time between those who uphold the dominance of heredity and those who maintain that environment is more important. The scientists of the Soviet Union are just now attacking vigorously the Mendelian laws of heredity, asserting that contrary to the consensus of biologists, environment does affect the germ plasm and that acquired characteristics can be transmitted to the offspring, as Lamarck taught. This is not the place to carry on this debate, but a clarification of this problem is essential to the correct understanding of man; consequently I shall analyze briefly the situation.

The first thing to bear in mind is that all the qualities and complicated mechanism of the cell, genes and chromosomes are the result and product of a dynamic substance, protoplasm, acting and reacting and adapting itself to a changing environment. Secondly, we must assume that neither the environment nor protoplasm of today are the same as they were a billion or more years ago when the cell was emerging as the result of a long chemical evolution into the bit of organized protoplasm that it is today. At that time, protoplasm was in what the chemists call nascent stage, that is, a period in which a substance is being formed and acquiring stable properties. The division of labor and the specialization of the cell, that made possible higher organisms including man, was also the result of reaction and adaptation to a new environment created by the aggregation of cells into colonies or multicellular organisms. From the new relations between the cells and the new positions in regard to each other and to the external environment emerged differences in metabolism and function that became fixed and stable, so long as the internal environment in which they developed and lived remained chemically and anatomically constant and identical to the original.

Biologists have proven with experiments that by transplanting cells from their normal position to another part of the organism in the very early stages of the fetus, they can change the course and development of those cells; but once differentiation of the cells has appeared, the characteristics of those cells are fixed and determined for a lifetime and changing their environment does not change their characteristics any more. The enormous differences and diversity in mental capacity, attitudes and creative ability found in men born and brought up in the very same environment, from the same parents and having the same teachers, is ample evidence that the culture of the group is not everything and that the germ cells have acquired certain qualities that although needing a favorable environment for its blooming, are not the product of it. This is what we call heredity. All the study and the best teachers in the world cannot make a person intelligent, nor make a genius out of the average individual, no more than a change of environment can change a connective tissue cell into a neuron. Thousands of children are studying music and pounding the piano, but how many of them equal a Beethoven, a Mozart, or any other genius, not only in music, but in literature or art? Very few or none.

What combination of genes or what other ingredients lift a man out of an ordinary family into the sky and make him shine like a radiant star? The answer to this important and challenging question has to wait for the future; but already in animals and in primitive men we can observe leadership and variations in mentality. Thus, although the experiments of Müller and other biologists seem to show that the germ plasm is not affected by diet, environment and other factors, it must be affected by something, and there are, no doubt, protoplasms able to store the experience of the group and project that experience with a force and brilliance that astonish their fellow men. Is it, perhaps, mutations produced by cosmic rays, which in turn produce a greater sensitivity and activity of brain? The study of the effects of the atomic explosion in Nagasaki has shown that under the same conditions individuals are differently affected by radiation. The psychological man cannot be properly understood, nor evaluated or wisely directed, unless we get well acquainted with the structure and development of the brain and the nervous system which are composed of billions of the most complex and specialized cells found anywhere, and make man an individual with the widest range of behavior, from the saint to the criminal. It makes possible men like Francis of Assisi and Torquemada, Lincoln and Hitler, Beethoven and ordinary musicians.

It is the fore brain or the new brain that sets man apart from the rest of the animals and makes him lord and master of animals much stronger than himself; it is in this enormous and practically unexplored jungle, with its fifteen billions of cells, where the alchemy of his dreams, artistic creations, love, inventions, spiritual and mystical longings take shape and sometimes become a reality or are mistaken for reality; through this jungle, hatred, envy, greed, jealousy and other destructive emotions blow like a hurricane from the hypothalamus and put out, at least temporarily, the tiny candle of reason, plunging man into the darkness, sinking him lower than the beasts he despises and making his life miserable and tragic. Damage or removal of some of those microscopic cells rob man of his God-like attributes and can alter his personality, as shown by cranial surgery.

Nature is beautiful and awe-inspiring, even in its most angry moods, but man is ugly and horrible when he indulges in his tantrums of anger and violence. Since the new brain, with its critical, analytical and restraining power is a new-comer, its marvelous and unique faculties are too often undeveloped or easily drowned by the emotions and instincts of the animal brain. It is in this exclusive duality of man that lie the basis and causes for the titanic struggle that has been raging within him since religious reformers, ascetics and priests, long in good intentions but very short in biology, tried to make a god out of him, and branded as evil some of his most deeply-rooted and primeval instincts. The complete defeat of the god-men and of their herculean attempts to crush the Flesh are discussed elsewhere in this book. Yet, man must exercise control and direction of his biological instinct if he would live in peace and friendship with his fellow humans.

The foundations and structure of the Psychological Man are laid down with the union of the two germ cells, usually in the Fallopian tubes, and become reality in the grown-up man. When the genes and chromosomes of the male and female cell embrace themselves like long lost brothers, several physiological, anatomical and psychological qualities and characteristics such as the color of the skin, of the eyes, of the hair, stature, facial features, mental capacity, creative ability, imagination, sexual potency, longevity and, of course, sex, are determined usually for life. It is all too obvious then, that those who claim that the stars and the planets, in combination with the time of birth, determine the character and qualities of man, are either ignoramuses or charlatans who exploit the ignorance and credulity and cosmic vanity of people.

Thus the child is born with all the raw material for the formation of the mind; but just as the sleeping Princess needed the kiss of the Prince Charming to awaken her to life, so the neurons need the kiss of external stimulations. The ego or personality is formed under the impact of the environment. At birth the neurons are like a virgin forest, a jungle without pathways; the impressions and stimulus that constantly come from the outside elicit responses and discharges of energy, and the flow of this energy is what opens pathways through this jungle, thus beginning the formation of habits, traits, patterns and peculiarities that make up man an individual different from every other man. Since protoplasm is very plastic at birth, the child learns quickly, habits are formed, the first lines of the psychological man are traced. Energy will travel easily along the pathways opened and formed in those early years; that is why it is so difficult, if not impossible, to eradicate many habits and peculiarities, both physical and psychological, acquired in infancy. Long before modern psychology discovered this, the Jesuits realized that whomsoever had the education of the child could claim his loyalty for the rest of his life. "Give me the child until he is seven years old, and then you may have him," they say. People born Catholic or Moslem stay with that faith and die in it. After more than three hundred years of Catholic propaganda, education and domination, the Indians of South America still cling to their old religion, and though they pay lip service to Christianity, they are pagans at heart. The activities of missionaries in China, India and other countries have failed to win an appreciable number of people, even with the glowing promises of spiritual and material benefits; of course, there is always a minority that gets "converted" or become atheists, but the great majority stays within the walls erected by tradition and absorbed with their breast milk.

What, if any, are the mental differences between man and woman? Is man mentally superior to woman? This is really a hot question. No answer would be wholly acceptable and agreeable to all concerned, nor would it be completely true. It does not matter. I am bound to tell the truth as I see it in the light of biology and of accomplishments in the artistic and intellectual field. There is no doubt that the mind of man possesses some qualities lacking or found rarely or in meager quantity in the mind of woman; there are biological and physiological causes for these differences since the mind derives its properties from the brain, from the nervous system, from the endocrine glands in general and from the gonads in particular.

I would say that creative imagination and analytical power are two outstanding qualities found in man that are absent or scarce in woman. The history of religion, art, music, poetry, painting, sculpture, literature and politics, gives us ample proof of that statement. It cannot be said that women did not have the opportunity to create, and that opportunity has been greater in the last couple of hundred years. It seems that the secretion of the testicles acts like a catalyzer or spark on the brain of man, fires his imagination and drives him to create or to conquer. If the testicles are removed from man in his childhood, he will develop some feminine characteristics and will lack the imagination and aggressiveness which are his birthright as a male. Castration in animals has the same well known effects. Experiments with hens have shown that injections of testosterone propionate, the male hormone, will make a hen more aggressive and make her the leader of the flock. Moreover, in woman her energies are usually directed towards the creation and care of the child which is just as important or more, than anything the artist may create. Menstruation, pregnancy, nursing (though this is becoming a lost art, unfortunately for mother and child) and menopause are physiological functions from which man is free, and that affect powerfully the mind of woman, producing limitations over which she has no control. Therefore, women must not feel inferior, only different and with different functions to perform in our society.

It can be stated that man is more cosmic and universal in his thinking; his mind, like the sperm and like himself, is a wanderer, the explorer ever restless, ever seeking the beginning and an end of the universe and the causes of the phenomena he perceives. The mind of a woman, like the egg and herself, is more passive, usually centered around the home and the children, as it should be. Her womb is the center of her universe, and every physiological and even psychological function revolves around the uterus and its capacity to shelter and nourish the expected guest who may never arrive; but whether the guest arrives or not, it does not change the psychological characteristics of woman.

Man often leaves his wife and his children to fight and sometimes die for an ideal in some remote corner of the globe. Very few women do that, fortunately; her children and her home come first. History records the martyrdom of many men who rebelled against tyranny, of men who created worldwide religions and who "saw" God; very few women can lay claim to these things. It is a curious fact that even the classic cradle songs and lullabys have been composed not by a woman rocking the cradle, but by men. Contrary to popular belief, man is emotionally more unstable than woman; consequently he is more often neurotic and maladjusted. In order to cover his own instability and amorous fickleness, he has invented the myth that it is woman who is fickle; his tantrums and outbursts of violence make hysterical women seem insignificant. Man is more beset and tormented by contradictions, seldom finding the necessary and desired balance; he is the revolutionist, the rebel fighting for freedom and the tyrant who destroys liberty and grinds his fellow men into the dust of slavery. Man is the high priest, the creator of religions, rituals and ceremonies, the weaver of complicated and voluminous theological treatises, the maker of icons; he is also the iconoclast, the skeptic to whom nothing is sacred, and like Prometheus, challenges

the gods. Man is the mystic who preaches chastity and proclaims the union with God as the highest pleasure and the only
goal of life; he is also the most lascivious creature on the face
of the earth. Man is the ascetic who abhors pleasure as a sin
and tortures his body; he is also the sybarite, the gourmet, the
glutton ever seeking new pleasures, unconcerned with the price
he may have to pay. Man is the most selfish and greedy and
proud and the most unselfish and meekest of all animals. Man
is ever restless in search of adventure, exploring the earth, the
depths of the sea and the vastness of the space, or the hermit
who can live on a pillar or in a cave for many years. Man is
the boldest and most fearless animal and the most servile, the
greatest coward who trembles with fear before danger, real or
imaginary. All these contradictions, and perhaps others, are the
product of his biological and physiological structure and of the
culture in which he lives.

Woman is the stabilizer, the patient and understanding
mate, the mother of his children, ever ready to listen to his
troubles or his achievements and to encourage him in his creative labors, to console him with praise when he feels discour-
aged, to soothe his violent depressive moods, to keep a home
for him. Behind every great man there is usually a loving and
understanding woman or the vision of a woman who, though
unattainable, represents an ideal from which he derives inspiration and courage.

If the theory that the mind is the product of the body is
correct, the mind must be influenced and conditioned, among
other things, by the physiological changes brought by age. That
this is the case can be easily ascertained by a brief analysis of
the different psychological patterns and wide variations, and in
the power and quality of the mind at different ages. For the
purpose of this analysis, we can divide man into five major
ages: Infancy, Adolescence, Youth, Menopause and Senility.

INFANCY: This is the formative age of the mind, when
habits are traced, beliefs rooted into the unconscious and pat-

terns of behavior crystallized. At this age the mind is avid for sounds and pictures; it is the age of assimilation and integration. Information about the world keeps coming to the brain at a very fast pace, so fast that often the infant cannot digest and catalogue it, with consequent confusions and totally or partially wrong evaluations being formed, thus creating future maladjustments and conflicts, both with the ego and with the outside world. Here is where the wise guidance of the parents is so necessary to aid the child in establishing correct evaluations and proper relations with the self and with the environment. Gradually the ego is hammered into shape by the constant stream of impressions entering the brain by the five doors that are the senses, and by the reactions and discharges of energy which follow, in answer to the stimulus.

Infancy is the age of wonder and discovery when the trivial and the prosaic for the adult is new and marvelous for the child. It is then that the infant begins to explore his body in general and his genitals in particular; the difference between the I and the others is established slowly and through experience. There is nothing supernatural about the formation of the I, as supernaturalists claim. Adults are prone to think that all is clover for the infant, but a careful analysis will show that growing, both physiologically and psychologically, does not come easy, without tensions and hard work, sometimes painful. The child has to learn to walk and to talk and must obtain control of many muscles for which he spends his time kicking and making frantic and sometimes funny efforts.

Infancy is the age of imitation because the child learns by imitating his parents or guardians, or other children with whom he comes in contact. There is a good amount of awe in the child as his eyes roam around his immediate world and sees people, giants to him, moving around in a hurry, talking in loud and strange voices, laughing, crying, fighting and loving. He tries to understand all these things, but is not equipped for this difficult task; neither is he equipped to distinguish between good and evil, between moral and immoral, and right and wrong. Man is born without the slightest notion of sin and morality; for him, like for all other animals, life has only one yardstick to measure right and wrong. Whatever is beneficial for him and aids to satisfy his needs and to survive is good, right and moral. Whatever is harmful for him and endangers his security is evil, immoral and wrong. Animals live by this rule instinctively and defend themselves as best as they can. Man must learn the ethics and morals of the group in which he is born and lives and adapts himself to them.

I cannot pass the opportunity to point out how odd of God that man be born without the slightest sense of guilt or sin, and this must be drilled into him with great effort. The formation of conscience also begins in early childhood; this is one of the most delicate and far-reaching psychological processes and very often is arrested or detoured, thus preventing conscience from attaining a robust and healthy life. In the great majority of individuals, conscience leads a rather rachitic and anemic existence, fighting against great odds. A man with a strong and exacting conscience finds it very difficult to get rich, and since our present civilization, especially the American, measures success in terms of dollars, boats, houses and other material assets, the temptation to silence or ignoring the voice of conscience is mighty powerful; the result is that many people lead a double life. Outwardly they pay lip service to the moral and ethical code of the community of which conscience is the mentor and guardian; they go to church, give to charity, even becoming great philanthropists. But in their business, conscience is usually silenced with rationalizations like this: business is business; if I don't do it, the other fellow will or does it; my children and my wife come first and they must have the best, regardless of methods and moral price. In other words, the end justifies the means, as the Jesuits so well have taught and practiced, otherwise how could they have accumulated the immense wealth they possess? The result of this behavior is disastrous, both for the individual and for society.

The exuberance and enormous energy of the child is often

annoying to parents and to adults around him. Astronomers tell us that the universe is expanding and this expansion seems to be how the galaxies and universe are formed. This expanding process is also a basic characteristic of protoplasm. The cell is a universe and the child is a galaxy with billions of cells growing and expanding rapidly; when the two cells get together, they seem to release an enormous amount of energy and the cells multiply with amazing speed: that is why the child wants to grow faster. He looks with envy toward his parents, and wants to be big like them in a hurry. Therefore, he indulges in wishful thinking, in day-dreaming and fantasies in which he fulfills his wishes; his high metabolism is greatly responsible for this great mental and physical activity, because it produces enormous quantities of energy. The child can be compared to a transformer loaded with high voltage electricity; this energy is under great pressure and must be expended and discharged, or tensions will develop and grow to the breaking point. That is why the child is active, ever doing something; he tears things, breaks objects, pulls the tail of the dog or the cat, and does many other mischievous things. Psychiatrists usually give wrong interpretations to this destructiveness, investing it with a psychological meaning it does not have. The causes are, usually, physiological. In these violent activities and strong reactions, the child uses his surplus energy thus relieving tensions, exercises his muscles, tests his strength, seeks attention and asserts his personality. It is therefore wrong and harmful to suppress these discharges of energy; they must be encouraged and directed into harmless or constructive channels, but never stopped.

Strong and powerful attachments to persons, to words, to ideas, to things and beliefs are formed during infancy; fixations that may last for life also take place. Since the brain is getting organized and the mind is in its formative stage, higher reasoning, critical and analytical functions are still far away; consequently, the thoughts of the child are concerned only with the satisfaction of his physiological needs and with gathering information about his environment. The hypothalamus, or animal brain, plays a dominant role in the child, that is why emotions flow violently and unrestrainedly. No attempt can be made at first to control them, and it will be many years, if ever, before these emotions are mastered. This is one of the great tragedies; so many men grow up, never learn to direct and control their emotions, and to make them their servants, instead of being their slave.

Imagination begins to appear, and like a fledgling trying to leave its nest, takes short flights; later this imagination will soar to the confines of the cosmos and weave beautiful dreams and illusions, or crawl in the gutter, scheming and knaving under the influence of the belly. Curiosity appears in the infant as soon as he opens his eyes because it is closely related to security. From Amoeba up, every animal explores and gets acquainted with his immediate surroundings, to avoid danger and enemies. Infancy should be a very happy age, free from frustrations, fears and bitterness. It should prepare the child for adulthood by fortifying him to face reality and withstand the fierce passions and emotions that the increasing activity of the gonads will bring upon him.

ADOLESCENCE: Adolescence is ushered by the progressive formation of the personality and by the growing activity of the glands. The child is on the threshold of manhood; he becomes more and more aware of his own self in general, and of his sex in particular; he begins to feel attracted toward girls. Primitive man sensed the great importance of the psychological and physiological changes that bring the child into manhood, and took the boy away from the mother to live with the men of the clan; he believed that Nature needed help to make a man out of the child, and for this purpose he developed certain initiation ceremonies which he thought would usher the boy into full manhood. These ceremonies still survive among "civilized" people: the Christians have confirmation and the Jews have no less impressive ritual to receive the boy as a man.

[91]

Strange as it may seem, the increasing awareness of sex differences and the growing activity of the gonads, produce a negative attraction toward the opposite sex; the boy withdraws or tends to withdraw from the girls, just as primitive boys do and seek the company of other boys. The main reason for this peculiar behavior is fear: primitive man was afraid of woman for reasons already discussed in another chapter. The man and the boy of the twentieth century have not changed much in this respect, and they feel both attracted and repelled by woman; they sense some danger in woman and try to avoid it. There is another ingredient to this fear. Since woman has been branded as the weaker sex, forced into slavery and menial tasks, the boy, as he becomes conscious of his manhood, feels too proud and too shy to be seen with girls; he is afraid that his friends will call him a sissy; therefore, to hide his feminine leanings, he becomes more aggressive, rough and tough than he is in reality. He believes, in common with men, that these are the attributes of manhood, the mark of masculinity: man must be hard, brutal and even cruel; tenderness, humility and crying are alright in women, but very unbecoming to man; therefore he plays rough and hard, fights easily because the mere thought of being called yellow and a coward frightens him more than the possibility of getting a beating and even killed. He must show that he is strong and courageous, and not afraid of anything or anybody, for he wants above all to win the respect and admiration of other boys and men, and girls too. Loyalties to the group or gang and to the country are formed and strong friendships are forged. Loyalties to the gang can be so strong as to overcome loyalties to the home; a boy is expected not to tell anything about the gang; thus the ties with the family begin to get thinner and weaker. The adolescent gets wanderlust and dreams of far-away places, and like the young bird, wants to leave the nest; he also begins to think about his future and his work. As for the infant, time goes slow for the adolescent; he is in a hurry to grow up and be a man, not realizing that before long he will wish to push back the hand of time.

The onset of puberty and its immediate post-period are also characterized by more intense religious activity—it is the age of conversion; mysticism flares up with visions of angels, fairies, virgins, witches and other mythical creatures accepted by the culture in which the boy or girl lives. We have no record, however, of any adolescent who has claimed of seeing God. The reason for this interesting phenomenon is not hard to find; the adolescent has not yet formed a complete picture of God, and the sketches he has received are too austere, too severe and confusing for his mind. Playful fairies, angels and virgins are visions more in harmony with his mind. To the adolescent, these visions are very real, so real that often he succeeded in convincing adults of their reality. The visions and voices of Joan of Arc and apparitions of the Virgin of Lourdes are typical; there is not the slightest doubt that Joan of Arc and the other adolescents saw virgins and angels, but these were products of their own imagination. Consider these facts; no virgin or angels have ever appeared to the non-Christian people who really need apparitions to convince them, because the mind cannot create images that have not come through the senses; no recognized apparition of angels, virgins, witches, etc., has occurred in the United States of America and neither in the rest of the world since the development and use of photography and modern means of communications; the latest apparition of the virgin took place in one of the most backward countries, Portugal.

If we examine the case of Joan of Arc we shall find further arguments against the supernaturalism of apparitions, for if we accept that the voices and visions of Joan were real, then we must admit that God behaves very much like a farmer who burned the barn to roast his pig. Why should God select a simple maiden to unleash a bloody war between two Christian people merely to place upon the throne a moronic scoundrel who no sooner was crowned than he was betraying his savior?

More yet, fighting with the pure Maiden of Orleans was the infamous Giles de Rais who was found guilty of murdering nearly a couple hundred children; then when she needed the voices and visions, she lost them and was burned at the stake by the same church that had pronounced her a child of God, and later, realizing the blunder, made her a saint to please the outraged Frenchmen.

The brain of the adolescent is not yet capable of higher thinking, but the analytical faculties are already being organized and dawning. Play is the main concern and interest of the adolescent because it provides the easiest outlet for his surplus energy, both physically and mentally. Most boys like to play with guns because of the feeling of power and omnipotence these weapons give them, and for the same reason they identify themselves with Superman and other mythical entities for whom there is no impossible feat. This intense desire to escape from reality has been the subject of much discussion since Freud placed it for the first time under the microscope. For Freud and for the psychoanalysts who followed in his footsteps, escapism is the result of the Pleasure Principle, that is, human beings are mainly concerned with Pleasure and try to avoid unpleasant things. This explanation is not supported by facts; I will go further and say that it is contradicted by facts.

Escapism is a universal phenomenon already found in the Amoeba; yet the Amoeba is incapable of pleasure. Escape in the Amoeba is purely a psycho-chemical reaction to a disturbed environment. As the organisms grow more and more complex, all their functions also grow more complex and the means of escape, so limited in the uni-cellular creatures, become more adaptive and nearly conscious, but only in man do they reach full consciousness. The Pleasure Principle, however, is a myth, a hypothesis invented by Freud to explain phenomena that can be better explained by the rational interpretation of biological facts. When faced by danger, practically all animals try to escape; man is no exception. Do they want to escape because they seek pleasure? Not at all. They want to escape because it is the line of least resistance, the easiest way out of a situation that involves danger and from which they do not know how they will come out. Escape, then, is an instinctive reaction, which, of course, can be modified by several factors, but it has nothing to do with pleasure; in fact, pleasure is hardly known to animals because it is the product of consciousness. Animals seek satisfaction of their needs and security, but not pleasure. Only man seeks pleasure—and not always. Man seeks primarily the satisfaction of his biological needs, but in satisfying some of those needs he finds pleasure, at least sometimes. Eating and sex have developed into the two main pleasures, but originally had nothing to do with pleasure. Because of his creative imagination, escapism has acquired in man qualities, methods and mechanisms so amazing, so contradictory and so harmful that even men like Freud have been led astray.

YOUTH: Bernard Shaw has somewhat truthfully said: "Youth is wasted on young people." Who has not said to himself many a time: If I could only be young again with the experience that I have now! Youth has vitality, strength, energy to spare, optimism, faith and opportunity to choose its own destiny to some extent; but youth lacks the wisdom because this has to be bought at a very high price—years of bitter disappointment. Youth is like a traveler standing on a beautiful valley; his vision of the road he has to travel is hidden by the mountains that he has to climb, while the older man has already crossed the peaks and looks down upon the road and the country he has traveled, and he sees the detours and blind alleys he mistook for smooth and straight roads that have made his journey hard and painful, and perhaps a failure. He sees how he could have traveled the royal and beautiful Road of Life.

Youth is too sure of itself, too optimistic about its own powers and abilities to listen to the voice of experience, for the simple reason that Youth is hungry for experience, for conditions and situations in which it can try its strength. The analytical and critical faculties of the mind begin to unfold and usually reach their peak during youth.

Youth is the age of rebellion against established authority and the age of conquest. Man sets out to conquer the world in general and woman in particular, only to be conquered by her. Sexual hunger, disguised with the colors of romantic love, blooms like a flower whose first sips of its nectar are sweet and intoxicating—but only too often bitter gall is hidden at the bottom of its chalice. It is not my intention to be cynical, nor to deny love; there is such a thing as pure and unselfish love, but as stated in other chapters, what passes for love in the majority of the cases, is nothing but sexual hunger. Marriage and the creation of the family, a career or profession, are serious tasks which Youth takes in its stride and sometimes carries to a successful stage.

MENOPAUSE: Most men still believe that menopause is exclusively associated with the stop of the menstrual flow and therefore it happens only to women; but more and more men are becoming aware that the male is not immune from the physiological changes brought on by advancing age. When man approaches the half-century mark, the sun of life hangs over the horizon, and though it may take still a few years before it sets completely and darkness descends upon the individual, the heat and radiance of youth are gone forever.

Sexual potency, so greatly valued by man and woman, begins to decline and with the diminishing activity of the glands in general, and of the gonads in particular, the mind also begins to lose some of its vigor and boldness. Man becomes more conservative, and even reactionary, and more than ever seeks power, political, religious and/or economic. It is interesting to note that practically all dictators come to power around the onset or during the menopausal period. This is not mere coincidence. Young people seldom wish to wield great power or to become dictators; they are too interested in making "love", building a home, starting a family and bursting with energy and sex potency. The man around the menopause begins to feel the appearance of impotency; he feels the fire of youth cooling, and though his desires are just as strong or more so than ever, his phallus no longer responds to his wishes with the promptness and vigor of yore. Therefore, to make up for his sexual weakness and to hide his inferiority, he seeks money and political power as never before; he may become ruthless and cruel as a result of his impotency and his frustrations. For the same reasons the menopausal man may become a mystic seeking in God power by proxy because by identifying himself with God, who, in his belief, is the source of all power, he elevates himself to a superior plane and shares, vicariously, of God's power. There is no doubt that the same forces that operate in the mystic also operate and move the political dictator, and the results can be harmful and destructive in both cases, for the individual and for mankind.

In man, like in woman, the climacteric is characterized by greater irritability, nervousness and emotional instability. Hot flashes and sudden sweats, followed by chills, are likely to occur. Men who in their youth were rather careless about their appearance, become self-conscious and consult the mirror more often, trying to hold on to their vanishing youth. The man of the twentieth century, however, has within his reach a vast amount of knowledge of nutrition, hygienic care of the body, vitamins, and other things that can tide him up over the rough road. He also has testosterone propionate, the male hormone, without doubt the most effective lift for his menopausal doldrums.

On the other hand there are reasons to believe that primitive and less primitive man glided over the menopause more easily. With the complexity of "civilization" and the growing sensitivity of the brain and of the nervous system, man's sexuality has become more acute and its changes more noticeable.

The menopausal man, like the menopausal woman, deserves more care, kindness and understanding than they usually receive.

SENILITY: As man approaches the biblical mark of three score and ten, he witnesses with sorrow, and often with despair, the rapidly increasing ravages time inflicts daily upon his body and mind. I invite those who speak so enthusiastically and praiseworthily about the wisdom of God and Nature to contemplate for a moment an old man or woman and to tell me frankly and honestly if they see any wisdom in a plan that brings man to such pitiable and tragic condition. Here we have a man who not so many years ago was handsome, strong, daring and bold, physically and mentally; a man whose thinking powers challenged every problem and probably solved many. He had women at his feet, and his dreams soared to the stars. Now, look at him; he is full of wrinkles, shrivelled, weak, dried up and wilted like a flower left in the sun. His hearing is partially or totally impaired and his eyes find it hard to see what is going on around him, even with the aid of glasses. He is plagued by pains and aches; his mind has lost its vigor and analytical faculties, and behaves very much like a child. Nothing can stop the deterioration of his brain and a form of involution takes place. The cells lose their elasticity and shrink, and his glands, tired and depleted, no longer pour into the blood stream those vitalizing and vigorizing secretions which fired his body and his imagination. Like a ship wrecked and battered by the angry sea of life and thrown upon the shore with a last wave of contempt to disintegrate there, thus lies man in his last years upon the earth. Is this the masterpiece we are told God created in his own image? This most wretched piece of work is a credit to nobody, much less to an intelligent and powerful creator.

I hear pious people say: It is not God's fault; man has brought all this upon himself by sinning against his body and soul; by disobeying God and Natural Laws. Come, come, gentlemen. Let us be honest and quit evading the issue. In the first place, man's body, for all its complicated and wonderful mechanisms and marvelous structure, is an imperfect and ill-made machine full of faults and flaws. The great physicist Helmholtz once said that if someone would bring him a human eye, he would return it as very poor workmanship; the same thing could be said of the other organs and of the body as a whole. Even the most holy men and those who claim to know how to live and take care of their bodies, get old, wrinkled and weak. Animals, whether domestic or living in their natural environment, also get old and suffer the disabilities of old age. Moreover, the "Creator" sends man into this world incapable and ignorant of taking proper care of his body, and the people who assume that responsibility very often are also ignorant. Is it fair then to blame man for things over which he has no control? It is true that a few men reach an advanced age with fairly strong mental faculties and a body in good physical condition, but they do not escape the ravages of time, neither mentally nor physically.

Although this picture of senility is very dark, it has a few bright spots. I believe that man and woman can grow old gracefully, free from bitterness and frustrations and relatively free from disease and ailments. The man who has led a happy and useful life grows old like the weary traveler who has had a wonderful and exciting journey; he is tired, but pleasantly tired; his mind is well stocked with sweet memories, and his life is like a vast canvas on which, with his deeds, he has painted a beautiful picture, for he has made his life a work of art, admired by his fellow men. Now that Father Kronos has curtailed his activities, he can sit down and closing his eyes, he can relive again some of the past exciting moments or years. Death has no terrors for him, and he is ready to fall into that sleep from which nobody awakens.

I cannot think of more appropriate words to express my

sentiments and to close this chapter, than the last lines of *Thanaptosis*:

> So live that when thy summons come to join
> the innumerable caravan, which moves
> To that mysterious realm where each shall take
> His chamber in the silent halls of death,
> Thou go not, like the quarry-slave at night
> Scourged to his dungeon, but sustained and soothed
> By an unfaltering trust, approach thy grave
> Like one who wraps the drapery of his couch
> About him, and lies down to pleasant dreams.

Man and Marriage

And Jehovah (the Lord) said: It is not good that man should be alone; I will make him an helpmeet for him.

And the Lord God caused a deep sleep to fall upon Adam and he slept; and he took one of his ribs, and closed up the flesh instead thereof;

And the rib, which the Lord God had taken from man made he a woman, and brought her unto man.

—Genesis

For this cause shall man leave his father and mother, and shall cleave to his wife; and the two shall become one flesh. So that they are no more two, but one flesh.

—Matthew

What therefore God hath joined together let no man put asunder.

—Matthew

A man finds himself seven years older the day after his marriage.

—Bacon

God has set the type of marriage everywhere throughout the creation. Every creature seeks its perfection in another. The very heavens and earth picture it to us.

—Martin Luther

Marriage has a biological basis, and would be far more often a success if its biology were generally understood and the knowledge acted upon.

—J. B. Haldane

Marriage is a very sea of calls and claims, which but little to do with love.

—Ibsen

Marriage is the bloom or blight of all men's happiness.

—Lord Byron

It is better to marry than to burn.

Wives, be in subjection unto your husbands, as unto the Lord.

—St. Paul

Marriage always demands the greater understanding of the art of insincerity possible between two human beings.

—Vicki Baum

[101]

MAN IN NATURE AND BEHAVIOR

There is nothing a man of good sense dreads in a wife so much as her having more sense than himself.

—Fielding

To continue love in marriage is a science.

—Mme. Reyband

The keys to a man's heart are words of praise and food well served.

—B. E. R. Turner

One of the most prolific causes of the breaking up of marriage is indigestion.

(I'll agree to that if indigestion is given a broader meaning.)

—Bishop Dover

Men dream in courtship, but in wedlock they awake.

—Pope

Marriage is one long conversation chequered by disputes.

—Robert L. Stevenson

Marriage is the Keeley cure for love's intoxication.

—Helen Rowland

Married in haste, we repent at leisure.

—Congreve

The wise woman will reform her prospective husband before she marries him. After that there is no hope.

—Anita Dawson

Love, like ice cream, is a beautiful thing, but nobody should regard it as adequate provision for a long journey.

—Robertson Davis

Marriage with a good woman is harbor in the tempest of life; with a bad woman, it is a tempest in a harbor.

—J. P. Senn

Marriages are made in heaven.

(Perhaps that is why so many marriages are so ill made and last such a short time.)

—Anonymous

Men marry to make an end; woman to make a beginning.

—A. Dupuy

Marriage is, today, the green light to heaven or to hell. More often to the second.

Getting married is like sailing in a boat called Love, with oars made of Good Intentions; but the two sailors know little or nothing about navigation; therefore the boat, battered by the Winds of Passion very often is wrecked on the rocks of Ignorance, Selfishness and Misunderstanding.

Marriage is slavery that can be sweeter than freedom.

Marriage means one thing to woman and another to man; when they find this out there is trouble for both.

Marriage is the key to the pantry given to two hungry people who unfortunately cannot distinguish between sex hunger and love. A bad case of indigestion usually follows.

Marriage can be and should be the beginning of a beautiful friendship. Marriage is a contract from which each of the contracting parties expects to get more than each puts in.

Marriage usually is poison to romantic love.

Marriage should be the art of living together. But so far in most cases it is limited not even to the art—but to the common routine— of bedding **together**.

I HAVE quoted extensively from different authors, and have added a few definitions of my own to show how diverse and contradictory are the opinions about marriage. There is one point, however, in which everyone will agree; that marriage is very ill with many grave ailments, and that a lasting and happy marriage is a rare flower. Divorces are increasing, leaving behind a trail of wrecked homes and broken hearts, bitterness and suffering. This breakdown of marriage presents a serious problem to our civil and religious society. We may as well realize that this problem cannot be solved ostrich-like by illegalizing divorce and forcing two human beings to live together "till death do us part"; nor by good intentions and wishful thinking. A scientific analysis of marriage, its meaning, its enemies and forces that bring man and woman before the magistrate or the priest, is imperative for a correct diagnosis and treatment.

What is marriage? Is it a "sacrament" instituted by God, as the religionists claim? Is it true that "What God hath joined together let no man put asunder"? What is the real purpose of marriage? Procreation? The formation of a home and family? The satisfaction of the sexual urge?

If the hypothesis of the divine institution of marriage were true, we should expect God to have given man and woman the necessary intelligence and freedom to choose the right mate, for without this intelligence and freedom to choose the right partner, marriage for life is a most cruel joke perpetrated upon helpless human beings by an alleged All-Powerful, All-Knowing and All-Loving God. This may sound blasphemous and irreverent, but it is true, and the sooner we face reality, no matter how unpleasant, the better it will be for marriage and for society.

Think for a moment of the millions of human beings who have been forced to go through life chained by the bonds of marriage, living under the same roof, perhaps sleeping in the same bed, yet hating each other; the woman suffering brutalities and degradation because of this weird superstition that one cannot put "asunder" what another human being has joined together, and that a mistake or error of judgment in choosing a mate cannot be corrected. And what about the millions of human beings who have never been informed that marriage is a "sacrament", and have not been married by a Catholic priest, or any kind of priest for that matter, and therefore must live in adultery and sin?

Leaving aside this metaphysical nonsense, let us examine marriage as a human institution in the light of modern knowledge. No clear and complete understanding of marriage is possible without at least an elementary review of the sociological and biological factors that bring man and woman together to form a home and raise a family. When anthropologists began the study of primitive tribes, these already possessed the rudiments of a culture that placed them above the really savage level. Nonetheless, those tribes have given us invaluable knowledge concerning the origin and development of our society in general and of marriage in particular. From these investigations have emerged several facts about marriage; this institution is unknown among primitive people, and in its stead there is a period of unorganized gregarious life—the horde. The wife (usually there is more than one) is obtained by capture from another tribe or horde. This exogamy is practiced whenever possible. There is no priest or magistrate to sanctify or legalize the "marriage", nor are there courts to grant a divorce. Man can repudiate his "wife" at will, reduce her to a secondary role and take another woman; nobody has been informed that marriage is a "sacrament" and that polygamy and divorce are contrary to "natural" or divine laws; evidently God must have been busy with other matters.

Gradually the horde grows larger and under the impact of changing economic conditions and means of obtaining food, relations between man and woman also change. There is group marriage; in many tribes a man marrying a woman also marries all her sisters and vice versa, thus appears polyandry. Men live in separate houses and occupy themselves mostly in hunting, while women do all the work. Since primitive man is unaware of the part he plays in the procreation of the child, this belongs to the mother and she gives him her name; this, in combination with the appearance of the rudiments of agriculture, brings forth matriarchy and raises the woman, in many tribes at least, at the head of the family, and even to Olympus. The Goddess of the Corn and the Goddess of the Rice are much older than Jehovah and all the other gods, because primitive man identifies the fertility of the earth with the fertility of the woman.

As the tribe and the complexity of relations between human beings grow, tabus that regulated behavior appear and also grow. Every act is regulated by some kind of tabu, either based in some superstition produced by fear, ignorance and imagination, or in some experience of the individual and/or the group. Thus tabus are either completely foolish and irrational, or are mixed with wisdom. Tabus about marriage are primarily concerned with the protection of property, including the wife who is considered a chattel. Marriage by barter in which the wife is bought or exchanged, appears whenever and wherever marriage by capture is no longer possible; if a man has no money and nothing else to give in exchange for a wife, he can sell his services to his father-in-law for a period of time. The Old Testament offers examples of this.

Polygamy and monogamy have nothing to do with morals, nor with religion; both are a question of economics. If a man can afford more than one wife he has more than one. The Patriarchs of the Old Testament are all polygamous and God seems very pleased about it; nowhere in the Old Testament is found a condemnation of polygamy. Jealousy is unknown and virginity has no value whatsoever. Romantic love is still very far away. It is quite a bitter irony for religion, but prostitution appears first as religious prostitution; in Babylon every woman had to go to the temple and there offer herself to the first stranger she met, at least once in her life. Herodotus says that "nearly all people, except the Egyptians and the Greeks, have intercourse with women in sacred places";[1] but he was wrong because Greece and Egypt also had sacred prostitution, and the Greek courtesans were the direct successors of the sacred hierodules. Even in Rome prostitutes were honored.

Even after the tribe has grown into a city, sexual hunger still plays a rather insignificant part in marriage because a man can satisfy his sexual hunger without marrying and because that sex urge is not too strong yet. Why do men marry them? Man is a gregarious animal, and like animals he has a mating instinct: man needs a kind of shelter, a place to hold his possessions, a home. He needs some one to work for him and serve him, to give him children and raise them; but he does not marry for love nor for sexual enjoyment. For this the Greeks had the Hetaira or Courtesan, and the Romans followed in their footsteps.

We are told that Christianity was a form of New Deal for men and women, that it swept away the vice and corruption of the pagans, that ended polygamy, imposed monogamy, and thus did away with adultery and with prostitution. It is true that Christianity raised to the heavens the value of virginity and chastity, making them the most precious virtues; so

---

[1] Herodotus, *Corpus Inscriptionum Semiticarum*, vol. I, page 86.

much so that marriage was at first opposed by the Christian leaders and later was tolerated because they realized it could not be eliminated completely. Men and women insisted on marrying, despite the high and great reward offered to virgins of both sexes; most people seem to have thought that a pleasure here was better than a hundred in heaven.

St. Paul, with the typical casuistry that was to follow and engulf Christianity, proposed a compromise to compensate for the loss of virginity, stating that: "It is better to marry than to burn." In other words, it is better to satisfy sexual hunger after man and woman have been blessed by the priest, than to commit adultery and go to hell. There is no doubt that many Christians made honest, sincere and vigorous efforts to live up to the demands of their ascetic leaders; but virginity and chastity, and even monogamy, are usually harsh and often impossible demands upon the body. It was not long before, while preaching virginity, chastity and monogamy and condemning adultery as a most grave sin, that the pagans seemed virtuous beside the Christians; instead of the Hetaira or the concubines, the Christian man had the mistress or the paramour, one or more, depending on the financial means and the sexual potency. This corruption reached up to the Chair of St. Peter (?). For the poor, who could not afford to keep a mistress in proper style, there was always the brothel and the street walker of whom there was such an abundance that no man, no matter how poor, need go without his good share of sexual pleasure, especially if he was fairly young and handsome.

Christianity made marriage respectable and sanctified, only in theory. Polygamy did not exist, only in theory too; monogamy was praised as an essential Christian virtue, but which few men observed. Matrimony became binding and indissoluble for life for man and woman, in theory again; in reality matrimony was binding only upon the wife. The honor and the sanctity of marriage were loaded upon the fragile yet strong shoulders of the wife, who must be virtuous and above suspicion. Stripped of all its religious tinsel, this meant slavery, sexual and economic slavery for life, often to a selfish, brutal and cruel "lord and master." Man could run around and have as many love affairs as he could, not only without soiling, but enhancing his honor. The wife had become the repository of his honor; this situation still prevails to a great extent in Catholic countries, like Spain, Portugal and most South American republics, where the man who can afford a mistress and does not have one, is an exception and is looked down with scorn and a kind of pity by his fellow males; he is not "muy hombre" nor "muy macho", that is, he is not very manly nor male enough—in other words, he is a sissy. For these people, manliness resides in the genitals and in their potency and not in the cerebral cortex, nor in the use of intelligence in human relations.

Marriage in the higher level is still, to a great extent, a business transaction in which prospective partners have very little or nothing to say; the parents of the bride and of the bridegroom usually arrange the marriage, sometimes while the future husband and wife are still in diapers, for business and economic reasons. Love and happiness of the prospective partners are completely ignored. The motives of marriage are: a dowry, to get rid of an unwanted female, to unite two families, property and money, everything but love. In the lower level, although marriage transactions are not conducted with the same amount of etiquette and red tape, the motives and methods are about the same; parents have been and still are very reluctant, if not altogether opposed, to concede that their children have a right to live their own lives and to choose their own life partner.

The United States is a paradise for woman. Here she has obtained freedom, economic and political, dignity and equality, seldom equalled; here she refuses to accept the other woman and to share her husband with her. But man's nature is not different here, and since he is generally polygamous, the number of divorces is alarming and appalling; yet divorce alone is

not an index to the failure of marriage, as I have shown elsewhere. There are many marriages that although they hit the
rocks long ago, are kept afloat because the partners cannot or
do not want to break up the home for one or more reasons, such
as children, religious scruples, etc. If we take this into consideration, as we must, then the number of happy marriages that
have weathered the storms and tribulations of living together
is very small indeed.

What are the causes of this enormous number of failures
of what is supposed to be a "holy sacrament" instituted by
God and upon which His (?) ministers bestow their blessings?
Many and varied are the answers given to this vital question
by psychologists, psychiatrists, priests and marriage experts;
many also are the cures offered by them, many of which are at
best palliatives or worthless nostrums. Firstly, we must recognize that monogamy is an ideal state, a utopia seldom fully
and completely achieved. Polygamy is the rule throughout Nature, and man is not an exception. From sixty to seventy per
cent of divorces can be traced to sexual causes. Secondly, mismating is a most common occurrence, even when man and woman are allowed to choose their mate; both are too emotionally immature and too much under the influence of sexuality to
be wise and objective in selecting a mate, and they too often
confuse sex hunger with love, as shown in another chapter.
Moreover, living together for a long period of time demands
and requires patience, understanding, tolerance and self-
control, qualities usually lacking totally or partially in the
majority of human beings.

There are two kinds of sexual mismating, the general or
natural, and the particular or specific. By natural mismating I
mean the great differences in the sexual urge and in its manifestations in man and woman, and by particular sexual mismating we must understand the individual variations, idiosyn-
crasies and requirements to which both mates must adjust
themselves. We can best solve these problems by making a
careful analysis of men. For the purpose of marriage we can

divide men in three broad categories: 1—Men who are or can be monogamous with little or no effort at all; these men have a weak sex urge and their monogamous tendency is helped and strengthened by mating with a woman who is a good sexual and psychological partner. 2—This category comprises men who, although possessing a more or less strong polygamous urge, can under favorable conditions, keep them under control. A good wife, lack of opportunities, fear of being discovered and lack of financial means to indulge in their promiscuous sexuality can hold these men to the strict and narrow path. 3—Here we deal with a type of man that includes the majority; this type possesses a very strong sexual urge and is strongly polygamous. Dr. Kinsey's report has merely corroborated with factual statistics, what every student of human nature already knew about extra-marital relations. These men seldom are satisfied with one woman and often risk everything to satisfy their overwhelming sexual urge. Some psychiatrists have condemned and ridiculed these men, placing the blame for their promiscuous sexual activities upon some feature of their childhood and accuse them of infantilism, while moralists, priests and religionists have thundered against them and branded them sinners and adulterers; but their preaching has never had any appreciable effect in diminishing polygamous activities because, among other things, men know that preachers do not practice what they preach, and have feet of clay. Yet these men want a home and children and usually they love their wives to whom they are problem children. Those men who can afford it, marry and divorce with the greatest of ease. Women who marry this type of man find themselves in the horns of a dilemma, literally and figuratively, for which nobody can offer a solution; each woman must solve her own particular problem, or leave it unsolved. A wise woman who loves her husband and knows that he loves her, will be tolerant and give him a certain amount of leeway, and thus keep her marriage going as long as possible, especially if there are children.

This classification of men applies to women also; it can

be stated that there is a good number of both men and women who should never marry, or if they do marry, should not bring children into the world, because they cannot stay chained to each other; they like change and variety—in other words, they want to eat the cake and have it too. For all these reasons, it is very important that man and woman know each other well before getting knotted together. Today we have means and methods to examine and discover the character and qualities of human beings, and many tragedies, divorces and even crimes could be avoided if men and women would avail themselves of this scientific preventive. A good analysis would also show whether love is one of the forces that brings man and woman before the judge or the priest, or if it is merely sexual hunger and physical attraction. If love were the force that brings husband and wife together, marriage would have far greater chances to succeed because love is a durable emotion not subject to sexual satisfaction and petty irritations.

Just as in nutrition we cannot depend on the kitchen or on the vegetable market, but must go to the soil for good and nutritious food, thus with marriage we must not dilly-dally with superficial causes and must go to the infant. The first thing is to have the home produce *men*, responsible, emotionally and mentally mature; men who are free from frustration and do not run away from facts; men who are capable of correct evaluation and clear thinking. Since sexual relations play such a vital role in the success or failure of marriage, sex problems ought to be discussed by prospective mates, but not alone; this should be done in consultation with a competent physician or counselor. I believe that a physician would be better because even if the prospective parties have read extensively on sex, there are always some things they cannot evaluate and take into consideration, such as the size of the phallus and of the vagina, the position and anatomy of the clitoris and the strength and quality of the sex urge. There are many women who seldom or never have an orgasm and thus are robbed of that sexual pleasure so necessary for the good functioning of the nervous system, because of the peculiar position and formation of the clitoris and because men do not know the proper technique to arouse women. Many women have come to me complaining about their frigidity and lack of orgasm, even after years of married life. A good physician can, in most cases, correct this tragic and troublesome condition.

Generally it is advisable to postpone children for a couple years to give marriage a trial before forging more and stronger chains. Parents must realize the tremendous responsibility they assume when they bring children into the world; they practically forfeit their right to divorce, at least until the children are able to take care of themselves. The welfare and happiness of the children have priority over the happiness of the parents, and only in cases where the children would be harmed more by their parents living together than by divorce, should the breaking of a home be considered, but both must try first to stay married and live at least as friendly enemies for their children's sake.

Man should be taught that menstruation, pregnancy, child-birth and menopause are physical functions that often affect greatly and adversely woman's emotions and behavior, and require much patience and understanding; he must take into consideration that these functions modify, to some extent, the sexuality of woman, making it more periodic and infrequent. Fear of pregnancy alone has a pathological influence in her sexuality. Although woman is physiologically capable of coitus at any time, while man is not, she is psychologically ready less often than man.

Jealousy is a most treacherous enemy of marriage and very often gives it a mortal blow; it is a symptom of fear and inferiority and that the individual stopped growing mentally and emotionally when he was a child; it is also greed of the ego, pathological selfishness.

Quite often marriage is wrecked by in-laws because husband and wife lack the wisdom and courage to keep their busy-body, snooping, interfering and trouble-making parents out of their lives. Before the knot is tied, both partners ought to inform their loving and well-meaning parents that they are marrying only each other, and that no interference whatsoever will be tolerated and that if they cannot cooperate with them in making their marriage a success, they better leave them alone.

Difference in age should not be great; yet a marriage may succeed where the husband is much older than the wife, but not the other way around. The reason is that youth and physical attractiveness are very important to man on account of his sexual make up, while to woman are much less important. The Spaniards say: "El hombre y el oso cuanto mas feo mas hermoso."[2] When a woman marries a much older man she usually does it to find a solid economic shelter, and she may also have a father complex; the maternal instinct of woman is also an ingredient.

Prohibition of divorce is the result of a backward mentality and a fallacious metaphysical concept of life that refuses to face the facts of life and the real nature of man and woman, and it will never contribute to the success of marriage nor to the happiness of men and women. Neither secular nor civil powers have the right to force two individuals to live together for many long years, nor to keep them chained to each other and prevent them from seeking happiness and love in another marriage; since no one is infallible, even in choosing a mate, everyone has the right to have more than one chance at happiness. Where children are concerned, however, the State has the right and the duty to do everything possible to keep the marriage from breaking down, and thus leaving the children stranded in a sea of bitterness without the care and protection of both parents; otherwise divorce should be made easy to obtain in every state. Outside of scientific education of the child, the most important medicine against divorce would be what I have proposed at the beginning of this book and which I believe must be emphasized and repeated: there ought to be

2 The man and the bear the uglier the more beautiful.

a law providing that in order to obtain a marriage license, the applicant must present proof that he or she has attended a seminar for five or six months, at least once a week, in the course of which man would receive an elementary knowledge on the psychology, physiology and anatomy of woman, concerning her sexual and reproductive organs; woman on the psychology of man, and both on the art of educating children and living together. Besides the invaluable knowledge this course would give to prospective parents, it would serve as a cooling off period, which would give them a good opportunity to know each other better and thus prevent many hasty marriages and tardy regrets. The establishment of such schools would cost a good sum of money, but it would save much more money that is expended in fighting crime and it would pay good dividends in happiness, stable homes and more ethical and law abiding citizens; the family is the foundation of our present society and every effort and expense possible to protect it is one of the best investments. Since most of the States already demand a premarital certificate, there is no reason why they cannot require another far more important.

With radio, movies and newspapers at its disposal, the government could easily educate and convince the people of the necessity and benefits they would receive from the small inconvenience and effort required from them. Marriage can be and must be saved from divorce as much as possible, but this cannot be done with Middle Ages methods; only the skilled application of knowledge and scientific methods can save the home from destruction. Let us have the courage and honesty to admit the failure of our laws, both human and "divine" and give science a fair trial. Nothing else will do.

Man, Religion and Morals

Religion is the fear and love of God; its demonstration is good works; and faith is the root of both, for without faith we cannot please God; we cannot fear and love what we do not believe.

—*W. Penn*

Religion—a daughter of Hope and fear, explaining to Ignorance the nature of the Unknowable; Impiety—your irreverence toward deity.

—*Ambrose Bierce*

What I mean by a religious person is one who conceives himself or herself to be an instrument of some purpose in the universe which is high purpose, and is the motive of evolution—that is, continual ascent in organization and power and life and extension of life.

There is one religion, though there are a hundred versions of it.

—*G. B. Shaw*

Religion is the opium of the people.

—*Karl Marx*

Credo quiam absurdum.

—*Tertullian*

No creed is final. Such a creed as mine must grow and change as knowledge grows and changes.

—*Sir Arthur Keith*

All religions die of one disease, that of being found out.

—*John Morley*

They profess that they know God; but by their works they deny Him, being abominable, and disobedient, and unto every good work reprobate.

—*Tit. 1:16*

Religion: Man's joint quest for the good life.

—*C. Hagdon*

Religion is an escape from reality and the projection of an illusion into reality.

Religion is the offspring of: Imagination, Fear, Ignorance, Hope, Vanity and Egotism.

There is no religion: There are religions; that is, responses and reactions to external and internal stimulus.

[115]

Religion is the art of explaining mystery by creating more mystery, of explaining the unexplainable with words that explain nothing and create confusion.

Religion is big business, the business of "saving souls" at the expense of the bodies.

FEW SUBJECTS are so loaded with emotional dynamite as religion; and few efforts can be so fruitless and antagonizing as a discussion on religion. The believer does not want to be disturbed by doubt and criticism of his faith; he stands firmly and resolutely on his right to believe what he has been taught to be true, regardless of how absurd and contrary it may appear to modern knowledge. This is what William James called: "the will to believe". But the believer usually refuses the same right to the unbeliever. Why should those who believe that an Omnipotent and Omniscient God is on their side be afraid of atheists? The inconsistency is obvious. But who expects religious people to be consistent?

Since religion forms a very important part of man's life and has influenced his behavior from the moment he stood erect and looked interrogatively at the stars and has played a major role in the development of our culture, it must be subjected to a careful analysis. The study of religion at once poses these questions: What is religion? What is the origin of religion? Is it a revelation from God? What has religion done to man and for man?

The definition of religion in the dictionary will not help us to understand it; nor will the claims of the theologians and religionists give us a clear and rational idea of this chain-reaction emotion we call religion. Whether the word religion comes from the Latin word "religio" or from "relegere" or "relegare" which means to gather and to bind together, does not throw any light upon the meaning and effects of religion; if anything, these terms confuse and mislead because it is all too evident that religion also divides people in innumerable groups and sects.

Scientifically speaking, religion is an emotional attitude

toward the universe and its phenomena. Religion is also a behavior for specific purposes and in specific occasions; this emotional attitude, in common with all other emotions, is conditioned by a number of material factors, as we shall see later. I believe that we can get a clear view of what religion is and what it means, in relation to man, by comparing and contrasting it with science. Religion is dogmatic and authoritarian; it commands man to believe. Science is liberal and anarchic because it does not recognize dogmas nor established authority. In religion, hypothesis comes first, and all subsequent reasoning is used to support it, even when that hypothesis is contradicted by facts. In fact, religion uses hypothesis as the gallows in which reason and criticism are strangled. In science, hypotheses arise as the result of painstaking study and observation, and are used as a temporary tool to help in the explanation of phenomena and things beyond our analysis; but science sacrifices and discards a hypothesis or theory gladly and quickly for a better one more in harmony with newly discovered facts.

Religion seldom discards a hypothesis and maintains it often by force at the cost of rivers of blood and enormous suffering. There is, for instance, abundant proof of the evolution of man from lower organisms, yet religion still teaches the myth that man is a special creation of God, and that we descend from Adam and Eve. Religion proscribes doubt, investigation and criticism of its dogmas. Science thrives on doubt and investigation, and criticism is its blood. Science takes nothing on faith nor accepts anything on the authority of another person; everything must be subjected to verification. Religion holds there is more than one road to knowledge and that divine revelation is one of those roads. Science does not admit the existence of divine revelation and recognizes only one road to knowledge—that of the senses. Science is cold, yet dynamic and objective. Religion is emotional and passionate, yet static. Religion is totalitarian and intolerant. Science is tolerant and democratic. This should be enough proof that religion and science are irreconcilable and incompatible, regardless of what religionists and part-time scientists may say to the contrary.

Let us now answer the question: What is the origin of religion? Anthropologists have, through many years of painstaking investigation and study of primitive people, accumulated a great quantity of factual knowledge, and based upon this knowledge, we can state that primitive religion, from which our present religions stem, consisted of a system of magic ceremonies, rituals and tabus whose purposes were: 1—to protect and defend man against evil spirits; 2—to expel from the body those evil spirits that cause pain, disease and death; 3—to increase the fertility of the earth and of woman, both being considered intimately related, and to protect crops and food; 4—to obtain the help of the spirits and gods in defense or offense against enemies, individual and collective; 5—to propitiate and thank the gods for favors and benefits received and to ask for more; 6—to explain Nature and its phenomena; 7—to give man security in a hostile world. The religion of primitive people was formed on the principle that everything living and non-living was animated by an invisible being identical to man. Out of this animism whose vestiges are still abundant, evolved polytheism and monotheism. Primitive man was amazed at his own powers of speech and believed that some words had a magic power over things and could change the course of events and produced phenomena. Thus he constructed invocations, exorcisms and prayers, still believed to be efficacious in this age of atomic power.

The ethical and moral commandments, so numerous in our religions, are lacking in primitive religion; in their place there are tabus based on real or imaginary fears. I shall give only one instance of this lack of morals and ethics. Sir James Frazer tells us in *Psyche's Task* that the treatment of the murderer has nothing to do with any moral condemnation of the act, but arises from the dread of the murdered man's ghost, which renders it unsafe to associate too closely with the object upon which the spirit may inflict his revenge. A tabu is a categorical imperative that sets an act or a thing as sacred and holy or as dirty, evil and contaminating; in either case it is untouchable. An analysis of the menstrual tabu, the oldest and the most universal of all tabus, will illustrate the point. Primitive man soon found out that the loss of blood was always followed by weakness and very often by death. Therefore blood became synonymous with life; but when primitive man saw that a young woman would all of a sudden start to lose blood and then lose it periodically for many years without apparent weakness or injury, he was compelled to conclude that woman possessed supernatural powers and that the menstrual woman was dangerous. Obsessed by this fear of the supernatural, man forced the menstrual woman into isolation. As soon as the first drops of blood appeared, the menstrual woman had to retire to the seclusion of a hut and remain there completely alone until she was clean; then the hut and the garments she had used were burnt. A savage would rather meet a tiger or an enemy than a menstrual woman because he knew what to expect of and how to defend himself from this beast; but he did not know how to deal with a menstrual woman, whose magic and supernatural powers were far beyond his comprehension and for which his spear was no match at all.

But in some instances primitive people believed that the menstrual woman was good magic. The American Indians believed that a menstrual woman, with her hair down, walking at midnight through the corn fields, would kill the pests. The Hindus believed that menstrual blood had magic powers for good. The Jews codified this tabu in the Old Testament: "And if a woman have an issue, and her issue in her flesh be blood, she shall be put apart seven days: and whosoever touched her shall be unclean until the even". Lev. xv. 19.

Child-birth also was tabu, and the pregnant woman had to endure child-birth in complete isolation, because man was afraid of being made unclean. Judaism and Christianity developed rituals and ceremonies of purification for both the menstrual and the child-bearing woman because they were considered unclean and dangerous until they were purified. Few people realize the enormous and tragic consequences these tabus have brought upon woman and also upon man; they have degraded both and started a cold war between man and woman that was intensified by the Judeo-Christian prophets and mystics.

Of the already mentioned elements that enter in the making of religion, two stand out as the most important: the search for security and fertility or sex. Most of the religious symbols, ceremonies and rituals are of sexual origin. The genital organs of man and woman have been worshipped, crudely or symbolically, by the Persians, Greeks, Egyptians, Hindus, Hebrews, Romans, Phoenicians and are found in Christianity. Religious dances and religious prostitution had for object to stimulate and increase the fertility of the earth and woman, both being intimately related in the mind of primitive and "civilized" people.

The cross itself is of phallic origin, symbolizing the phallus and the testis, and was worshipped by the Egyptians as the god Ptah, by the Phoenicians as "Asher", meaning "The Upright, The Powerful, The Opener". The Old Testament speaks of Jehovah as the Opener: "And God remembered Rachel and God hearkened to her and opened her womb". Gen., xxx, 22. " . . . And when the Lord saw that Leah was hated he opened her womb". Gen. XXIX, 31.

The genital organs of man were considered the holiest part of the body by the Jews because they took oaths by laying the hand upon the phallus of the man to whom the oath was given. But the translators of the Old Testament evidently felt ashamed of the language used by God and improved (?) His vocabulary by translating phallus into the innocuous English word "loin". The Hindus also worshipped the phallus under the name "Lingan" and it has been found in the Aztec temples. There is also evidence that the death and resurrection of Jesus are myths borrowed from the Egyptians, Persians, etc., and whose original meaning was the death and resurrection of life, observed in Winter and Spring respectively, and that the Sacrament of Eucharist or Communion can be traced to the eating of the Totem or the king by primitive people. Christmas was taken from the birth of the Sun, celebrated by the Mithraic religion during the solstice of the Winter. The truth is that nobody knows when Jesus was born and that the date of his birth has been celebrated the sixth of January, the nineteenth of March, etc.

The Christian religion is nothing else but a rehearsed paganism. A great Spanish statesman expressed this very eloquently in the following words: "Cristianismo: ultimo dia del paganismo y primero de lo mismo."[1] If religion were a revelation from God, as religionists still claim, we should expect a unity of belief in all ages and in all people. Why should God give one revelation of religion to Buddha, another to Moses, another to Jesus, another to Mahomet, still another to Arius and another to Luther, to mention only a few of the innumerable religions?

We have seen men and women like Mary Baker Eddy, Father Divine, Robinson (I talked with God) I AM, and others start new religions that from the business point of view have been a tremendous success, at least for the founders and a select group. In fact, the easiest way to get rich is by starting a new religion; no taxes to pay and no accounting of the profits is necessary and the capital is all provided by God and the suckers.

Now it would be a most cruel joke on the part of God to give different and contradictory revelations to people and thus confuse them and sow the seeds of hatred, intolerance and fratricidal wars that have cost rivers of blood and have made a hell out of this fairly good earth; and it would be a no less stupid and sadistic joke on the part of God to send his only Son to save mankind and atone for its sins, into a corner of the earth where only a handful of people could see Him.

1 Christianity: Last Day of Paganism and the First of the Same Thing.

Surely, God must have known that there were other lands besides Judea and other people besides the Jews. Yet God left all these millions of people in complete ignorance of the coming of the Savior and of His plan for salvation.

This extremely absurd and inefficient method of saving humanity has proven very costly. Think for a moment of the brutal and cruel efforts made by the Christians to bring Jesus and salvation to the infidels; the Crusaders killed, raped and looted their way across Europe and into Arab lands to save people who did not want to be saved or who had their own way of salvation. But despite all the zeal and fury of the Christians, after almost two thousand years of fanatical efforts, only about three hundred million human beings of the two billion that inhabit this planet are Christians, or at least call themselves Christians, because very few men and women really practice the teachings of their God-Man Jesus.

There is still more conclusive evidence that religion is a natural process originated in a material plane and influenced and determined by material factors, such as: 1—the ways and means of obtaining food; 2—climate and geography; 3—culture and experience of the people. In other words, hunters will have a religion different from that of agriculturists; again, people living in the tropics will have a different religion from that of people living in cold or temperate climates; and people living in the mountains will have a religion different from that of those who live on the plains or on the sea.

There is a story of the priest who went to preach to a very cold village, and in his sermon described very eloquently the burning heat of hell. After the sermon, the local priest took the visiting preacher to task for his sermon saying to him: "Don't you realize that you have made hell so attractive to these freezing people that now all will want to go there?"

What has religion done to man and for man? It would be wrong to deny that religion has done some good; it has brought peace, solace, consolation, hope and some security to many people. It has produced a few saintly men and women who have practiced Christian virtues and have valiantly tried to stop the tides of greed, cruelty and lust; and it has inspired many artists, poets and writers to create beautiful works of art. But against these meager benefits let us place in the balance: the first mass persecution in history, the expulsion from Spain of the Arabs and the Jews, carried out by their most Catholic Majesties Ferdinand and Isabella. Hundreds of thousands of Spaniards were robbed of their property, terrorized and thrown into the roads to die or to seek asylum in other countries. How many men, women and children died from hunger and hardships in the road to exile, nobody knows.

Place also in the balance the Holy (?) Inquisition that burned at the stake, tortured and jailed countless people without any legal process, merely on suspicion of heresy. Let us place the Children's Crusade in which thousands of children who did not die in the rotten ships were sold into slavery to the Turks; the massacre of the Albigenses and of the Huguenots the night of St. Bartholomew; the Thirty Years war; anti-Semitism, whose latest tragic effects was the massacre of six million Jews by the Nazis and by Monsignor Tiso; the "civil" war in Spain, in which about a million people were killed, and many other wars, cruelties, hatreds, intolerances and persecutions, too numerous to mention.

Place also in the balance the filth, corruption, disease and ignorance of the Middle Ages and the war upon science. What has religion done to increase the food supply, to feed starving millions, to cure disease and alleviate pain? Nothing, absolutely nothing, outside a few so-called miracles. If religionists had any sense of proportion and any respect for truth, they would be ashamed to claim that one particular person was saved by praying to God, the Virgin or some saint, while millions of other human beings with as much faith and praying with the same zeal the same prayers, have died or continue living crippled by disease. Certainly such a favoritism is unworthy of an Almighty and Just God.

Yet, despite this poor record of religion, we are exhorted

[123]

to have faith and are told that religion is essential to good education; without religious education, the religionists say, man cannot be good, ethical and moral. If their claims were true then, during the Middle Ages, when the only education available was religious education, men and women should have been shining examples of goodness and morality; but this is not the case. In the golden age of religion and religious education, corruption, dishonesty and cruelty were rampant from the pope down to the serf.

It is no different now. In his book, *Religion and Roguery*, Franklin Steiner presents the following facts: Catholics are 15% of the population of the United States, but 42% of its prison population. Protestants are 42% of our population but 40% of our prison inmates. Jews are 3% of our population but 6% of our prisoners. Non-church goers are 52% of the population but only 12% of the prison population.

Dr. Albert E. Wiggam, who conducts a syndicated column entitled "Let's Explore Your Mind", received this question from a reader: "Does a large church membership in a city indicate it is a good or a bad city to live in?" Here is the answer:

"A bad city. A staff under Psychologist E. L. Thorndike found from a study of 37 factors that make for general goodness or badness in 310 cities, that those cities with most church members were above the average in infant death rate, child labor, and illiteracy, and below average in school attendance and persons who owned their own homes."

Father George B. Ford, Roman Catholic Chaplain of Columbia University, admitted that more than three-fifths of the juvenile delinquents recently arrested in New York were Roman Catholics. As quoted in the newspaper *P. M.* of February 29, 1944, he declared: "During the first four months of 1943, 64 per cent of the juvenile delinquents in Children's Court were Catholics. This means the Catholic Church has something to be greatly concerned about."

The same conclusions are reached by another Catholic

priest, Rev. Leo Kalmer O.F.M., in his book: *Crime and Religion.*

At the Ninth International Congress of Psychology held at Yale University on September 6, 1949, Professor Hightower of Butler University, read a paper reporting an examination of thirty-three hundred children. *The New York Times*, on the following day, reported his address with this caption: "Students of Bible Found Less Honest." Professor Hightower said: "People have been saying for years that if you give children a knowledge of the Bible they will walk the straight and narrow way. The results show that they will not walk the straight and narrow way."

I hear Christians say: It is not religion, nor Christianity that has failed. It is the people who have failed to apply Christian principles to their lives; Christianity has not been given a chance. Although this is a flimsy evasion for two thousand years of failure, let us accept it for a moment in order to ask a very pertinent question: Why is it that not only the average man and woman, but even the clergy, both Catholic and Protestant, have failed to practice Christianity and to live up to the teachings of Jesus? The answer is not hard to find. The moral precepts and way of living preached by Jesus, by St. Paul and other founders of Christianity are too high, too impractical and out of relation with the nature of man; therefore he finds it almost impossible to observe those precepts. The founders of Christianity were ascetics who either had a congenital weak sex urge, or had become impotent and satiated after a life of pleasure, like St. Paul and St. Augustine. In addition to their weak sexuality, they developed self-denial of other biological necessities, no doubt as a defensive mechanism to hide their inferiority complex. Thus they became different from other men and were able to turn their inferiority into a superiority complex by claiming their ascetic life was not only most pleasant to God, but that it was the only way to salvation.

In this way, men otherwise weak, poor and unknown, acquired more power than the wealthy, and even the emperor.

Unable to enjoy the most sought and valued pleasure—sexual pleasure, they declared war on all pleasures and tried to impose their way of life, or rather, their way of dying, upon all the people, with threats of eternal punishment or with reward of eternal happiness. Why should God have given man a powerful and demanding sex urge only to punish him for using it, is another of those contradictions and mysterious ways we must not question.

Although the Christian Church was founded upon the principle of strict poverty, it soon became immensely wealthy. St. Francis of Assisi and Ignacio de Loyola both founded monastic orders whose members took solemn vows of poverty, their orders soon became greedy and rich with material goods; God's grace availed them nothing against biological imperatives.

Christian leaders realized before long that very few men and women were capable of loving their neighbor, of turning the other cheek, of remaining chaste or even monogamous, of giving everything to the poor, of being humble and of restricting their sexual activities to the procreation of children, and of forgiving their enemies, much less loving them. But instead of honestly admitting their error about human nature and their mistake in trying to impose upon men and women their strict code of morals and behavior, and making attempts to reform it more in harmony with man's biological needs, they persisted in preaching their morals, while practically every one, including the preachers, were doing the opposite.

The results of this colossal hypocrisy have been most disastrous for religion and for humanity. Religion has lost its spirituality and power over man; it has become an empty shell, a mantle with which many people, including the priesthood, cover their greed, their pride and their immorality. We hear priests thunder against secularism and materialism, while their own churches are sinks of iniquity. Every service performed by the priest must be paid just as well as the services of a plumber or a lawyer. Salvation has a price.

From all the aforesaid, it follows that religion offers to man two negative approaches to life. One: it counsels and commands complete and unreserved surrender to myth and dogma; this surrender means slavery of the mind. It also preaches resignation to whatever condition man is subject to, no matter how degraded and miserable, for that is the will of God. This earth is a valley of tears in which we must live and suffer in order to gain heaven. The other negative approach to life could be a positive one: religion gives man hope for a better life and for happiness, after he is dead. Religion sets before man several virtues, some of them good and attainable, and some impractical and practically unattainable; these are like stars, so high that the majority of people either make a faint try to reach them and give up, or never try at all. This failure produces negative and harmful results because it breeds hypocrisy and cynicism. Religion places before man a God who has come to embody the best that is in man, even the best he can ever hope to be and teaches him that he is the son of such a God. This makes man feel good and important; but again he finds out that he is just a weak human being and not a God. Thus religion, although it has some good in it, has defeated its own ends and produced opposite effects to those it set out to produce.

Those who prattle about the "moral law" are like those who spread the news that a child had been born with a gold tooth; everyone repeated the gossip, until a doubter went to see the child, opened his mouth, and there was no gold tooth. Morals are a matter of geography and time. In one province of Holland a girl must become pregnant before she can marry. In our country it is a terrible disgrace. Among the Eskimos a man offers his wife to a visitor and feels insulted if he refuses her. At one time it was a sin to drink coffee because it was the beverage of the infidels—the Arabs. A few years ago no one would have dared to go to the beach in the scanty attire of today; anyone attempting such an "immorality" would have been arrested and severely punished. There is only one immoral thing: hurting or harming in any way another human being, except when the security and welfare of the community so demands.

Mysticism is another example of the negative and destructive approach of religion. Much has been written about this subject, but most of it is pure fantasy and unadulterated humbug; there is nothing supernatural in mysticism and nothing mysterious about the mystic. The basic ingredient of mysticism is sex; the secondary ingredients are frustration in love and in the world and imagination. The results of these ingredients produce, in some cases, mysticism which is a powerful desire to escape from the world in general and/or from some person in particular, and find security. The mystic withdraws from the world for almost the same reasons that compel a man to commit suicide; in both cases the elements of escape and self punishment are present. The mystic punishes his body by depriving it partially or totally of some of its biological necessities and escapes the world and himself, to some extent, by submerging his personality in God. In the mystic union with God, the mystic seeks a substitute for the union with woman. His visions are but the visualization and distortions of images stored in his brain, but they are so vivid and clear that he mistakes them for reality. Those visions do not have more reality than the visions and dreams induced by opium or some other drug. The mystic has the advantage over the drug addict in that he can enter the world of dreams and illusion on his own power. The artist can do the same thing; that is why we can say that a mystic is an artist gone wrong, because the artist usually creates and plasms his visions and illusions into material forms that can be inspiring and beautiful. Mysticism is intellectual masturbation leading to "spiritual" orgasm. Since few men have a powerful and vivid imagination, there are few artists and few mystics. Mysticism appears as a forerunner of Christianity as a revolt against the Flesh and the World. Mysticism is practically unknown among pagan people; it is not exclusive to Christianity for it is also found in the East, but the motives and causes are the same.

The climacteric and adolescence are the two critical ages for conversion and for mysticism, because of the activity of the gonads. Young men full of vitality and with a strong sex urge are poor soil for mysticism. Women are also very poor candidates for mysticism, that is why there are so few women mystics. And when a woman becomes a mystic, like St. Theresa of Jesus, her mystical experiences are plainly materialistic and physical; Theresa speaks to Jesus as if she were speaking to her sweetheart. This is not the moment to analyze the mechanism by which she sublimated her strong sex urge and transferred it to the mystical figure of Jesus, but there is nothing supernatural about it.

Women are too earth bound, too concerned with procreation, too attached to life to betray it by becoming a mystic. Menstruation and menopause are also enemies of mysticism, not to say pregnancy and child birth. No woman who has been pregnant ever becomes a mystic, because maternal experiences are far superior to mystical. Old age is also an enemy of mysticism because the gonads no longer produce the spark that fires the imagination.

What is the future of religion? Sigmund Freud expresses a pessimistic view in his book, *The Future of an Illusion.* There was a time when I also thought that religion would be eliminated by science before long. Today I am not so sure, for although science has taken away from religion many of its functions, like the protection of the crops, the cure of disease, the explanation of the universe and its phenomena and has rendered unnecessary the expulsion of devils and the burning of witches, religion still persists and has a powerful hold, not only on ignorant people but also on intelligent persons as well. The reasons for the survival of religion from vigorous attacks of science are the following: (a) there is still much mystery in the universe, and this provides the soil for the maintenance of religious hypotheses; (b) the great majority of men grow up physically but not emotionally nor mentally, and just as the child seeks the protection and the security offered by the father so they still seek the protection and security of a cosmic father; (c) there is a core of irrationality in most men; that is why we find scientific men who in the laboratory take nothing for granted, but when they come to the interpretation of facts they step out of character and talk like the average believer; they seem to keep two compartments in their brain, one for science and the other for religion, and never the twain shall meet. I call these people part-time scientists. Religion gives man cosmic importance and tickles his ego, while science reduces him to an insignificant and incidental cog in the wheel of life, a piece in the gigantic jig-saw puzzle that is the universe.

Religion is also a very solid and respectable pillar of the "status quo", acting as a stabilizing and conservative force, that is why it has always obtained the wholehearted support of the wealthy and the powerful. It cannot be denied that religion had, and still has, a soporific effect upon the people, instilling in them fear and obedience to the tyrants and resignation to their misery and suffering, while a small minority lived in luxury at the expense of their hunger and labor. Since religion persists and will probably persist for a long time, the problem is not how to suppress it or uproot it, but to direct this emotional energy toward a constructive and beneficial goal. To accomplish this religion must be taken out of the hands of the priestcraft and cleansed from all its superstitions; it must cease being big business. If man has to worship anything, let him worship the sun, as he did in more primitive and sensible days; the starry heaven, sunset and sunrise, the mountain and the shore of the restless sea should be both its church and its ceremonial. Man must return to Nature as much as possible; his temples cannot match the beauty, the vastness and the power of Nature. Those who feel the need for worship and for adoration of God or some unseen power, where can they find a more inspiring and beautiful ceremony than in the rising or setting of the sun? Here, before the giver of life, man can kneel without degrading himself. Where can man find more inspiration and feel a sense of strength and power than under the starry sky, in the towering mountains, by the mighty sea or contemplating the flowers, the trees or even a blade of grass? Nature is beautiful and inspiring even in its most ugly moods, but man is not. Cold and lifeless statues, altars and walls, no matter how beautifully painted and decorated, cannot give man the idea of an all-powerful deity nor the cosmic feeling found in the communion with Nature.

Man needs meditation to develop his inner life and to digest and assimilate the stream of sensations reaching his consciousness, and this should be part of religion; but this meditation must be free from superstition, from supernaturalism and from ritualism that leads to bondage. Most men lack inner life; they never take time off for introspection, never stop to look at themselves in the mirror of their own minds. Consequently, they are extroverts, always seeking pleasure, stimulation and excitement outside themselves. These people are afraid of solitude, afraid of being alone. This is due to the emptiness of their minds and to the lack of high constructive thinking; therefore these people go about like robots, rushing and getting nowhere and feeling the burden of frustration and the lack of a constructive goal and purpose in their lives. A few minutes dedicated to meditation every day can work wonders for us; opening new vistas and giving us a factual sense of values about ourselves and about our fellow men.

There is no sense in denying that man is a creature of faith; from his very beginning he has had faith in something. But his faith has suffered many and such big blows that it has almost been shattered. Man has misplaced his faith, that is why he has been disappointed so many times. He has become suspicious, cynical—not trusting even his own God. Man must have faith in himself, in his ability to solve the problems of life with the help of fellow humans; faith in his capacity for good; faith in his strength of which he had no idea until science discovered it for him.

A humanist religion, such as I have briefly sketched, will heal those ugly sores of suspicion and cynicism and give man faith in himself and humanity; it will take up where science stops and fill the gap between the known and the unknown, and provide that necessary outlet for the religious emotions and for the cosmic longings of man.

But when will man wake up from the horrible nightmare which is present religion? When will man open his eyes and see that the gods he worships and the dogmas he holds as eternal truths are figments of his own imagination and hold him in bondage? When will he break those puny, powerless and often ugly idols or place them in his museums as relics of his ignorance? When will man burn all the labels that divide men into Catholics, Jews, Protestants, Mahometans, Hindus, Unbelievers, etc., and realize that we are all children of the sun and of the earth, and that everyone wants to enjoy life?

Oh men and women, I implore of you, I beg of you to listen to this call: this earth is not a paradise, but we can make it one if we apply to this task only a small part of the zeal and energy man has applied and used in destroying, hating, killing and making it a miserable and squalid hovel and a battlefield.

For the first time in the history of humanity man has the knowledge and the means to control his environment and change this earth from a hell into a heaven. This must be the purpose and goal of religion.

Man and Violence

Homo, hominis, lupus.
—Latin Proverb

Vengeance belongeth unto me; I will recompense, saith the Lord.
—Rom. 12:19

Love your enemies, and pray for them that persecute you.
—Matt. 5:44

But if any harm (mischief) follow, then this shall give life for life, eye for eye, tooth for tooth, hand for hand, foot for foot, burning for burning, wound for wound, stripe for stripe.
—Ex. 21:23-25

Resist not him that is evil: but whomsoever smiteth thee on thy right cheek, turn to him the other also.
—Matt. 5:39

Violence is the easiest and the most costly manner of settling our problems.

Violence started as an individual sore. It has gradually grown into a collective cancer that threatens the existence of the social organism.

The eradication of violence and cruelty should be the immediate and supreme task of Science.

Man is the only animal that is cruel and kind consciously and that inflicts pain with pleasure.

A man with a gun feels like a superman.

History is mostly the history of violence; the history of man's inhumanity to man.

MAN is conceived and born in violence and lives under the sign of violence; and he walks in the company of hatred and cruelty ever ready to use his fists. A very large part of man's energies are used, or rather misused, in the creation of weapons and instruments with which he can multiply many times his violence, both in quantity and quality. Instruments for destruction seem to have a hypnotic power over man; a mind with a gun feels like Jupiter with the bundle of lightning in his hand. How easy it is to destroy, to kill and to strike fear and submission into man's heart; one flip of the finger and one or many lives may be snuffed out like a candle by a gust of wind.

Destroying and killing was once a rather slow and difficult task; but the conquest of atomic power has solved this difficulty and enables man to kill and destroy on a global scale never attained before. The man with the bow and the arrow and even the man of the Middle Ages with sword and musket could kill only a few people; but the man of the atomic and poison gas age can destroy a city at one stroke and kill thousands of human beings with just one blow.

Violence is a disease that alternates between chronic and acute stages, and for which so far only religious poultices of holy water and theological exorcisms have been used; that these remedies are worse than failed is amply proven by the enormous increase of violence and cruelty. There is more violence in the world today than before Christianity came upon the earth to implant an era of love and compassion. The history of the world for almost two thousand years is the history of Christian nations fighting among themselves, persecuting, burning, torturing and robbing Jews and other heretics. Christian leaders displayed a gross ignorance of human nature when they attempted to exorcise violence with beautiful words and commands to "love your enemies". Only a scientific study of violence, of its causes and mechanisms, can give us ways and means to cope with it and bring it under our control.

Violence has played an important part in the formation of the earth; it is found throughout Nature, and it is part and parcel of life, of its evolution and self-preservation. There is violence in animals and in primitive man, but it is limited to the obtaining of food and mate, and for defense. This is a basic and necessary violence and it does not brutalize, nor does it become cruelty. As man advances toward a more complex and "civilized" society, violence and cruelty increase by leaps and bounds, both in quality and quantity.

Since everything in man has a biological origin, violence is not an exception; self-preservation, sex and fear are the springs from which all violence flows. Man and animals fight for their lives, for food, for a mate, for their offspring and for security. This type of violence disappears when the factors that make it necessary no longer operate; if an animal has food and a mate and is not being attacked, it feels secure and at peace with the world. The same thing goes for primitive man. Children, being close to the primitive, use only basic violence; secondary or unnecessary violence is the product of the environment.

Why do people, individually and collectively, resort to violence at the slightest provocation? Why do people like war? How is the cruel man made? What are the causes and forces that compel man to hate, to kill, even himself, and to destroy with sadistic pleasure? There is ample evidence that the first seeds of cruelty and neurosis are planted in early infancy; the child is primarily concerned with the satisfaction of his biological needs and with the pleasure derived from them. Thumb sucking, defecating, urinating and playing with his genitals become pleasurable because they relieve tensions, besides the sphincter muscles involved in those functions are erogenous. But along come the parents and attempt to regulate his biological functions, and order him to stop playing with his genitals, under the threat that it is dirty and very bad. The child cannot understand why something that gives him pleasure can be bad, but he is afraid to displease his parents, therefore he usually stops, and submits to defecate and even urinate on schedule. Thus the first seeds of resentment, bitterness and frustration are planted. The child feels that he is unjustly treated and deprived of his right to pleasure; moreover, by blocking the release of energy that accompanies the orgasm and the other pleasures and tensions, both physiological and psychological, frustrations begin to take form and grow daily with more blocking and more suppressions, thus laying down the basis for neurosis, unconscious revenges and cruelty.

The first critical age of suppression may last three or four years, followed by a short period of negative quietness until the onset of puberty, which ushers another critical period again. The activity of the gonads create new and stronger tensions, for which the sexual act is the natural release; but in our civilization the boy is blocked and deprived from obtaining normal satisfaction, and must content himself with masturbation, which, of course, is also injurious and a sin to be avoided by all means; at least, that is what he is taught. The sexual needs of the boy are thus ignored, and thus the seeds of frustrations and bitterness planted in his infancy are watered and fertilized, and it will not be long before they will bear abundant and poisonous fruit. Sex in itself, already violent, cruel and egotistic, is made worse by suppression and branding it as impure and immoral. I have already pointed out that coitus is an act of violence rather than of love, in which the male derives pleasure from biting, crushing and mauling the female. From this natural and temporary fit of violence in which the male feels that his phallus is a weapon with which he must assert his superiority and subjugate the female, there is only a short step to sadism or pathological cruelty.

The pleasure derived from bull fights, cock fights, boxing bouts, hangings, burnings at the stake, lynchings and other spectacles of violence, is closely related to sex and often brings a tumescence of the sexual organs. The suffering and pain of the victims are unconsciously associated with the pain and subjugation of the sexual partner, and bring in another important ingredient: masochism. Thus the spectators identify themselves either with the victim and its punishment or with the victor or executioner, obtaining an unconscious revenge and satisfaction for their sadistic or masochistic feelings, by proxy. In either case, every spectator gets a big thrill with discharges of energy that relieve some of their tensions.

It is interesting to note that young people, although ready to indulge in basic violence at the slightest provocation, do not as a rule go for deliberate cruelty, which is found, commonly, in men approaching or going through the menopause, for reasons discussed in another chapter. Most cruel people are very

religious: Torquemada and the Inquisitors who invented instruments and methods of torture and who used them with an
art (sic) never known before and seldom surpassed, were very
religious men, and killed and tortured in the name of God.
In our own time we have witnessed the unspeakable cruelties
and sadism of Hitler, Mussolini, Franco, Salazar and Peron, all
religious people, or at least the product of a religious education. Even Stalin and the Communist leaders, who are imitating, to some extent, the Inquisitors, are the product of religious
education.

In his book: *The Sexual Life of the Savages*, Malinowski
offers us corroboration of the theory that the seeds of neurosis
and cruelty are sown in early infancy by the suppression and
blocking of the sex impulse. He tells us that in one of the
Trobriand Islands, where children are left alone and in complete liberty in their sexual play, they grow healthy and free
from neurosis and frustrations. It is true that we find a certain
amount of cruelty among primitive and much less primitive
people, like the Mayas, Aztecs, Incas, Egyptians and other cultures who offered human sacrifices to their gods and punished
offenders with a certain amount of torture; but this violence
was sporadic and lacked the deliberation and organization of
the Holy (?) Inquisition—it was carried out merely to please
the gods and to enforce obedience to the ruler.

There is no doubt that the intense struggle for life and
for the obtaining of wealth, contribute greatly to the growing
quantity of violence and make man more cruel and ruthless.
The criminal is motivated by two factors, one physical and the
other psychological. Money is power and the means to obtain
many things, but it is hard to get. Violence opens the door to
easy money, but the criminal also labors under frustration and
desire for revenge; he feels that society is unjust to him because while some men have plenty of everything, he has nothing, and working hard and long only brings him a pittance.
Consequently, he is willing to risk his freedom and even his
life in order to get the coveted wealth and to revenge himself,

consciously or unconsciously, against real or imaginary wrongs, and to appease hidden frustrations.

It is easy to see that crime can never be eliminated by laws and punishments, no matter how cruel. In the Middle Ages, pick-pocketry was punished by hanging, but this supreme penalty did not stop pick-pockets from plying their trade right under the shadow of the gallows; no more than the burning and tortures of the Inquisitors stopped heresy, or our jails, electric chairs and gas chambers stop criminals from their anti-social behavior. Violence begets more violence in an unending and vicious circle that can only and must be broken by the application of our newer knowledge of man and of the forces that motivate his behavior and his misbehavior.

Revolutions also illustrate how violence from the top provokes more violence from the bottom; violence that once unleashed, is like a Juggernaut that crushes blindly anyone who stands in its path. There was a time when I looked upon a revolution as a laudable and beneficial act of collective violence; today, after more mature, objective and careful study of violence, I am tormented by grave doubts, for I do not see how tyranny can be overthrown without violence. On the other hand, the leaders of the revolution who climb to power on a ladder of ideals and good intentions but whose rungs are red with the blood of friends and enemies, once on top feel just as insecure as the former tyrant, and beset by enemies who constitute a serious threat, not only to themselves, but to the ideals for which they have fought, suffered and risked their lives. Hence, revolutionists have only two alternatives: to continue the use of violence until the complete extermination of their enemies or to admit defeat and lose the opportunity to create the new social order which they have dreamed; no revolutionist ever considers the second alternative, therefore violence only changes hands, hands that tremble with the fear of losing the sceptre, and this fear makes them more ruthless.

The French revolution sent Louis XVI and his nobles to the guillotine and destroyed the Bastille, but it brought new waves of terror with Robespierre and Napoleon. The Russian revolution wiped out with one stroke the Czars and their tyrannical regime, but it has brought the political Commissar and the NKVD which is far more effective and ruthless than the secret police of the czars. Revolutions fail for the same reasons that Christianity has failed; a revolution is a social upheaval produced, on the one hand, by the exorbitant wealth and the tyranny of the few, and on the other hand, by the hunger, discontent, poverty and slavery of the masses. But though made by the masses, the revolution is directed and integrated by a small minority of men who are the catalysts and the ferment and whose ideals and goals are not shared or even understood by the multitude. For the masses, the revolution has only two immediate objectives: (a) to get a greater share of the wealth possessed by the few and satisfaction of their biological needs; (b) to take revenge upon their masters for the many wrongs and injustices suffered.

Another important reason for the failure of revolutions is this: revolutionists are idealists with an over-optimistic and fallacious opinion about human nature which they believe can be changed over-night by just overthrowing a king and by distributing the wealth of the rich, and by promulgating new laws and reforms. The Christian leaders made the same mistake. Beliefs, age old traditions, habits and customs become a part of human nature, and people cling to them very stubbornly, even when the new methods and the new social order promise to bring a happier and more abundant life.

The Russian revolution offers us a very striking example of the people's resistance to change. Far be it from my mind to deny that the Communist leaders were, and still are, animated by the best intentions to bring an ideal social order to their people, and that they have done many good things, which I doubt balance the evil ones. The fact is that those leaders, no sooner had climbed into power, when they were forced to compromise and gradually have brought back many of the bourgeois things they had sworn to destroy forever, medals, decorations, nationalism, unequal wages, and above all, religion. The State and its violence have grown instead of decreasing. The fact is that Russian leaders are caught in a web of violence, just like a fly is trapped in the spider's web, from which they cannot attempt to escape without endangering their rule, and many of the reforms they have forced upon the people, and this would mean to them a betrayal of the revolutionary principles and a confession of failure, something they will never do.

History teaches us that every revolution is followed by a counter-revolution. The Russian revolution has been attacked, but their leaders have so far succeeded in exterminating their known enemies at hand; whether they will be that successful in the future, is hard to predict, but I fear a disintegration of the power machine they have built because it is based upon violence and maintained by terror.

The American revolution is about the only successful revolution that did not produce a counter-revolution; perhaps I ought to take that back because the civil war was a form of counter-revolution against the principles of freedom and equality promulgated by the Fathers of our country. Moreover, the American revolution was also a rebellion against a foreign power and political tyranny that was not produced by hunger and poverty, and the people had a vast continent of rich and fertile land where to expand and grow rich.

The Reformation was both a revolution and a counter-revolution; it can be called a draw, with no complete victory for either side. Nailing the religious thesis at the door of the Cathedral of Wittenberg was not an act of violence, and no doubt Luther was animated by peaceful intentions, but his knocks were heard around the world, and followed by more wars and violence than the world had ever seen.

People do like war; at least many people, very important and influential people do, and those who are neutral on the subject, or even peaceful, can be rather easily convinced of the necessity and benefits of war. No other conclusion can be drawn from the innumerable wars that have bled mankind and caused suffering and destruction beyond calculation, and from the costly preparations for another war that will make other wars look like a tavern brawl. Why do people like wars? Here is a question that should be included in all our quiz programs, but it is conveniently ignored; yet it is a most vital question because with the correct answer obtained and acted upon, we would set in motion the machinery for lasting peace. People like wars for two reasons: economic and psychological. People have gone to war to obtain food, loot, slaves, land and strategic bases, or to defend those very things against aggression. But psychological reasons are no less important; men have fought to prove their strength and courage, to gain admiration and mastery over their fellow men, to get the thrill of physical combat, to discharge pent up energies, tensions and accumulated bitterness, to get revenge for frustrations and injustices and to impose their beliefs or religious dogmas. Physical combat is the supreme expression of the struggle for life, the supreme test of strength and valor in which many people find a great thrill, either by engaging in it, or by witnessing it.

Fear and hatred are two powerful emotions present in the great majority of people that can be aroused and brought to white heat by those who have a lot to gain by war. We isolate those we know to carry germs of contagious diseases like typhoid carriers; war and violence also are contagious diseases and those who preach and advocate them by their deeds, if not by their words, should be isolated on some island and given swords and shot-guns, so they could release their violence and fight to their hearts' content, without dragging into war those who want peace.

Let us now examine the causes and mechanism of violence against the self. I have looked for light on this subject in: *Man Against Himself*,[1] by Dr. Karl A. Meninger, without appreciable results, only a few sparks and much misinformation.

[1] *Man Against Himself*, by Dr. Karl A. Meninger, page 71.

Dr. Meninger follows Freud and accepts his theory of the death instinct. I have said already that there is no death instinct; I do not say that the wish to die does not come upon some people sometimes, but this wish to die is not instinctual. Rarely is it found in young people who are overflowing with vitality and the will to live; therefore, very few young persons commit suicide. Frustration, fear and the overpowering desire to escape what seems to be a situation from which there is no other door than the destruction of the self; these are the forces that sometimes overpower the strongest of all biological urges: the will to live. Heredity, health, age and the chemistry of the endocrine glands, determine, to a great extent, whether the individual will keep on fighting and living or whether he will give up the sponge. No doubt there is a chemistry of courage and of fear and of aggression. We know that when animals, or man, are in danger, the adrenal glands are stimulated to produce more adrenalin in the blood stream that enables him to fight with greater courage and strength or to escape with more speed than under ordinary conditions.

In manic-depressive people the wish to die appears rather often and with varying degrees of intensity; these people alternate between states of euphoria, in which everything is rosy, and periods of depression, in which everything looks very dark. It is at this time that they feel a compulsion, a powerful urge to escape this life of struggle and frustration. There are cases in which the individual wishes to hurt someone by hurting himself, or seeks sympathy and attention or, burdened by a sense of guilt, wants to punish himself; but in the majority of the cases of self-destruction, it is fear, loss of face or failure, lack of love, frustration and the wish to escape that motivate suicide. To these people death offers the only way out, the solution to every problem and security beyond the reach of anyone or anything.

Are people who commit suicide cowards? What requires more courage, to go on living and struggling or to put an end to life? These questions have been debated extensively with many arguments, pro and con, but as far as I know, no one has adduced the argument that it really does not require courage to go on living, for the simple reason that the instinct of self-preservation takes care of that. But it does require courage to overcome self-preservation and to plunge into the unknown. In most cases, suicide is preceded by a period of incubation and inner struggle between the instinct of self-preservation and the wish to escape, what it seems, an intolerable and insoluble situation. Under the title: "The Wish to Die", Dr. Meninger says as follows: "Anyone who has sat by the bedside of a patient dying from a self-inflicted wound and listened to pleadings that the physician save a life, the destruction of which had only a few hours or minutes before been attempted, must have been impressed by the paradox that one who has wished to kill himself does not wish to die."

"The popular assumption is that having yielded to a sudden impulse the patient has 'changed his mind'. It leaves unanswered why the act should have brought about this change. The pain is usually not great. The prospect of death is actually less than before the attempt since 'while there is life there is hope'. One gets the impression that for such people the suicidal attempt is sometimes a kind of insincere histrionics and that their capacity for dealing with reality is so poorly developed that they proceed as if they could actually kill themselves and not to die."[*]

Dr. Meninger and other psychiatrists are baffled and stumped by a problem the solution of which stares them right in the face, but which they cannot see because they are dallying with the branches of the tree instead of the roots, studying effects instead of causes, and wasting much of their mental energy in the formulation of neo-mystical hypotheses instead of applying themselves to a scientific interpretation of the biological urges that motivate all our behavior and misbehavior. The change of mind of the would-be suicide is no

[*] *Man Against Himself*, by Dr. Karl Meninger. Page 71.

mystery at all and very easy to understand, and to call it "histrionics" is rather in poor taste. The change of mind is brought about by the instinct of self-preservation asserting itself again, after a momentary lapse. There is no reason to doubt the sincerity of a would-be suicide, even if the attempt is a feeble and misdirected one, because we must take into consideration the terrific struggle that takes place between the will to live and the wish to die. Dr. Meninger himself gives the clue to the mystery, and then fails to develop it. He says: " . . . as if they could actually kill themselves and not to die." That is precisely what the suicide really wants, to kill himself, that is, to escape, yet to live, to be able to come back after he has left behind the situation and circumstances which force him to take such a drastic solution. Moreover, a brush with death, whether intentional or accidental, increases the appreciation of being alive; this is seen in patients who have been very close to death and recover, or in those who have had an accident.

Dr. Meninger echoes Freud in stating that people who come upon fortune kill themselves sometimes because of a very strict conscience. I do not find this explanation satisfactory; in my opinion, those people are driven to suicide by fear, rather than by a very strict conscience—fear of being unable to cope with a situation that entails new responsibilities, which they think are unable to fulfill, and not the thought of getting something they do not deserve, is what drives them to shirk the responsibility of fortune. People who refuse to accept wealth when it is handed to them on a silver platter have not learned to enjoy life, because life has been presented to them as a duty, austere, ascetic and full of privations. If these evaders were investigated, it would be found that they are very religious people, with a very distorted and wrong conception of life; a pagan or an atheist would never commit suicide because Dame Fortune empties her horn of plenty on his lap, for he knows how to enjoy life and is not afraid of pleasure and happiness. Only ascetic people burdened with a guilt and sin complex, see danger behind every joy and good fortune, and are afraid of them.

Dr. Meninger also states that: " . . . the death instinct is probably much more evident in the activities of daredevils than in the pessimistic musings of melancholy patients and philosophers. As Alexander points out, nothing else can so well explain the pleasure of mountain climbers, automobile racers, building scalers in exposing themselves unnecessarily to great dangers."[2]

Psychiatrists often reason like theologians: they usually seek and find (?) "explanations" for many problems by postulating some hypothetical instinct, of which there is no proof, when a rational explanation is at hand. People who risk their lives and court death in some sport or voluntary fighting for an ideal, do not wish to die—quite the opposite. They seek danger and risk their lives because they are so very much alive and live intensely. They are typical extroverts who seek admiration and attention for which they reluctantly are willing to pay the highest price; but they always hope to cheat death. They want to live and listen to the applause which is music to their ears and gas to their ego. I would not say, however, that only hunger for applause and admiration drives them to perform dangerous feats: these people are conquerors, and to them the conquest of a difficult acrobatic or maneuver on the trapeze, or climbing a mountain presents a challenge they cannot resist. Moreover, these people crave strong stimuli, both physical and psychological; their urge to challenge death and Nature is typical of young people overflowing with vitality and with a high metabolism. It is interesting to note that very few women go for mountain climbing, auto racing and other death-courting situations. Women have a lower metabolism, and as the guardians of life, they are more attached to it, more passive and conservative, and their conquests are rather directed toward other fields.

Asceticism and martyrdom are also forms of violence

2 *Man Against Himself*, page 77.

against the self. Asceticism is characterized by mortification and deprivation, partially or totally, of things that are necessary for the normal human being. The forces behind asceticism are: (a) belief in the supernatural and in immortality; (b) a sense of guilt (c) belief in sin and in the evil nature of the body; (d) belief in the necessity to punish the body to obtain greater happiness or reward; (e) a wish to escape from the world in general and from some people in particular; (f) fear of the passions and biological demands of the body; (g) a wish to obtain superiority and power, and to win admiration by mastering emotions and demands of the body that rule most human beings; (h) to obtain physical and ‚psychological security. In India many Fakirs and ascetics make their asceticism pay by providing food to keep alive. The ascetic is repulsed by the mere thought of committing suicide, for this would be a terrible sin against the Creator, but he has no scruples to commit slow suicide and to betray life with his chastity. Most people try to avoid pain and seek pleasure, but the mechanism of these two sensations is not identical in every human being. In the ascetic there seems to be a short circuit and pain is sought as a way to pleasure; it can be said that the ascetic is a masochist who enjoys what other people dread and consider painful. Contrary to popular belief, the ascetic is very selfish, and expects to be rewarded generously.

Like the ascetic, the martyr is a product of religion in general and of Christianity in particular. The Christian martyrs who sought martyrdom and death at the hands of the pagan emperors were intoxicated with "spiritual wine" which gave them a sense of cosmic importance never felt before, and were convinced that only death kept them in this "valley of tears", away from the joys and happiness of heaven; consequently, they thought it worthwhile to be thrown to the lions, since by killing themselves not only would they forfeit the heavenly reward, but would be punished with eternal fire. Thus they also were very selfish.

From the aforesaid, it should be evident that violence,

whether individual or collective, cannot be legislated out of existence nor prevented by severe punishment, or exorcised into good behavior, and peace by prayers, commands, fear of God and holy water. Only a scientific attack upon violence can produce positive results. The following three things I consider essential to bring to a minimum, if not to eliminate, violence; a certain amount of individual violence, we will always have: 1—Elimination from the life of the child every situation and element that may produce deep anxiety, frustration, bitterness and desire for revenge. 2—A more equitable distribution of wealth, so that every human being who can work has employment that provides him with more than the bare necessities of life. 3—Complete universal disarmament. 4—A complete reform of our penal system, with emphasis on rehabilitation rather than on punishment or revenge. The elimination from our culture of those factors that glorify violence. Here is where the movie industry could be of great help; at present the greatest part of the movie energies and activities are directed to the presentation and glorification of violence. This is both a symptom and a cause of our disease. This catering to the lowest and most brutal emotions and passions is a tragic degradation of one of the most potent forces for good and for the education of human beings. It should be stopped, but not by an ukase of the government, but rather stopped, or much curtailed, by consciousness of the great responsibility of the movie makers. People should be educated into a more wholesome entertainment. This task would not be an easy one nor profitable as giving the people what they want, but in the end it would pay great dividends for the nation and for the world. Think of the millions of dollars wasted punishing the violence we create, and of the billions worse than wasted in armaments and preparation for another war, both on this and on the other side of the Iron Curtain.

What the suicide seeks in death, humanity seeks in war; but those who survive must face the same and more problems: death of loved ones, greater taxes, loss of freedom, etc. Mankind seems to be under the grip of a compulsion neurosis that leads it to destruction, and whose causes I have exposed. Sports and other forms of competition should absorb the aggressive and competitive forces and provide an outlet for that core of aggression that resides in man. Violence has grown too costly in blood, tears, money and property. A civilization that indulges in violence as easily as we do does not deserve that name, for civilization means, above all, the use of our reason and intelligence in the solution of all the problems arising from our relations with other human beings. Let us prove that we are civilized by outlawing violence from the face of the earth; the violence of Nature should suffice unto ourselves.

Man and Freedom

Promising them liberty, while they themselves are bondservants of corruption; for of whom man is overcome, of the same is he also brought into bondage.

—II Pet. 2:19

The greatest glory of the free-born people is to transmit that freedom to their children.

—Havard

Give me liberty or give me death.

—Patrick Henry

The Four Freedoms: Freedom from Want, Freedom of Speech, Freedom from Fear and Freedom of Worship.

—Roosevelt

In every age the priest has been hostile to liberty. He is always in alliance with the despot, abetting his abuses in return for protection of his own.

—T. Jefferson

No man is free who is not the master of himself.

—Epictetus

. . . That government of the people, for the people and by the people shall not perish from the earth.

—Lincoln

Freedom of religion, freedom of the press and freedom under the protection of the habeas corpus, those are the principles that have guided our steps through an age of revolution and reformation.

—Jefferson

Eternal vigilance is the price of liberty.

—Anonymous

Free will is an illusion that must be treated as reality.

Freedom is a luxury relatively few people can afford or enjoy even in small doses.

Under normal conditions one man's freedom must be limited only by another man's freedom.

Man is not born free. He must learn to be free, just as he learns to walk.

The word Freedom means different things to different people. In fact, to many people freedom means to be free to impose their dogmas or opinions upon other people.

[149]

Where economic slavery exists, freedom is only an empty word.
This is the meaning of freedom: To make the right choice at the
right time, for we have only the freedom to choose and not always.

"WE HOLD these truths to be self-evident, that all men
are created equal, that they are endowed by their
Creator with certain unalienable rights, that among these are
life, liberty and the pursuit of happiness", thus states boldly
and dogmatically our Declaration of Independence. Sometimes
it is a good thing that idealistic people are not too critical
and scientific, or many a good cause would have been born
with much less zeal and enthusiasm. Had the writers of our
immortal document stopped to analyze those famous words in
the light of modern knowledge, they would have held back
their pens or they would have qualified their statements.

The truth is that those truths are no truths, nor are they
self-evident; man is not born free nor equal, and in practice he
is endowed only with the rights that the group in which he is
born sees fit to grant him. Man is born weak and dependent
upon the good will of his parents or guardians, and for some
time knows nothing and cares nothing for freedom; he is only
interested in the satisfaction of his biological needs, and he
can be conditioned to be a robot, a slave. Millions of human
beings have lived and died in slavery without ever hearing
that magic word—Liberty. Man can be made to believe that he
is free, when in reality he is chained and a slave; such is the
power of words.

Man is born with unequal intelligence and with other in-
equalities, both physical and mental, that may handicap him
and place him at the mercy of other people. Finally, it certainly
would be most unjust and unfair on the part of the Creator to
endow man with "certain unalienable rights", and then leave
him in complete ignorance of those rights for thousands of
years, besides permitting the church, the state, the high priests,
the feudal lord, the tyrant and his own parents to trample
upon his rights and to reduce him to slavery. Theoretically,

man is born with the right to live, to be free and happy, but
these rights too often are not worth the paper on which they
are written, unless he fights for them and conquers them with
his own efforts, sometimes with his own blood. The long history of slavery and tyranny is witness to this tragic and bitter
reality.

We do not know how soon after man stood erect and
gripped his first club or stone axe with a threatening gesture
to frighten and beat another human being into submission and
slavery, but we have reasons to believe that long before the
Pyramids were built by slave labor, many men had already felt
the whip on their bent backs. The Greek civilization rested
upon the shoulders of slaves; freedom was a luxury enjoyed by
the privileged few. The Romans kept it and enlarged the slave
system and also reserved freedom for a limited number of citizens. Man's aspirations for freedom, however, were incubating
in the breasts of some slaves. The rebellion of Spartacus and
his fellow slaves against the Roman masters is, to our knowledge, the first battle for liberty in the history of mankind.

Prior to Christianity religion was not concerned at all with
the freedom and dignity of man, nor with his rights; the Creator, evidently, had neglected to inform man of his unalienable
rights. The pagan hierophants were not bothered with moral
ideas. But along came the Jewish prophets, and in the name of
a new god, promulgated new commandments and new moral
precepts, thus preparing the way for Christianity.

It is idle to speculate what would have happened if Christianity had really put across and carried into practical use its
ideas of freedom, brotherhood and equality of man, preached
by some of its leaders. The question is: Did Christianity really
bring freedom and dignity to man? In theory, yes; in practice,
no. Worse yet, Christianity forged new and stronger chains
for man and spawned a new crop of tyrants far more cunning
and worse than the pagan slave masters. Christianity raised the
slave to the level of the emperor, in the eyes of God, but it
did nothing, absolutely nothing, to give him a tangible proof

of freedom, to guarantee his rights, or to improve his miserable existence. Why bother with such trivial things as physical freedom, health and the pursuit of happiness when the end of the world was at hand, and with death, complete freedom and happiness in heaven? Why should the slave complain when he would be sitting at the foot of the throne of God equal to kings and emperors? This was the millennium, for the dead. No wonder it began to sour so soon. Very few Christians were willing to give up this miserable life for the spiritual freedom and joys of heaven, so they remained earth-bound. In view of the many misconceptions and false stories about the founders of Christianity, it must be noted that Jesus never attacked slavery, although there were plenty of slaves in his day; never spoke for freedom nor for democracy. And if we accept the Gospels, when confronted with a most vital question, he flunked it with an answer that has become a classic in evasion: "Give to God what is to God and to Caesar what belongs to Caesar." What part of the coin belonged to God and what part to Caesar he did not say, leaving people in the dark and as confused as before as to what belonged to whom. Moreover, this contradicted his teaching that everything was under God and belonged to God.

St. Augustine, whose words are considered inspired and binding, condoned and accepted slavery, and in his famous treatise, *The City of God*, he speaks of slavery as "a divinely ordered social arrangement".

Another Father of the Church whose words were also "inspired" and authoritative, St. Thomas Aquinas, says in his work, *Summa Theologica*: "Respecting heretics, we have two observations to make: In the first place they are guilty of a sin by which they deserve to be excluded not only from the Church by excommunication, but from the world by death." This was a tremendous blow against freedom because a heretic was anyone who refused the slavery of the mind and attempted to exercise the "unalienable rights endowed to him by the Creator". This reactionary and inhuman pronouncement still is the official doctrine of the Catholic Church, in spite of the fact that most of the vast knowledge we have, and the wonderful inventions we enjoy, have been brought forth by heretics, by men who claimed freedom and refused to believe or accept the dogmas and teachings of the Church about things and the universe.

The pagan slave masters at least were honest and consistent, because they did not teach that the slave was their equal before God or anywhere. The Christian slave masters were dishonest and hypocritical because, while teaching the brotherhood of man and the fatherhood of God, they kent slaves and exploited and mistreated them just as much, if not more, than the pagans. The new slave-masters used the name of God like an enormous club to beat man into submission and to chain him to the rock of ignorance.

The cry of freedom given by Spartacus anticipated by hundreds of years the famous words of Patrick Henry: "Give me liberty or give me death", but did not find an echo for many centuries. Strange as it may seem, it was a monk, Martin Luther, who echoed, in a way, the cry of freedom of the Roman slave; not that Luther was interested in freedom for freedom's sake when he nailed his rebellious theses at the door of the cathedral of Wittenberg, in defiance of papal authority

The Reformation, however, was the result of a long incubation, the dramatic explosion of the suppressed aspirations for religious freedom already articulated by Wycliffe, the Albigenses, the Jews and other heretics. But this liberating movement, although it was the precursor of good things, had serious defects; it liberated man from the authority and tyranny of the pope, but it chained him to the infallible authority of a book whose beautiful prose is only surpassed by its confused and contradictory statements. Were it not so, Christians would not be divided into so many sects, wrangling, quarreling and even killing one another and each sect claiming to possess the correct interpretation of the "Word of God". Can anyone show me anything more discreditable to God and to those who wrote down his words?

The Reformation, however, with all its short-cuts and flaws, was a tremendous victory for freedom, and set into motion further aspirations and conquests of liberty. Now, at least, man could interpret the Scriptures according to his own light and his conscience, or could doubt them and subject them to scientific criticism. But the Reformation did nothing to abolish slavery and to bring freedom to all men. Christian merchants, landlords and industrialists kept their slaves and raided the African coast in search for cheap human labor. Negroes, who according to the Christian teachings were children of God, "born equal" and "endowed by the Creator with certain unalienable rights", were violently and brutally kidnapped and torn out of their native land and their families and loaded like cattle, or worse, into dirty and disease-ridden ships where many died; those who survived were sold to toil in the plantations of America and Europe. Christian leaders, Catholic and Protestant alike, sanctioned in the name of God this brutal, cruel and most un-Christian degradation of man.

Sometimes I wonder what it is that robs men of the capacity for indignation at the sight of injustice and cruelty; what makes them remain silent when the very principles they preach are violated and trampled into dust. I believe it is fear and greed: fear of losing wealth, honors, privileges and pleasures; greed for more power, for more wealth and lust. These are the mortal enemies of freedom and the dignity of man. And what is man without freedom, without dignity and integrity, without honor? An evil worm that crawls upon the face of the earth, without seeing the stars, a sanctimonious hypocrite, a perverted liar, a greedy monster, a prostitute and worse, because the prostitute sells only her body, while he sells his "soul" and covers his degradation and his evil deeds with the mantle of respectability and religion. I have more respect for the thief who at the point of a gun takes my money, and for the whore who sells her body, than for those "respectable" robbers who steal under the immunity and impunity of their profession. The gunman at least risks his freedom and his life, and the whore also risks her freedom and her health.

True, some abolitionists were Christians, but they were abolitionists in spite of being Christians and because they possessed that rare quality, that capacity for moral indignation without which man is no better than a beast. In recent years, several attempts have been made by Christian leaders to take credit for our ideals of freedom and democracy, which they claim are part and parcel of religion in general and of Christianity in particular, but in view of the historical facts here briefly reviewed, it requires a lot of nerve to stake such claims. Moreover, I could fill a few pages with quotations from the supreme and infallible (?) authority of the Catholic Church condemning, anathemizing and cursing democracy, freedom and liberalism. Already Pope Innocent III condemned and excommunicated and "annulled" the Magna Charta, the basic document of English freedom. Pius IX in his famous or rather infamous *Syllabus of Errors* and his Encyclical *Quanta Cura,* asserted the totalitarian power of the Church and repudiated all our freedoms and democracy. The same categoric denunciation of freedom and democracy can be found in other encyclicals, like: *Mirare Vos, Immortale Dei, Humanum Genus, Vehementer Nos, Diuturnun on Civil Government,* and in many other official publications of the Church. During our civil war for the abolition of slavery, brought to a successful end by our immortal President Abraham Lincoln, Pius IX practically took sides with the Confederacy, sending a letter to President Jefferson Davis. This was one of the reasons why the Union broke diplomatic relations with the Vatican, and have remained broken ever since, though in recent years the late President Roosevelt established them again on a personal basis.

We have our first glimpse of democracy and freedom in Greece, but it lasted only a short time. The torch of freedom was later lifted by the French Encyclopedists and the English philosophers who prepared the ground for the French and the American revolutions that struck such powerful blows for freedom.

It would be most unfair to ignore woman, because she has suffered and still suffers, in many parts of the world, more slavery than man. Woman was probably the first slave and has been the slave of the slave—no lower state can be reached, no worse degradation can be suffered. She has lived in physical and mental slavery since the dawn of mankind; the fact that she has had times and places where she has ruled and been free does not alter, on the whole, the above statement. Christianity by making woman the scape-goat and loading upon her shoulders the myth of the temptation of Adam and the loss of Paradise, made her lot much worse than before, and sunk her into worse slavery than she had suffered under paganism. Practically all the Christian leaders, beginning with Jesus who repudiated his own mother, all the Fathers of the Church, have heaped abuse, slander and condemnation upon woman, seeing in her only the temptress, the lascivious creatures whose charms and pleasures lead the soul to perdition. Nor did the Protestant leaders improve her condition; woman was unclean, impure, the witch to be feared and often burnt at the stake or hung on the gallows. Ignatius Loyola, the founder of the Society of Jesus, an organization that has come to play a dominant role in the Catholic Church, compared woman to the devil. He writes: "Our enemy imitates the nature and manner of a woman as to her weakness and forwardness. For, as a woman, quarrelling with her husband, if she sees him with erect, firm aspect, ready to resist her, instantly loses courage and turns on her heel, but if she perceives he is timid and inclined to slink off, her audacity knows no bounds, and she pounces upon him, ferociously. Thus the devil, . . ." etc. With such an opinion of woman held by the most influential and powerful men, is it any wonder that she was considered a chattel to be bought and sold, a slave with no rights? Up to the eighteenth century women were sold in the open market in England. Even such progressive thinkers as the framers of our Declaration of Independence, omitted woman from their famous statement: "All men are created equal ... " etc.

Let us inquire now into the nature, meaning and mechanism of freedom. Freedom, as an abstract principle, does not exist among the savages; the savage wants freedom because being free he can best satisfy his biological needs and be free from hard work. The child, being close to the savage, has the same attitude toward freedom. Intellectual freedom comes into being with the growth and development of the mind and of the successive emergence of cultures, each one reaching a different and often higher level.

Physical freedom was appreciated long before the Greek philosophers, with their brilliant mind and high-reasoning powers, brought forth intellectual freedom, but the torch of liberty they lighted soon was snuffed by the wind of tyranny. The Greeks, however, had written an indelible page in the history of liberty, and the radiance of the torch of freedom would pierce the darkness of the Middle Ages, to guide men again in their fight against tyrants.

The meaning and conception of freedom is influenced and conditioned by time, age, experience, knowledge, wealth, sex, religion and social status. President Roosevelt, in a moment of inspiration, formulated the Four Freedoms, and I cannot think of a better way of presenting a clear picture of freedom than by making an analysis of these Four Freedoms:

FREEDOM OF SPEECH: For the average individual, this freedom has little meaning and less value because he has little or nothing to say, that is, important and worthwhile. The average man and woman go through life satisfied with the political and religious beliefs they absorbed during childhood; they seldom indulge in heavy thinking, nor do they try to change the world, and as long as they have a full belly, a house and perhaps a car, all is well with the world. But for the reformer, the idealist, for the scientist and for the thinker, who see ignorance, injustice and other evils, freedom of speech is supremely important, so important that he is often willing to fight and even die for it, if necessary. In most parts of the world, freedom of speech does not exist; the press, radio and the spoken word are controlled by the dictator, and no word of criticism can be uttered without bringing swift and severe punishment. Consequently, there is stagnation and intellectual death, because without criticism no progress is possible. Here in America, we boast of our freedom to speak and to criticize, but we must not fall asleep on our laurels; the picture is not as rosy and bright as it is painted. Editors, movie makers and radio owners have ways and means to close the door to heretical thoughts, to slant the news and distort facts. There exists a hidden censorship exerted by certain religious and economic powers who, by threatening economic reprisals, curtail this freedom to speak. Our schools, colleges and universities are far from free—this insidious censorship has found cracks in the armor of Miss Liberty, and like termites, are destroying it. Freedom of speech has helped to make America great, rich and powerful, but unless the modern means of communicating thoughts and ideas to our fellow men are free and open to criticism of any and every kind, political and religious freedom of speech will be just an empty word, and the mind will be chained to those age-old myths and superstitions that have held it for so long.

FREEDOM FROM WANT: All the freedoms and unalienable rights guaranteed by our Declaration of Independence and Bill of Rights are so much wet paper unless every human being who can work can find a job that provides him with a good standard of living. To a hungry and jobless person, freedom has only one meaning—the freedom to starve, and who wants this kind of freedom? The proclamation of Emancipation by our immortal President Abraham Lincoln and the bloody civil war to abolish slavery, were to a great extent annulled, because the victory of the Union armies left the Negroes in the same economic conditions they were before. In theory the Negroes were

[158]

free to do as they liked, to refuse to work for their former masters, but in practice they remained slaves; they were rooted and chained to their posts, because they had no money to move around and the landlords saw to it that they did not get more than what was essentially necessary to keep them working. It took many years and much struggle to really give meaning and substance to the Emancipation and to the sacrifices of the civil war, and even today there is much peonage and economic slavery, not only among the Negroes, but among the whites as well.

Can this present capitalist society bring freedom from want? It could *if*—it is no use to speculate about that *if* because those who really could bring about the millennium are too greedy and too blind to see the benefits that a change in methods and tactics would bring to everyone, including themselves. These people have the mentality of Marie Antoinette, and are courting the same tragic end. Other countries are in trouble because they do not produce enough; we have troubles because we produce too much, and could produce much more, if all the modern discoveries and ways to increase our food supply were used. Abundance, however, seems to be injurious to our capitalist system, that is based on scarcity; thus we have an artificial scarcity in order to maintain high prices and greater profits with less cost, and while millions of human beings are hungry and on the verge of starvation, potatoes, coffee, corn and other foods are burned or otherwise destroyed or kept in immense warehouses. We take gold from the depths of the earth, and after much work and fuss we bury it again in the hole in the ground. Can anything more irrational, more insane and absurd be imagined?

FREEDOM FROM FEAR: The world would be a wonderful place if men were free from fear; but fear is with us, and like a thick fog, obscures and limits our vision, isolating human beings in small islands in a foggy sea. Wisdom is the only road to freedom from fear. For a detailed discussion of this subject, see the chapter on Fear.

FREEDOM OF WORSHIP: This is a rather peculiar freedom. It could be formulated as follows: Each individual is free to choose his own chains, which may not be after all a freedom to be treated lightly; they are of different colors, some are gilded and very pretty, but still are chains. The very act of worshipping, as it is practiced today in our churches, is an act of submission and slavery, a negation of freedom, a declaration of dependence and weakness, a confession of inferiority before men, no better or worse than the rest, and before mythical beings created by fear and imagination. Worship also implies a body of dogmas and beliefs that tyrannize the mind. Man has never obtained freedom, nor anything worthwhile, by kneeling, begging and imploring; only when he stands on his feet and uses his intelligence and applies his knowledge, does man obtain some amount of freedom. Yet, freedom of worship is an important thing that has cost much struggle; it permits man to worship whatever god he wants and where he wants, or not to worship at all.

How free is man? Does he have a free will? Yes, answer theologians and many philosophers: man is free to choose between right and wrong, between good and evil. God has given him free will, therefore he is responsible for his acts, thus acting freely. Adam and Eve ate the forbidden fruit and were kicked out of Paradise by an angry God. Even if the punishment had been limited to the disobedient couple, it would be too severe and out of proportion with the sin. But when generations of children yet unborn are deprived of that Paradise and punished for an act for which they cannot, by any stretch of the imagination, be held accountable, the penalty becomes unjust, extravagant and absurd beyond words; any father who would punish his children so severely for a more serious offense, would be considered very cruel and hauled before the Society for the Protection of Children. The fact that God knew that Adam and Eve did not have the moral stamina to resist temptation minimizes the offense on two counts: one, Adam and Eve had just come out of the hands of the Creator, made in his own image; therefore it was not their fault if they did not have the will power to resist temptation; two, God knew in advance they were going to be tempted and that they would sin, so he really framed them very neatly. Why? Would it not have been to his greater glory if he had arranged things differently so that they and their descendants would have stayed in Paradise forever? Look at the trouble that could have been prevented. The whole thing is so absurd and incredible that its acceptance by intelligent people is one of the greatest wonders of the world.

Those who maintain that God has given man free will ignore another contradiction, since they claim that nothing, not even the leaf of a tree, moves without the will of God, and if this is true, then everything that man does, good or bad, is already predestined, planned, ergo, he is not responsible for his actions. Theologians evade this contradiction saying that although God has planned everything and controls everything, man is free to obey or disobey those laws and choose between right and wrong. This is like putting a man in jail and after locking the door, we tell him that he is free to go and do as he pleases. Moreover, what about the sixteen hundred millions of human beings born and living outside of the Christian religion who have never been told what is right and what is wrong? Even Christians are born without knowledge of good and bad, how then are they going to choose wisely and rightly? The only way to untie this Gordian knot is by cutting it with the sword of science.

We agree that animals have no free will, and that their movements are determined by a rigid system of instincts, reflexes and tropisms. A reflex is an automatic response to a stimulus. A good example of a reflex is touching something hot—the hand is jerked away from the fire before we know it. A tropism is an attraction toward something, like the flying of the moth into the light, the moth is positively heliotropic, that is, light attracts it. A potato growing in a dark place will grow towards the light, just as we, when lost in darkness, will move automatically toward a light, no matter how far away it is. There is also geotropism, attraction toward the earth, and chemotropism, chemical attraction.

Lacking fore brain or cortex, all perceptions and stimuli reaching the brain of the animal are automatically answered, thus they have no choice whatever; their movements and functions are completely determined by external and internal forces. But man has two brains, cerebrum and cerebellum. The cerebellum is the animal brain where the internal mechanism and functions of our organs are regulated and where reflexes and automatic responses take place. The cerebrum is a form of high court or supreme tribunal where stimuli and perceptions can be, and often are, detoured for decision and action. In this new brain is where thinking and other high functions take place. Will power, that is, control and regulation of emotions and behavior and "free will", are also functions of the cerebrum. Thus the phrase, free as a bird, has no meaning because birds are not free.

How free is man? Is a criminal responsible for his evil actions? From the above we can see that man has a certain amount of freedom of choice. For instance, a person can go to church or swimming instead; he can walk or run, go to bed and do many other things at will, or refuse to do many things. But everything that he does, even when doing nothing, is a link in a long chain of events, of causes and effects, and if we trace this individual chain, we will arrive at the union of the two cells that give birth to the new being. At the moment of this union color, glands and many other biological and physiological factors are determined; these factors will in turn determine how an individual will react to the environment. Besides heredity, there are elements that strongly influence and condition man's "free will", such as: climate, barometric pressure, temperature, education, geography, age, health, disease, food, sex, knowledge or culture, traditions, tabus, beliefs, and chemical and physiological changes constantly going on in the body. If we could correlate all these factors and others that

[162]

we ignore we would be able to predict what a human being would do in a given moment, what decision he would make, what he would choose, bad or good, right or wrong; but this knowledge cannot be obtained.

Let us take the case of stealing. A man sees an object he desires very much but has no money to buy it, and has an opportunity to take, with some danger of being caught. A struggle usually takes place between his conscience and the wish to take what he likes; the intensity of that struggle and its outcome will be determined by the factors above enumerated. It is obvious then that criminals are not really free and that the line dividing the sane from the insane is so thin in many cases that psychiatrists cannot tell us where sanity ends and insanity begins. In spite of all this, we must hold people responsible for their actions, good or bad, with the exception of those cases where there is a defined mental disorder and a compulsion clearly shown; otherwise life would be impossible and an awful chaos. Society could not exist if human beings were able to shirk their responsibility; but this society must take cognizance of the factors that lead a person to anti-social behavior and temper punishment with a correct evaluation of responsibilities, both individual and social.

If from man we pass to Nature, we will find that we live in a deterministic world. The discovery of the indeterminism of the electron by Heisenberg, has put wind on the sails of the free willers, and raised unfounded hopes. The position and velocity of the electron may be free from determinism, but the aggregation of atoms is not free, otherwise we could not predict eclipses, tides, chemical reactions, etc.; in other words, all our science would collapse. Thus the present is the offspring of the past, and the future is sired by both the past and the present. The future can be compared to a hurricane; we cannot with certainty predict its path because it is a dynamic thing in constant flux and affected by innumerable and unknown factors also in constant change. The behavior of man is also like a hurricane—we know it is determined, but cannot predict its path.

Since man lives in a deterministic world and he is an integrating part of this world, it would be impossible for him to be free, but he must keep on thinking he is free as a bird. The world is plagued by dictators, from the right and from the left, who threaten the little freedom that we enjoy; it behooves us then to look closely into the biological and philosophical causes and reasons for our liberties. The germs of authoritarianism are found in the very nature and structure of man. Already in the animal world we find the dominance of the group by one member. One male asserts his authority over one or more females, and over other males who are weaker. The club and the stone axe wielded by the strongest member of the clan or the tribe became the symbol of authority; later it lost its crudeness and became the gilded sceptre of the king, dainty and pretty like a toy, but no less brutal. At first there was only one source of authority and tyranny: might or brute force; but from the fear of the unknown and the belief in the supernatural emerged another source of authority, another tyranny—the witch, whose functions and importance gradually grew in quality and quantity to become the hierophant, the high priest who transmitted the will of the gods to the people. These two streams of authority, after running parallel for some time, merged together and the king became the supreme physical and spiritual authority of the tribe or nation: his word was law, from which there was no appeal. The priesthood, however, often tried to bring the king under their power, sometimes with success.

It was the Jewish prophets who promulgated the newer doctrine of spiritual authority and made Jehovah the source of all power. The Christian leaders took this doctrine of the supremacy of the spiritual over brute force and gave it the new look. Might took a temporary defeat before the spiritual "soldiers" of the new religion. The emperor Constantine recognized the value and power of Christianity and gave it his might, in exchange for valuable help; thus, through tortuous ways, the witch and the hierophant had triumphed over brute force and become the Pope—the Supreme Pontiff, spiritual and physical ruler of mankind, maker and unmaker of kings.

The Reformation was like a dam against the river of physical and spiritual authority, and divided again the two streams, probably forever. Democracy that had appeared in Greece, was revived and given a powerful shot in the arm by two new comers: capitalism and industrialism. Paradoxically enough, these two early allies of democracy that helped to batter down the feudal lord, the king and the papacy, became later its enemies.

The biological basis of authority are sexual, localized in the testicles and the phallus; if man is castrated in very early infancy, before the body cells have become saturated with the male hormone, he loses the urge to assert himself aggressively and to dominate his fellow men and women. Another corroboration of this is found in the behavior of asexual animals—no aggressiveness and urge for dominance is found in them. Of course this urge for dominance, like sex and other urges, displays enormous variations and even negative manifestations; there are men who like to be dominated and feel the weight of authority on their shoulders, especially "spiritual" authority.

It seems that the mind of man abhors vacuum and must have a point of support in which it can find shelter and security; also a supreme authority to make decisions, to give him unity in a conflicting and divided world. The child looks up to his father as the supreme authority; the adult looks up to God, to the Bible, to the Pope, to some religious leader, to the Supreme Court, to the dictator, rarely to science where he can find the authority that can free and guide him.

The development of Communism shows very clearly how strong this necessity for a supreme authority is to the mind of the average man. Communists started by rebelling against spiritual and political authority; they denounced the State as a tyrant to be overthrown and destroyed forever. This period of rebellion and struggle for complete freedom lasted less than one hundred years, and has given birth to the proletarian dictatorship in which the two streams of authority, the "spiritual" and the physical have again been reunited in a most strange and unholy alliance. Marx has become for the Communists what Jesus is to the Christians, and his writings have become the Gospels. At first anyone could interpret Marx's writings, and many Communists did interpret them differently, bringing divisions and schisms within the Party. With the triumph of the Bolsheviks, Lenin assumed the role of Supreme Interpreter; at his death there was a struggle between Stalin and Trotsky for the mantle of Lenin and Pontifex Maximus of Communism. Stalin won, and today nobody inside the Iron Curtain dares to challenge his interpretation of Marxism and Leninism without suffering severe and swift punishment, of course.

If tears had color, I would write these words with my own, so great is the sorrow that grips my heart when I contemplate this enormous defeat of freedom, this betrayal of an ideal in which millions of human beings had pinned their faith and their hope. I am fully aware that in the postrevolution period a good amount of control and surrender of liberty is necessary to insure the triumph of the new social order against its many internal and external enemies, to be followed by a gradual restoration of the freedom of the individual; but the State, instead of withering away as it was promised, is growing stronger and has become again a monster that devours anyone who rebels and challenges its authority. It is obvious then that freedom has nothing to hope and much to lose and to fear from revolutions, whether of the right or the left. The Founders of our country showed great wisdom and knowledge of human nature when they diluted authority and divided it between several institutions. The checks and counter checks they put around man's greed for absolute power are somewhat cumbersome and costly, but every effort and money we expend in maintaining them pay handsome dividends in freedom and security.

MAN AND FREEDOM

The dictatorship of the mind and of the body as a short cut to security is just as fallacious as it is injurious; people submit themselves rather easily to the dictatorship of the mind because it relieves them from heavy thinking and from the necessity to face unknown and unfriendly forces and thus ease them of much responsibility. Democracy, on the other hand, although it gives power to the people, also gives them responsibility, often beyond their capacity, and here is where politicians enter into the picture: they relieve people of heavy thinking, too and from responsibility together with the sweat of their brow. Even liberty becomes endangered by those who are appointed by the people to guard it.

I have said that freedom is a luxury few people can afford or ever taste. How much freedom has the average individual even in our own country? He is born and grows under the custody of his parents who more often than not are despotic. Then he goes to work and usually marries. Suppose he works eight hours, which in reality means ten hours, in which he is practically a slave. Let us allow eight hours for sleep, and he has only six hours of freedom daily, and Sundays to be with his children and wife. Yet many people misuse those few hours of freedom and get into heaps of trouble. I see the day when man will not have to work more than three or four hours—machines will do the work for him. Let us hope that by then he will have learned to use his newly gained freedom for constructive purposes; meanwhile we will do well to guard and defend the little freedom that we have because the best fruits of the mind: science, inventions, music, literature and the arts, bloom only in a soil watered with Tolerance and fertilized with Liberty.

The Anatomy of Love and Hate

Love is of man's life a thing apart; 'tis women's whole existence.
—*Lord Byron*

It is not decided that women love more than men, but it is indisputable that they love better.
—*Dubay*

I never could explain why I love anybody or anything.
—*Walt Whitman*

Love makes obedience lighter than liberty.
—*R. H. Alger*

All true love is grounded in esteem.
—*Buckingham*

Life is a flower of which love is the honey.
—*Victor Hugo*

Man, while he loves, is quite never depraved.
—*Lamb*

To love is to place our happiness in the happiness of another.
—*Leibnitz*

Love is a thing to be learned. It is a difficult, complex maintenance of the individual's integrity throughout the incalculable processes of interhuman posterity.
—*D. H. Lawrence*

Passion may be blind, but to say that love is, is a libel and a lie. Nothing is more sharpsighted or sensitive than true love, in discerning, as by instinct, the feelings of another.
—*W. H. Davis*

But love is blind, and lovers cannot see the pretty follies that themselves commit.
—*Shakespeare*

'Tis better to have loved and lost than never to have loved at all.
—*Tennyson*

Where love rules laws are unnecessary.
—*Anonymous*

Love that has nothing but beauty in good health, is short-lived, and apt to have ague-fits.
—*Erasmus*

THE ANATOMY OF LOVE AND HATE

Love is a new-comer among mankind, the youngest of all emotions; so young that most people have not yet met it and do not know what it is.

Even an ugly woman is beautiful when she is in love.

True friendship is the noblest expression of love.

Love and hate cannot be turned on and off like a faucet, nor can love be changed into hate.

FEW WORDS are more misused, abused and misunderstood and bring more unhappiness than the word love. For hundreds of years man has been told and even commanded to love God, his neighbors and his enemies by religious leaders and philosophers who evidently had a very confused idea about the nature of love, and a too optimistic opinion about man's capacity to love. The fact that in almost two thousand years of commanding men and women to love one another love has not increased by any appreciable amount, while hate has flourished exuberantly, is ample proof of my accusation.

Even men like Freud, who probed so deeply and critically into the dark caverns of the mind, have confused love with sex. It is not surprising then that people have such a distorted and erroneous conception of love. I love you; I want your love. These beautiful words man has repeated passionately innumerable times like music in the ears of the woman he wanted to possess. But in most cases man really says: I want your body; I want to possess you.

I have already pointed out that sex hunger is the very opposite of love; yet love often grows in this soil like a rose grows in the mud. It is not always easy, however, to distinguish between sex hunger and love. Even the classic love of Romeo and Juliet, sung by the poets and analyzed and expounded by psychologists as a shining example of pure and beautiful love cannot be accepted as such by a critical biologist; at the age of Romeo and Juliet it is very difficult to distinguish between love and sex hunger. Youth is like a boat tossed to and fro by the powerful waves of passion, while looking for the security of a harbor where that hunger can be satisfied. These conditions are most favorable for the fixation of passion upon a person who immediately becomes the synthesis and personification of all that is beautiful and good, either in womanhood or in manhood. A woman becomes the ideal woman, the only woman in the world; even if man has other women with whom he can easily satisfy his sex hunger, he usually scorns them, or if he uses them, he is not psychologically and "spiritually" satisfied.

Opposition to the possession of the ideal woman, as in the case of Juliet, only raises the intensity of passion as a dam raises the pressure of the water that it impounds; blocking the pleasure makes it more desirable and spurs man to conquer because that conquest is a challenge to his ego and to his vanity, and also acts as a powerful stimulant to his gonads. Romeo and Juliet, and other lovers like them, act and behave as if they were under the action of a powerful drug; and indeed they are because the secretion of the gonads is highly disturbing and intoxicating to the organism, as shown elsewhere in this book. People who believed that a person madly in love had been given some kind of witch's brew or love potion, were not very far from the truth. What they could not know is that the magic love potion is manufactured right inside of the body. The passion, violent and overwhelming, of Romeo and Juliet and other lovers, is not love; love flows evenly, quietly, like a rivulet and not like a torrent, trampling everything in its path.

What is love? Whence does it come? Are there different kinds of love? Why is love so rare and man's capacity to love so small? Can man love God, his neighbors and his enemies? Man has asked these questions many times without obtaining a rational and satisfactory answer. Even today, in this scientific age, when I ask people: What is love? they answer: God is love and love is God, believing that they utter a most profound and wise definition of love when in reality they merely have covered their ignorance with a play of meaningless words. The right answers to these vital questions has not been obtained, because people have not looked for it in the proper place.

The biology of love is not different from other emotions; love is an affective response to an external stimulus, and this response is characterized by a discharge of energy directed toward the living creature that elicits affection; but contrary to the popular belief that love flows easily and abundantly, the discharge of this affective energy is rather meager and weak in comparison to the tremendous discharge or discharges of energy we find in fear and hate and other emotions. The reasons for this difference are not hard to find, and are discussed in another chapter. Hate is the offspring of fear and therefore partakes its ancianity, its power and its abundance. Unlike fear, love has no survival value; this will be a great shock to those who parrot-like sing the praises of love and placed it on the Olympus as the one force that permeates the universe, and is the prime-mover of everything. The fact that love is not found in the animal world nor in primitive and less primitive human beings, attests to the veracity of these statements.

Animals care for their new-born, and so does primitive woman; but this is a biological instinct and physiological attachment that lasts only a short time, during the period of dependence from the mother. In the human species the period of dependence is quite long, therefore stronger ties are formed between mother and child; moreover, the human mother, even in the most primitive state, already possesses imagination and consciousness, which are essential for the development of love.

We know that a mother's love does not appear fully grown at the first sight of the new-born baby, although in some cases the imagination of the mother has been set afire by the thought of having a child, and she is ready to grasp him in her arms and pour upon him the love and affection with which her heart is overflowing. In the majority of cases, however, love comes slowly and quietly, growing with the constant association and identification that takes place between mother and child. It is not an uncommon experience of obstetricians to see the mother turn from her offspring with a shudder and refuse to look at it. "It is not strange," writes M. W. Shinn in *The Biography of a Baby*, "that if the mother has not followed Froebel's exhortations and come to love her child before birth, there is a brief interval occasionally dangerous to the child before maternal instinct is fully aroused." At that moment infanticide is common among savage and civilized mothers, whereas a little later it is difficult, if not impossible.

We have good reasons to believe that the long and defenseless infancy of man, during which he needs care and protection and the development and continuous growth of consciousness and imagination, have given birth to that emotion we call love, first in the mothers and later in man. Just as from sexual hunger and physical attraction blossoms enduring love, in some cases, so from biological instincts and physiological attachment between mother and child, flourishes unselfish mother love. We do not know when this transformation began to take place, perhaps four or five thousand years ago, and much earlier in woman than in man. The Hindu sacred books speak of love and so do the Prophets of the Old Testament; but the Hindus were great eroticists and much of their talk on love seems to be sexual hunger and the search for pleasure.

"Tender feelings," says R. Briffault in the great work *The Mothers*, "are one and all derivatives of the maternal instincts and products of feminine evolution; they are developed, that is, in relation to the reactions of the female organism, and are feminine secondary characters. But characters developed in relation to the functions of one sex are, nevertheless, transmitted in some form to both."

Man, however, has usually fought and even crushed those tender feelings whenever they have appeared, because of the contempt with which he has regarded woman for thousands of years. Woman was considered weak and inferior, cowardly and deceitful, therefore man must be hard and cruel; consequently most men are still untouched by those tender feelings

[172]

and never come to experience the thrill of loving and being loved. Love, like all other emotions, is influenced and conditioned by several factors, such as age, sex, culture, health or disease and by the chemistry of the endocrine glands and the nervous system; of these two last factors we know little yet, but they seem to play a very important part and determine the capacity and the intensity of love. There is no such thing as love at first sight. We can get a clear idea of what love is by analyzing the process of "falling in love". What happens when a man falls in love with a woman or vice versa? A man sees a woman for the first time and "falls madly in love" with her, and from that moment on his mind is filled with her and devotes most of his energies to her conquest. Why that particular woman and no other? What causes that attraction and that specific reaction we call falling in love?

Man and woman, in common with every living thing, have a magnetic field around them; the Hindus call it Aura. The Western scientists scorn this theory and usually ignore it, mostly because it comes to us associated with mysticism and other metaphysical mumbo jumbo. It is not necessary, however, to be a scientist to perform experiments in the laboratory to prove the correctness of this theory. A flower, for instance, has a magnetic aura around it formed by the very small particles it radiates as long as it is alive, and as we come within the range of that aura or radiation field, we feel its perfume and are attracted or repelled by it. The same phenomenon takes place in man and woman. The activity of the cells and the secretion of the glands form around us a field of radiation or aura with its own peculiar odor, just like in a flower; when a person comes within the radiation or magnetic field of another person, he may be either attracted or repelled or remain neutral, the particular reaction being the result of many factors, some known and others unknown, that we cannot analyze here. This magnetic field varies and changes with age and is influenced by health and disease, beside other elements. The radiation of a young girl, for instance, is very different from that of an old woman, and the same thing applies to man and the response is, of course, very different. When a man sees a woman who attracts him strongly, his first reaction is a conscious or unconscious desire to possess her, to be in her arms, to kiss and be kissed by her. This may be a superficial and passing desire or a very strong passion that remains; he may see in her something striking that appeals to a conscious or unconscious wish: her voice, her odor, her touch, her way of walking and moving her hands, her eyes, any of these things or all together have something very exciting and attractive that hold him like in an iron grip. Thus a fixation takes place, and that woman becomes the only woman for him. But this is not love yet; it is merely sexual hunger, physical attraction which may pass away when that hunger is satiated.

If the road to possession and sex satisfaction is blocked by obstacles, as usually is in our civilization, passion and desire grow by leaps and bounds. When people get married under these abnormal circumstances, two things will happen: sex hunger is satisfied and "love" flies out of the window, or the two individuals find qualities that complement their personalities and real love emerges and binds them with strong ties.

A woman need not be beautiful to get a man to "fall in love" with her; personality, charm and a powerful magnetic field can be more attractive and more powerful in holding a man than a beautiful face and body. Some flowers are very beautiful, but do not have any odor, while others are not beautiful but have a very strong and intoxicating aroma. One usually holds longer to the second.

Friendship is, in my opinion, one of the highest and noblest expressions of love, and its analysis can help us to understand love. Two men do not fall in love with each other at first sight; friendship begins slowly and grows as the two friends become acquainted with each other and discover qualities they admire and esteem. There is no violent passion here; love flows easily and smoothly like a brook, not like a torrent. Love does not usually flow from a very high source to a very low level; that is, if a person is very superior to the other, there may be respect and admiration but rarely genuine friendship. This love is not influenced by looks and appearances, nor is it destroyed by petty trifles, for it is the inner person that we love and not the external. Since friendship demands complete confidence and trust between individuals and the struggle for life is fierce and ruthless, with no quarter given, few men can be trusted or are willing to trust another, and friendship is a rare flower and real friends are scarce. As the proverb says: a friend in need is a friend indeed. Great differences in age are not favorable to the formation of friendship.

Although friendship is the noblest expression of love, there is some difference between them; there can be love without friendship, but not friendship without love. A person, usually a woman, may love another person without asking love in return, though she may crave for such love; this is love at its best, and is very rare in men. This love can stand abuse and even injury. The person capable of such a love is happy when she can do something for the beloved, even to the point of sacrificing oneself. Men feel this way for an ideal or a cause, more so than for human beings; that is why they often abandon wife, parents and children to fight and die for such an ideal. It can be said that man loves more abstractly, while woman loves concrete and tangible things.

It should be noted that friendship is still more rare among women than among men. Women's highest aspiration is to be loved by men and to hold that love; fear of losing it leads woman to regard other women with suspicion and to consider them as rivals, especially if they are young and pretty. Jealousy is an enemy of friendship and of love too, and it does not take much to arouse jealousy in a woman.

There is only one kind of love that manifests itself differently in different persons and in different situations. Is it possible to love God and one's enemies? Contrary to all the assurances and commands of the prophets, it is impossible to love God and one's enemies; one cannot love and fear at the same time a Being never seen and of Whom we have only contradictory descriptions. Moreover, love cannot be commanded; it must flow free, or it will not flow at all. No one can love his enemies either; one may feel compassion, pity and tolerance—but not love.

We can get another view of love by contrasting it with hate. Hate comes in violent outbursts at the slightest stimulus or provocation, or even without external provocation. A person with a strong prejudice against Negroes or Jews, for instance, may get into a fit of anger and hatred at the mere mention of those words. But nobody goes into a fit of love, except at the sight of a beautiful woman, and that is something else again. Love is a fragile and delicate emotion; hate is vigorous, exuberant, lasting and enduring; one can hate a whole group of people and even a whole nation or all humanity, but no person has such a capacity to love. Most persons can only love one or a few persons at a time.

Since love is not an instinctive emotion, like fear and hatred, and has evolved from our culture and the growing intimacy of the family, it has so many more enemies and usually gets rough going. People often say: he loves himself only, not realizing that this is not feasible. Love is an emotion that flows toward someone, an affection for another person. What these people mean is that such a person is very selfish, egotistic and incapable of thinking about another person's feelings and needs, and therefore unable to love.

Can we love animals? I believe that the dog and the monkey are about the only two animals we can really love, because they are so close to us, and they return some love and devotion.

Since love is so easily confused with sex hunger, are there any ways and methods to find out when it is really love and not a mere infatuation? This question was asked and answered recently in the syndicated column: "Your Marriage", conducted by Samuel G. and Esther B. Kling. Here is their answer: "Yes. Here are some of them. You will find greater happiness in the presence of your beloved than in any other person. When you are apart, you will want to be with him. You will want to look at him, to hear his voice.

"You will have countless things to say to each other and to do together. His very presence will stir you not only physically but mentally, so that life becomes more meaningful than you ever thought possible.

"You will want to share your experiences with him and you will want to have him share his with you. You will want to know the people he knows and participate in his interests.

"You will be considerate of his wishes, dreams, and aspirations, making them yours as well.

"You will begin thinking of yourself as his prospective partner, and you will make plans for a future life together in terms of home and children.

"You will take pride in your loved one, praising him to others and be eager to have others praise him.

"Finally, you will be anxious for his success, and you will do everything possible to further his welfare and happiness."

Most of the symptoms and qualities enumerated by these writers can exist, at least in man, without real love being present, because they can be the product of sexual hunger and of the passionate desire to satisfy it. Most men exhibit practically all the qualities and symptoms described by these two experts, during courtship and for a period more or less extensive after marriage, only to lose them afterwards, thus proving there was no genuine love. What Mr. and Mrs. Kling say applies to woman but not to man; woman has a greater capacity to love and sexual hunger, although strong, plays a less important part in courtship and marriage. For a very great number of men marriage is not an end, but the means to satisfy a burning passion. All this makes it rather difficult to make a correct diagnosis of love. There is, in my opinion, another test or symptom that helps to diagnose whether the patient is afflicted with that wonderful emotion we call love. If the lover is willing to sacrifice his own happiness and his pleasure for the welfare and happiness of the beloved, then it is genuine love.

Love is a beautiful but delicate flower that does not grow in any soil; it requires good fertilizer and constant care, for it can be easily injured and destroyed. For this reason love is a luxury still unknown to millions of people; many want love but few are capable to love. Hate, on the other hand, is an evil weed that grows almost anywhere and in any soil; it does not require care, no fertilizer and defies successfully most efforts to exterminate it from our garden.

A scientific offensive against hate is imperative, today, not tomorrow. Since it will prove impossible to eliminate hate from the field of human emotions, we must seek and find ways to direct it against objects worthy of the most intensive hatred; these objects exist and psychology has already shown us how we can build proper dams to tame the destructive forces of this powerful emotion. What we need is the will to apply the knowledge and thus also prepare the soil for the growth and flourishing of love in every human heart.

The Pursuit of Happiness

All who win joy must share it; happiness was born a twin.

—Lord Byron

Happiness consists in the attainment of our desires, and in having only the right desires.

—St. Augustine

We take greater pains to persuade others that we are happy, than in endeavoring to be so ourselves.

—Goldsmith

The Shirt of the Happy Man—Once upon a time the king was very ill and his physicians decided that only wearing the shirt of a happy man could cure him. Heralds went forth throughout the country from palace to farm. Nobody was happy. Finally in desperation the searchers called at the door of a shepherd's hut far up in the mountains. Yes, answered the man, I am happy. But he had no shirt.

—Popular Story

A full belly makes a happy heart.

—Spanish Proverb

Men of the noblest dispositions think themselves happiest when others share their happiness with them.

—Jeremy Taylor

The happiest life is that which constantly exercises and educates what is best in us.

—Hamerton

That all who are happy are equally happy is not true. A peasant and a philosopher may be equally satisfied, but not equally happy.

—Johnson

Happiness is the supreme object of existence.

—J. Gilchrist Lawson

Drink deep or taste not of the Pierian Spring
A little knowledge is a dangerous thing.

—Pope

The quality and quantity of happiness is affected by the methods and manner in which it is obtained, and by its source.

Happiness can be bought rather cheaply if you have the right kind of money.

Happiness has but one supreme commandment: it must never interfere with the integrity and welfare of another person.

Prescription for Happiness:—One glass of water from the River Lethe (to forget what must be forgotten). Add: one tablespoon of optimism, health, stoicism and understanding. Mix well. Drink A. M. and P. M.

The more things you need to be happy the less are the chances that happiness will be yours.

Happiness means different things to different people, and even to the same people at different age, different sex and different culture.

To obtain from life the maximum of happiness with no harm to others or to oneself is the supreme achievement of every human being.

There can be happiness without pleasure but not pleasure without happiness.

Happiness is to pleasure what wisdom is to knowledge.

IF THE WRITERS of our Declaration of Independence had any idea of the meaning of Happiness and how to carry out the pursuit of the Blue Bird, they kept it to themselves, unfortunately. But although Thomas Jefferson did not add an appendix to the Declaration of Independence giving us a blueprint to paradise, the statement that all men (were women omitted intentionally or included in men?) have a right to the Pursuit of Happiness, was a most revolutionary and far-reaching statement, never made before. Hitherto, happiness had been considered a rather mystical and metaphysical experience not to be obtained on this earth. I should be more precise and add that this was true since the appearance of Christianity because to pagan peoples happiness and pleasure were something to be had right here in this world, not in the next. Under paganism men and women took pleasure and happiness where they found them, without moral scruples. With the advent of Christianity, happiness became the most elusive bird—it was only to be obtained by suffering, through God's intermediaries. Thus the priest became the sole merchant of happiness or rather, unhappiness.

Recently, a national magazine conducted a Round Table discussion on the Pursuit of Happiness in which a selected number of men and women tried to interpret what the writers of the Declaration of Independence had in mind when they wrote those famous words. But the discussion failed to throw much light upon the meaning of Pursuit of Happiness. It behooves us then to ask: What is happiness? What makes people happy and unhappy?

Happiness is an emotive state and like all other emotions is a response or reaction to an external or internal stimulus, characterized by discharges of energy and physiological processes that are pleasurable. The quality, quantity and intensity of happiness is an individual equation and will vary even in the same person, that is, something that may produce happiness at one time may not do so at another time, because it is influenced and conditioned by: age, sex, climate, temperature, health, knowledge and culture of the group, and by chemical processes occurring within the body that are not subject to analysis.

There are three states of happiness: (a) the negative state, which means merely the absence of pain and discomfort. The lower animals do not know any other state which is easily obtained by the satisfaction of the biological needs. In its early stages, primitive man is not different from animals, but having consciousness, pleasure begins to appear as short flashes and pain becomes of age, that is, it reaches the psychological level. Since the life of the primitive consist in eating, hunting and sex now and then, the sources of pleasure and happiness, as well as pain, are scarce and of low intensity. Therefore, man craving already for stronger stimulus and sensations organizes dances and singing followed by sexual orgies. Later drink also enters the stage as an added stimulant.

With the above aids, man reaches the second or positive state of happiness, though for a short time; but the taste left by pleasure and happiness, no matter how short, demands repetition. There is no doubt also that under the impact of strong sensations and powerful stimulants the nervous system becomes more sensitive and more easily stimulated and aroused as it is the case with modern man. At this stage, happiness and pleasure still are one, and all happiness comes from purely physical sensations; but in this moment of pleasure and happiness the euphoric state is already adumbrated. The development of this higher state of happiness and pleasure is of course made possible by the constant growth of society and the ever widening circle of stimulus and sensations.

Christianity, by placing a tabu on pleasure and happiness and making suffering and pain the essential requisites for the attainment of their spiritual facsimiles, reversed the progressive march toward happiness that had taken place in the pagan world. The results of this absurd, anti-natural and short-sighted policy were most disastrous; after a short lull people went after pleasure with a madness and resolution unknown to the pagans, and while a small number of mystics sought happiness in meditation and the union with God, lust and sexuality became rampant. The convents, where men and women had retired to get away from pleasure and happiness, became aflame with lust and worse than brothels, and even the halls of the Vatican palace became the scenes of bacchanalian and sexual orgies that would have brought blushes to pagan emperors.

In studying these conditions we must take into consideration the fact that people lacked the many and varied sources of happiness and pleasure we enjoy today. They did not have music to speak of, no movies, no great books, no poetry, no theatre, no sports, no games, no newspapers, no radio and no comics, etc.

When people speak of happiness they usually mean that euphoric state in which a most pleasurable sensation permeates every cell; like the rays of the rising sun cover everything and make every object bright and beautiful. How often and for how long will the individual experience this blissful state depends on many factors, the source of the happiness, the capacity of the individual, age, etc. For instance, the happiness produced by sexual intercourse is of short duration and varies in people, while the happiness felt by the mother in the love of her child is much more lasting. Usually the euphoric state does not last long and there are also physiological reasons for this. The body is incapable of such sustained discharges of energy as used in intense happiness without getting exhausted, and that is why these states are followed by a feeling of depression, of sadness and even guilt. We hear people say that happiness and pleasure must be paid for with sorrow and suffering; these people are afraid of happiness—they have been frightened by religious teachers and mystical nonsense.

But such is the powerful attraction of the euphoric state once tasted even lightly that people want to taste it again in greater doses. To this effect man has developed numerous techniques and discovered new and more potent stimulants to bring it at will. The most primitive technique was the already mentioned dances, singing and sexual intercourse, followed by religious ecstasis. However, few people are able to attain the euphoric state through mystical experience and the road is too difficult and prohibitive.

But man's search for new ways and means of escaping pain, discomfort and suffering was rewarded by the discovery of herb brews and concoctions and later by alcohol that, like the Aladdin Lamp, opened the doors to happiness with the greatest of ease. Chemistry has given man new keys with which to open the doors of euphoria; but these keys are counterfeit keys that produce negative states of euphoria with harmful results and should not be used.

The artist is a lucky man, for he is gifted with the power of lifting himself to the Seventh Heaven by his own bootstraps, that is, he is capable of attaining periods of exalted happiness without using alcohol or drugs—his vivid and powerful imagination can do the trick. Yet artists are very unhappy people: Beethoven, Shelley, Chopin, to cite only a few. They were unhappy mostly in their love life and because they had not learned to master and to use properly their wonderful gift.

Love is, in our civilization, the most abundant source of happiness and unhappiness. Love may be given a much wider meaning than just sexual intoxication. A man may "fall in love" with an ideal and feel happy in sacrificing everything including his life for it. Many men and few women (they do not seek martyrdom so easily) have gone to their death courageously and even singing, happy in the thought that they were doing something extremely important for their higher self, happier in dying for what they believed to be right and good than in living and betraying their super-ego. This sacrificing of life and happiness has been the subject of much speculation and has been held as a definite proof of the "spiritual" nature of man, and of the existence of God or a higher Being. Only the crass ignorance of man and of the forces that move him to action are responsible for these fallacious theories. The sacrifices done for an ideal or a cause are nothing else but an extension, a sublimation of the will to live.

Other human beings, under the same motivation, dedicate themselves to a life of service to others and give up the ordinary pleasures and comforts of life for another kind of happiness beyond the reach and understanding of ordinary mortals. These people are happy when they dry a tear, soothe an aching heart, alleviate pain and change a frown into a smile. They are like the artist who feels happy when he creates something that will bring joy and happiness to others. The physician who feels happy when his patient improves or recovers his health under his care, also belongs to this category. The world has too few of these people, unfortunately, because they constitute a very advanced stage in the evolution of man. On the other hand, there are those who find pleasure in the suffering of others; sadism is far more common than it is believed to be. Behind this sadistic pleasure will be found envy, frustration, desire for revenge, fear and insecurity, and all these things are in reality a degradation and supreme frustration of the will to live a happy and abundant life. We may obtain further light on the meaning and nature of happiness by analyzing what makes people unhappy.

There are few things that make a child unhappy: lack of food, pain, discomfort, lack of affection or love, and jealousy. In other words, if the child is healthy, has love and food, he is happy. As the child grows into the adolescent the field of unhappiness becomes larger; yet the problems of the adolescent are relatively small in quality and quantity. Moreover, he has too much vitality and optimism to feel unhappy and depressed for long. Youth sees the future with rose colored glasses that hide the dark clouds in the sky or gives them a silver lining.

With the entrance into adulthood and marriage the field of unhappiness again grows, this time to major proportions. The fear of want, of losing the job, dissatisfaction with the job itself, relations with the wife and with the children, with relatives, with the boss, with his fellow workers, envy, jealousy, failure in business, unsatisfactory sex relations and disease—all these things can be, and very often are, an inexhaustible source of unhappiness.

Since the average individual is sent into the sea of life without correct navigation charts and with a defective compass or no compass at all, he cannot cope with the many storms and enemies of happiness. Consequently, instead of facing these problems with intelligence, reason and stoicism, he gets frightened, panicky and seeks escape in religion, drinking, gambling and violence, neurosis and perhaps insanity. The young man or woman who saw everything so bright and the sea so calm, finds himself now blocked by what often seem to be insurmountable obstacles from which he takes a detour to sink in the swamps of escapism and unhappiness. The appalling number of neurotic and insane people, the alarming increase of delinquency and divorce are tragic testimony to the failure of our educational and economic system to prepare human beings for the Pursuit of Happiness.

Advancing age adds new problems and obstacles to happiness. Some of these are physiological—loss of virility, disease, and deficiency of glandular secretions with corresponding loss of mental vigor and optimism.

. I have hinted that happiness and pleasure, although they can and often go together, are different things. Let me make this clear with some illustrations. A person eats a delicious food and finds pleasure in eating; but that is not happiness. Even coitus with its intense thrill is not happiness, and sometimes not even real pleasure. To know that one is loved by the person he loves, to win a coveted honor or prize, the mother with her child, the appreciation of music, art, Nature —these are happiness. It can be stated that pleasure has to do more with the physiological and happiness with the psychological.

If the report of Beatrice Gould, editor of *Ladies Home Journal*, gives a correct picture, the people of the United States are the happiest in the world. In our country 46% were "very happy", 45% "fairly happy" and only 8% were "unhappy". But in France only 9% were "very happy", 52% were "fairly happy" and 35% were "unhappy". The members of Life's Round Table in their discussion on happiness felt this picture of happiness in the good United States does not correspond to reality, and I fully agree with them. Three marriages out of five end in divorce; certainly people who are happy do not break up their homes. Our jails and insane asylums are overcrowded, and who can count the neurotics and maladjusted people in the streets? And the American people spend many millions of dollars for liquor, gambling and tobacco, which really are attempts to escape reality and find some happiness. Moreover, since happiness is a transient visitor, perhaps the people interrogated were happy at the moment, or they did not want to admit their unhappiness.

On the other hand there is no doubt that the enormous industrial development and the spectacular progress of science that followed the American revolution gave a new and positive meaning to the immortal words of our Declaration of Independence. Men and women have been presented with new sources of pleasure and happiness, hitherto beyond the reach of kings. The former and exclusive merchants of happiness are facing very stiff competition in the many discoveries and inventions of science, and are being forced to adopt new methods and ways to hold and to attract the people to their counter; and let us not forget that psychology is discovering the causes of unhappiness and mapping the roads that can lead us safely to the coveted treasure.

Since I have shown that the Pursuit of Happiness means different things to different people, does this mean that there are no basic foundations or requirements for happiness? I do not think so. There are, in my opinion, several basic requirements. Economic security for oneself and for the family is one of those requirements; yet, paradoxically enough, people with plenty of money and economic security often are very unhappy, while others who live under the shadow of poverty and lack many necessary things are relatively happy. The reason for this contradiction is that those poor-rich people do not have money; it is money that has them; they do not possess things, they are possessed by things. They also lack psychological security. The richest man is not he who has more money, but he who has less necessities. Diogenes living in a barrel was happier than Alexander.

Health is a most important requirement for happiness; without this priceless ingredient we cannot enjoy fully of the banquet of life. People with bad digestion, with bad livers, with aches and pains, are not happy people, and usually make other people unhappy. Yet health, as a contributing factor to happiness, has been greatly neglected until recently.

Religion was considered at one time the only road to happiness, and many millions of people have traveled this rough and thorny road to find only bitter disappointment; but fortunately for the purveyors of happiness in the other world, none ever comes back to tell us about it. It would be wrong to deny that religion brings some happiness to some people, but it does that in a negative and not in a positive way—more like aspirin that relieves pain but does not cure it; it is the "happiness" of resignation to suffering and the anticipation of a reward which may never be won. It is true that a few men and women can whip religious fervor into a kind of mystic ecstasis, as already pointed out, but the immense majority of people never tasted that exalted happiness. The causes of the failure of religion to bring happiness to mankind are evident to the student of human nature, yet they are ignored by those who are duty bound to tell the truth without compromise and prefer the appeasement of error. Religion is based on fear and fear is one of the mortal enemies of happiness; it is also based in submission to hybrid monsters, half god and half human, and happiness requires freedom; religion means escape from reality, but just because the believer walks with his head up in the clouds, his feet will not avoid stumbling over the rough facts of life, nor does it isolate him from the bitter struggle for self-preservation. This breeds contradictions and inner conflicts that are "suppressed" and hidden in the unconscious by the simple process of double book-keeping. But hypocrisy, no matter how well practiced and how good the intentions, is also an enemy of happiness.

Here in America several Christian (?) leaders, dissatisfied with the somber and ascetic aspects of orthodox Christianity, have founded several sects which, in spite of their exalted spiritualism, are nothing but psychological efforts to cash right now and here on the benefits and happiness promised in the other world, and there is no doubt that many of the members are successful in that enterprise, but their benefits are mere crumbs in comparison to the wealth and privileges obtained by the leaders. However, these sects fail to have mass appeal because human beings resist change and because their crass materialism, although disguised with the flaming robes of spirituality, produces a negative reaction. To deny matter while living with and from it and dying when it is withheld, and to pretend to have tapped "that infinite reservoir of Cosmic power" while working and begging for dollars and cents, are hypocritical gestures the failure and hypocrisy of which cannot be hidden by metaphysical balderdash and the effects of which upon the integrity of the personality are clear to the psychiatrist. Integrity, honesty and the intelligent adaptation to reality are the pillars upon which happiness must rest; any other foundation will prove to be shiftless sand upon which no safe and secure shelter can be built.

Knowledge in small doses is, as the poet said "a dangerous thing" to happiness. Ignorance can be a bliss, a negative and limited kind of bliss that man is trying to leave behind. Knowledge in small quantities brings confusion, misunderstanding and cynicism, but in large amount, it increases the sources and the capacity for happiness. For instance, the ignorant looks up to the stars and sees only bright points without meaning, or tramples through the forest blind to the hidden mystery and wonders around him, in a blade of grass and in the bacteria working silently under his feet, or remains indifferent and cold before the incomparable beauty of the sunrise or the sunset.

To the wise, the starry sky is a thing of beauty in which he finds endless inspiration as he contemplates the universes on their nightly parade, and the blade of grass and the vast armies of microscopical soldiers are no less mysterious and wonder-inspiring than the stars and the galaxies. Yet all these things pale before the majesty of the sun as it ascends or descends over the horizon painting the clouds with the most beautiful colors.

All these things and more are inexhaustible sources of positive happiness within the reach of all yet enjoyed by relatively few. Knowledge enlarges the vision of man, and naturally he sees more of the good and of the bad; injustice, cruelty and the colossal stupidity of mankind fill him with indignation and with unhappiness, but he can find compensation in his understanding of those phenomena and in his greater range of sensation. The problem of the cultured man is to realize that he cannot change the world without becoming cynical and despairing; he must understand that pulling his hair and going into fits of anger will make him unhappy without bringing a bit of happiness to anyone. And he must consider it a privilege to be able to contribute even the proverbial grain of sand toward a better and happier humanity. This can, and ought to be, a great source of happiness.

Man, Death and Immortality

Therefore, as through one man sin entered into the world, and death through sin; and so death passed unto all men, for that all sinned.

—*Rom. 5:12*

For the living know that they shall die; but the dead know not anything, neither have they any more a reward.

—*Eccl. 9:5*

In a moment, in the twinkling of an eye, at the last trump; for the trumpet shall sound, and the dead shall be risen incorruptible, and we shall be changed. For this corruptible must put on incorruption and this mortal must put on immortality.

—*I Cor. 15:52:53*

It is as natural to man to die, as to be born; and to a little infant, perhaps one is as painful as the other.

—*Bacon*

Be of good cheer about death, and know this of a truth, that no evil can happen to a good man, either in life or after death.

—*Socrates*

For the wages of sin is death; but the gift of God is eternal life in Christ Jesus our Lord.

—*Rom. 6:23*

Yea, though I walk through the valley of the shadow of death, I will fear no evil; for thou art with me; thy rod and thy staff, they comfort me.

—*Ps. 23:4*

But now he is dead, wherefore shall I fast? Can I bring him back again? I shall go to him, but he shall not return to me.

—*II Sam. 12:23*

> Why if the Soul can fling the Dust aside
> And naked on the air of Heaven ride,
> Were't not a Shame—were't not a Shame for him
> In this clay carcass crippled to abide?
> Strange, is it not? that of the myriads who
> Before us passed the door of Darkness through
> Not one returns to tell us of the Road
> Which to discover we must travel too.

—*Omar Khayyam*

The soul is the first creation of the mind; with this hypothesis man explained things and phenomena he did not understand. With the soul, man also "defeated" death and obtained immortality.

Death is the Great Equalizer; it cannot be bribed, nor frightened; everything alive must die. There is some consolation in this.

Death is chemistry in reverse.

The wish to die can become, under certain conditions, the will to die.

Death has always seemed unnatural to man, that is why he has never reconciled himself to it.

Life is the Great Thief, ever greedy and stealing from Nature. Death is the Law; it always catches up with the Thief, stops him from stealing and forces him to give up everything he has "stolen".

Life is a dream; more often it is a nightmare from which we usually awaken to fall into a sleep from which there is no awakening.

CONTRARY to the "Inspired Word", death was already an old visitor before man could even pick any fruit at all; life and death were born twins. But in all the millions of years in which life and death played hide and seek before man entered the stage, no creature had possessed the consciousness necessary to ponder over the mystery of life and death to really fear the silencing Scythe or to cry over the loss of a loved one. No brain had accumulated enough gray matter to think and to attempt an explanation of life and death and no imagination to defy the second with the beautiful illusion of immortality. Consequently, to animals, death still is an incident of little importance soon forgotten by the living. But to man, death can be the greatest tragedy. To see a person full of life and movement one moment and cold and inert like a stone the next, is a phenomenon that still baffles and shocks man today as much or more than it did the savage when his eyes, shining with the light of consciousness, saw the work of death.

How can a human being stop living and cease being so suddenly? Why is a human being we love and who means so much to us taken away forever from our company to be seen no more? Impossible—it cannot happen, said primitive man to himself as soon as he had recovered from the shock of his first encounter with death. Yet there was the body, a moment ago throbbing with life, perhaps sweet and loving, working, wishing and talking, now rigid, deaf to entreaties, the lips silent forever, the eyes dull and extinguished like a candle snuffed out by the wind. These, the dreams and the visions of the dead, constitute the psychological basis for the belief in immortality and of its popularity.

We have no way of knowing how long it took man to "solve" the mystery of death, nor whether the solution was the work of one or many persons. We do know, however, that the mystery was "solved" quite logically, if we take into consideration the ignorance and inexperience of the new member of the animal world, *homo sapiens*. Man refused to accept death as the end of life and he escaped from the horns of the dilemma by formulating the first and most successful hypothesis ever to come out of the brain of man. Everything around him was alive, animated by an entity just like himself, only invisible. The rivers, the clouds, the mountains, the animals, the trees, the seas, every object animated by an invisible human being and every phenomenon was the result of the activity of those gods. Thus were animism and immortality born. This egocentric and anthropomorphic conception of life and death formulated by ignorant savages, scarcely emerged from animality, has withstood the test of time and the attacks of philosophers and today, as in the past, it is cherished by millions of human beings, learned and unlearned, ignorant and wise.

What happened to the soul after the body no longer sheltered it was no mystery to primitive man; he felt sure the dead were very much alive and that they remained around him. This belief was strengthened by visions and dreams in which he saw the dead and heard them talk to him. It probably took man thousands of years to develop sufficient imagination to conjure soul-dwelling abodes, such as Hades, Elysian Fields, and more yet to invent heaven, hell and purgatory, and to web more logical hypotheses, like re-incarnation.

The cult of the dead grew with "civilization", assuming

many forms. The Egyptians went to great trouble to make their dead content and comfortable in their journey through the unseen world. The cadaver was embalmed and wrapped in costly garments and jewels, and buried with pomp and cere- mony, amply provided with food and slaves, in sumptuous and imposing tombs—the Pyramids. But the pagans never made serious attempts to communicate with the dead; they left them alone and the dead responded to this fair treatment by staying in their sarcophagi or plain graves. Witchcraft was in the hands of the High Priests, therefore no witches went around flying through the air on a broomstick with the greatest of ease to their Saturday meetings. Being free from original sin and from the sense of guilt for having been born, the pagans did not condemn their dead to the temporal or eternal torture of burning. It was left to Christianity to trans- form the restful soul-dwelling places of the pagans into hell and purgatory. True, the Christians also invented a better heaven, but they made its entrance so difficult and uncertain that people are never sure they will get there.

Under the baneful influence of ascetics who had reneged life, living became a preparation for death. How to die be- came even more important than how to live. The most useless and sinful life could be wiped out and erased from the Book of Judgment in a few moments by dying according to the rules and regulations laid down by the Christian leaders; thus the very people who taught and demanded a virtuous life as essential to salvation and entrance into heaven placed a pre- mium upon wicked living. For what was the use of leading a good and virtuous life at the cost of sacrificing pleasure and other things when by a mere act of repentance and the magic words of the priest all the sins could be forgiven and the sinner handed a passport to heaven? In case of doubt, the soul would only go to purgatory, but it could be brought out of that imitation of hell by masses and prayers. No wonder that in the Christian society a virtuous life became a rare flower, while vice, lust, corruption and cruelty became rampant. The Middle Ages were the Golden Age of Witchcraft and thousands of women paid with their lives for a superstition, not always unwelcomed, that endowed them with supernatural powers and thus lifted them from weakness and anonymity.

How was one going to know whether a friend or a relative was in hell, in heaven or in purgatory? The Christian leaders, for all their boasted divine revelations, were just as ignorant as the dumb. Under these circumstances it was to be expected that people would make attempts to communicate with the dead with the help of the witches. The Church frowned severely upon those practices, perhaps because the leaders were afraid the people might learn the truth that their purgatory was a veritable gold mine.

When I was a boy I heard many stories of apparitions of the dead, and was told how sometimes small villages were terrorized by souls that later turned out to be bodies exploiting the ignorance and credulity of the people. I myself "saw" the dead draped in long white sheets with burning eyes, when passing by the cemetery after dark. I remember my father telling me the story of a man who, on a bet, went to a cemetery at midnight and "saw" the dead and died from the fright. What the poor fellow never learnt was that the "dead" he had seen were his own living friends who, masquerading as dead, played a prank on him. People believed that those souls were doing penance and that they wanted help to get to heaven. This meant more masses and prayers, and more money into the pockets of the priests. I was an altar boy for a few years, and during that time I collected plenty of "pesetas" for the "souls in purgatory". I saw people in rags, without shoes, who did not have enough for their children, give their hard-earned "pesetas" or cents for masses, and I saw the priests live on the fat of the land and laugh at the credulity of the poor people. If a person with money died, we sang "Requiems" and masses with great enthusiasm and brought the cadaver right to the grave with great pomp and ceremony;

the more money we got, the more prayers and better funeral. But if the family of the dead had no money, we just mumbled reluctantly a few prayers and left the soul alone, perhaps to 'stay in purgatory forever". This callousness and hypocrisy hit me so hard that I rebelled against it and refused to study for the priesthood, to which my parents and one of my cousins, who was an Archbishop, had destined me. I vowed that some day I would expose this most cruel and vicious of all rackets.

There is evidence that the first leaders of Christianity were sincere and honest, though mistaken in their views of life and death, and that they never dreamed the dead would be so cleverly and ruthlessly exploited. The resurrection of the dead was unknown to the pagans for the simple reason that they were honest about their beliefs. Since there was no death, how could anyone resurrect? If Christ did not die, how could he resurrect? He was alive all the time and his "resurrection" is no miracle at all. The contradiction is so obvious that it has been ignored and conveniently overlooked. We are also asked to believe that on the Day of Judgment the Angel Gabriel will sound the trumpet and all the human beings will resurrect and walk to hear their final sentences. I am afraid that somebody is not going to find his body because there will be not enough material in the earth. Moreover, who knows where Joe Doe's atoms are after thousands or even dozens of years after being buried or cremated? Nobody, not even God, can put Humpty Dumpty together again. True, the pagans celebrated the dead and resurrection of life in their Spring festivals, along the Mediterranean Sea where, during winter, life seems to die out and disappears from the fields. The sprouting of the seeds and the resurgence of life with a new vitality and exuberance brought new hopes of abundant food and with it, laughter and joy. In the tropics, where life is ever exuberant and the fields remain green all year round, the myth of the dead and resurrection of life is unknown.

It is really strange that although man has believed in the

immortality of the soul, it was not until 1848 that the dead began to rap messages and make noises to attract the attention of the living. It all began at Hydesville, N. Y., at the home of Mr. and Mrs. J. D. Fox who lived with their two young daughters, Kate and Margaret. Suddenly, unexplained knockings were heard, and when investigated, the knocks revealed a pattern and answered questions. "Soon it was found out that they were made by the spirit of a murdered peddler". Later the Fox sisters moved to Rochester, N. Y., where communications with the dead were "established" and Spiritualism got in full swing. "Clairvoyants" and mediums appeared everywhere and the spiritualistic movement spread like an epidemic. Mediums would contact the spirit of a dead friend or a relative and obtain messages from them; they also interrogated the spirits about the future, business and other worldly subjects, for a consideration, of course.

The works of Allan Kardec (France) and Madame Blavatsky, who claimed to be a medium and in communication with the Mahatmas, founder of the Theosophical Society, became very popular. Even scientists like Sir William Crookes were taken in by the mediums. But doubters and sceptics are never lacking, very fortunately for mankind, and they began to investigate mediums catching many of them, including the famous Eusapia Palladino, cheating. However it was not until Harry Houdini went to work on them that the mediums got real tough going. Houdini challenged mediums to produce a psychical or "supernatural" phenomenon he could not duplicate by purely physical and natural means and offered a reward of ten thousand dollars to the medium who would accomplish this feat. No medium ever collected that reward. Knowing that after his death the mediums would try to smear his reputation and defeat his work, he left a secret code that had to be given by any medium claiming to have established contact with his spirit, if there was such a spirit. Several mediums have attempted to communicate with Houdini but have been unable to give the secret code. His own wife kept a candle burning for ten years waiting for him, but in vain; she put out the candle and gave up all hope of ever hearing from her famous and beloved husband whose feats and tricks amused and amazed thousands of human beings.

Even if a medium could give the code, it would not be conclusive proof of immortality and communication with the "spirits". Madame Blavatsky was also accused of cheating by the London Psychical Research Society, which after a careful investigation in India, stated that the letters from the Mahatmas were fraudulent and the supernatural phenomena she performed were nothing else than magician's tricks. But the greatest blow to the Theosophical Society was given by J. Krishnamurti a few years ago. While still a young boy, Krishnamurti became a protégé of Mrs. Annie Besant who inherited the mantle of Madame Blavatsky and was president of the Theosophical Society. When Krishnamurti became of age, he was presented to the world in general, and to the Theosophists in particular, as the re-incarnation of Lord Maitreya, that is, Christ—the long-awaited Messiah who would lead humanity to salvation. There was great enthusiasm among the Theosophists and The Order of the Star in the East was formed to recruit and train people who would be the disciples and assistants of the Master. Our textbook—I was a member of that organization—was *At the Feet of the Master,* a little booklet written by Krishnamurti himself. All went well for a while; the Messiah had come again and mankind was going to be saved after all. But one day Krishnamurti threw a bomb into the ranks of the Theosophists by declaring that he was no Messiah, no re-incarnation of Lord Maitreya, no Master, that he had not come to save mankind or anybody and that each human being must save himself. With these words the Order of the Star in the East, so laboriously built by Mrs. Besant, was destroyed and its members left without guidance. I do not know of any other man who has refused to be God and denied himself the privileges, admiration, honor and wealth that go with that exalted state. Thus, from being a Master and prospective Savior of humanity, Krishnamurti has become an agnostic who denies the immortality of the soul!

The amazing long record and popularity of animism does not, as some people claim, prove that it is true. People have believed for thousands of years that the earth was the center of the universe, that the sun and the stars moved around it, and many other superstitions completely disproved by science. So far science has been unable to offer similar irrefutable proof of the fallacy of the immortality of the soul, but neither has it found the slightest evidence of that entity. This refutation by default, instead of discouraging people, is used as a pillar to support the hypothesis of immortality. I believe that even if science would succeed in proving that death ends everything, the belief in an immortal soul would not lose its hold upon the majority of the people. Science has proven the theory of evolution, yet millions of people, many of them learned and intelligent, refused to admit it and stick to religious superstitions. There are few instances in which the will to believe operates more strongly than in the presence of death. Belief in the survival of the soul persists in the face of contradictory facts because it is the expression of the will to live, the supreme assertion of the law of self-preservation extended beyond the grave, the protest of protoplasm and personality against disintegration and nothingness. To rob man of his soul is to rob him of cosmic importance, to deprive him of a world where justice cannot err, where it cannot be bribed and where reward and punishment are dealt out justly and swiftly. Without these things, life has no meaning, say the religionists.

What does science say about this matter of soul, death and immortality? Before biology and psychology flooded with their light the darkness of man's mind, the ghost of dualism, of soul and body, working at cross purposes, ruled supreme and unchallenged. Now it has vanished, at least from the realm of science. We know now that the "soul", ego or personality is the sum of the physiological and psychological activities of the body, the result of the integration of all the cells and functions correlated into a coherent whole after millions of years of trial and error. When a vital link in this integration is damaged or destroyed, consciousness disappears, the personality melts away like smoke, and death is a reality.

Strange as it may seem, we begin to die the moment we are born, and even before, because millions of cells die every day. Nor does death come all at once to all cells. The brain cells die first and with them dies consciousness; the other cells die at varying rates, some remaining alive for hours, especially in some animals, like the frog. There seems to exist a close relation between the rate of living and the rate of dying; the brain cells have the highest metabolism and therefore are more alive; they also die first and quickly; while cells with lower metabolism, like osseous and connective cells, die later.

Since both life and death are, in the last analysis, chemical phenomena, we must seek their solution in the science of chemistry, not in the lucubrations of the theologians and other purveyors of illusions. There is already enough evidence to state that life is the result of a special and exceptional integration and combination of atoms whose dynamic struggle to maintain their unstable stability is the primary cause of their adaptation to the environment and other elementary phenomena manifested by living creatures. The chemistry of life is a special kind of chemistry, but the elements and laws involved in those chemical processes are essentially the same as those found in inorganic chemistry.

Some scientists with one foot in the laboratory and the other in the metaphysical world, where, as scientists, they have no right to enter, have tried to prove that this combination and integration of atoms could never have happened accidentally. Life, however, gives the lie to these mathematicians. These part-time scientists do not seem to realize that in denying matter the power to lift itself by its own power to life they jump from the frying pan into the fire, and that instead of solving the problem, they complicate it beyond solution.

MAN, DEATH AND IMMORTALITY

If life is the work of an intelligent being called God, how can they reconcile His intelligence and power with the millions of years of innumerable trials and errors and failures it has taken to produce even simple organisms? Or with the enormous waste of life and the ruthless struggle for survival that has existed since the beginning of life?

Twenty-four hundred years ago Heraclitus likened life to a flame, and no analogy more fitting has ever been proposed. Life is sustained by the same sort of combustion as that in the flame; the contour of the flame, like the outward aspect of the body, is always the same, but the contents of both are continually changing. In the flame, atoms of carbon and oxygen are constantly combined to form carbon dioxide and energy is constantly released in the form of heat, while in the body energy is derived from the oxidation of carbon contained in food. Life is fire without flame, slow combustion of fuel; life is matter with metabolism. No human brain, not even a *Univac,* could calculate the number of chemical changes and processes and the atomic combinations that took place before the right combination that produced the spark and lit the fire of life; but once started, life—like fire—will go on, provided sufficient fuel is available. Yet the slightest disturbance of that atomic combination, if produced in the right place, can be sufficient to put out that fire. Death means disintegration, chemical confusion, a break of one or more links of the chain that holds the atoms together and their return to the original pool of Nature whence they came.

Death from natural causes, that is, from old age, seems to be due to the reaching of entropy. Under the magic touch of the sperm, the egg starts its growth with an enormous expanding power as great, or even greater, than that of a Nova star or an expanding universe, if we take into consideration the difference in size, and reaches a critical limit beyond which expansion is not possible. Then comes the period in which the loss of energy is greater than the production, and the organisms can no longer reverse the entropy. In this phase of greater diffusion of energy that follows the phase of concentration, the cells pass from a state of dynamic activity characterized by great aquosity, elasticity and turgescence, into one of static quiescence during which dehydration and hardening takes place and a kind of involution begins in the organism.

The second law of thermodynamics is based on the observation that the universe is "running down", that is, energy is being distributed throughout the space in an increasingly random manner so that eventually there will be nothing but disorganization where once there was an organized accumulation of matter. For a time, living matter in general and the human body in particular is able to defy and reverse the second law of thermodynamics, but it finally reaches entropy and succumbs to it like the earth and all other universes.

The earth itself acts and behaves like a giant cell, and no doubt, at one time had a very high "metabolism" and the dynamic qualities of youth. There is evidence that "the old mare is not what she used to be" and that the earth is following the same aging process of living creatures and that one day it will get cold, die and disintegrate; it will have reached entropy. Matter is ever in constant flux, ever becoming and passing through new forms. Long before western science could find this out, Hindu philosophers saw that matter and energy are eternal, that only form is transient and temporal.

This chapter would be incomplete without a brief analysis of the sociological consequences of the fear of death. The history of development and growth of the fear of death is strange and paradoxical. To the child, death has no meaning and no terrors, neither for the primitive man. When the savage saw another savage dead or dying he thought of it as a matter of witchcraft, the work of evil spirits that paralyzed the body, and naturally enough, the witch of the tribe was at first asked to counteract the sorcery and the evil spirits which brought harm. It probably did not take long for the savage to realize that no magic words, no gestures and no amulets were strong enough to bring the "soul" back to the body and to find out more logical causes of death, like disease.

But since the disappearance of the body meant only that the spirit had entered an invisible world very much like the visible one, death was accepted without abnormal fear. The Jews, being a relatively small community in which the loss of one or more members meant less defenders against hostile peoples, resented and feared death, but without the abnormal and pathological fear that would come later on the wings of a hybrid offspring of Judaism.

Socrates drank the hemlock with serenity and stoicism, and the pagan world as a whole accepted death with the same stoicism. It was Christianity, religion of "life", of "spiritual and eternal life" that gradually filled the minds of the people with a pathological fear of death—the reasons have already been pointed out. I should add that the gory and ugly picture of a man hanging from a cross found everywhere, haunting everyone like a horrible nightmare and reminding every Christian of his guilty part in the alleged tragedy of the Calvary, contributed very much to magnify the suffering of dying and the possible punishment in the other world. Those ascetics who had betrayed life and renounced all pleasures, found a sadistic pleasure in carrying the crucifix and in flaunting it in everybody's face to still laughter, to frighten away pleasure and to scare people into submission; they were, and still are, dangerous killjoys. Thus the crucifix that originally was presented as the "spiritual life-saver of the soul" and the step-ladder to heaven, became a symbol of persecution and intolerance, a heavy rock hung around people's necks that gradually dragged them into the lower depths from which it was supposed to lift them. Before anyone accuses me of blasphemy and extreme exaggeration, let him read the history of Christianity with an objective and impartial mind, as a scientist examines an object under the microscope. In fact, there is no need of turning the pages of history; let him look around and observe with a cold eye what is happening in the Christian world right now, and he will see that the crucifix is used as a club to enslave people, as a shield to hide an enormous greed for power and for money.

The Spanish people, out of their misery and suffering, have concocted the following doggerel:

> En tiempos de las barbaras naciones
> colgaban de la cruz a los ladrones
> pero ahora que vivimos en el siglo de las luces
> de los ladrones cuelgan las cruces.[1]

Blasco Ibañez, the famous Spanish novelist, wrote a book entitled: *Los Muertos Mandan,*[2] in which he shows how the dead tyrannize the living. The truth is that we live under archaic laws, senseless traditions and fallacious beliefs that may have seemed logical hundreds of years ago, or even before the development of modern science, but today they are worse than useless—they are downright harmful. We are tied to the dead by a sort of umbilical cord; let us cut it out and leave the dead alone. It is the living who deserve and need all our attention and our love. While a relative or a friend is living, we must do all we can for him, but once he has ceased living, the sensible and pragmatic thing to do is to put the empty vessel away with a minimum of fuss and ceremony. Funerals are nothing else but macabre and largely hypocritical gestures, as wasteful as they are foolish. If there is the kind of immortality and God those people believe in, how silly and ridiculous are all their ceremonies and their prayers, and if there is nothing, as the facts seem to indicate, they are still more foolish and useless. In fact, I should think that God would resent the chattering, begging and bewailing as an insult to His Justice and His Love for a soul who, after all, is His child.

I feel sure that if the dead could see their relatives and friends crying and despairing, they would order them to dry their tears and be of good cheer. I certainly would not like to

---

[1] In those times when people were barbarians
from the cross they hung the thieves
but now that we live in the century of the lights
from the thieves they hang the crosses.
[2] *The Dead Command.*

see my children, my wife and my friends in tears and in deep grief because I had reached the end of my journey, which is just as natural and necessary as the beginning; I will want them to stay happy, their lives bright and unclouded by my departure from the stage of life. And if my wishes are heeded, I do not want them to see me dead; I want them to remember me alive and to carry that image in their minds.

If we want to honor the dead and pay homage to their memory, there is one sensible and useful way—a way that would be pleasing to them if they could see, and that is, by living up to their teachings, by emulating their heroism, their courage, their unselfishness and their idealism; all the rest is merely a salve to soothe our conscience, to hide our failure and our hypocrisy.

Since the craving for immortality is a natural phenomenon, it is foolish and unnecessary to uproot it from the minds of men. What must be done is to give it a rational and pragmatic meaning and to direct that hunger toward constructive manifestations. Let man seek immortality in his children and in a useful life studded with good deeds that will shine like stars after his body returns to the dust whence it came; that is the "soul" that does not die, that is real immortality.

Man's Quest for God

(The following quotations are from the book:
My Idea of God, A Symposium of Faith, edited by Joseph Fort Newton)

Destroy the free personality of God and the possibility of fellowship with Him is gone; we cannot love a God of whom we are parts.

> —*J. Gresham Machen, D.D.*
> *(Presbyterian)*

The Catholic Church believes that there is one true and living God, the Creator and Lord of Heaven and earth, Almighty, Eternal, Immense, Incomprehensible, Infinite in intellect and will and in all perfection; Who, being One, Individual, altogether simple and unchangeable Substance, must be asserted to be really and essentially distinct from the world, most happy in Himself, and ineffably exalted above everything that exists or can be conceived.

> —*Vatican Council*

God is one but has three Persons, The Father, The Son and The Holy Ghost.

> —*Catholic Catechism*

I think of God, not as a Being who occupies space, not as seated on a throne in the sky, nor as working like an architect or builder, using tools and building-stuff. I think of Him as Spirit—which does not mean something vague, vapory, ghost-like.

> —*Rufus M. Jones, D.D.*
> *(Quaker)*

The Christian Science God is universal, eternal, divine Love, which changeth not, causeth no evil, disease nor death.

> —*Science and Health*
> *Mary Baker Eddy*

Hence God is not the Creator of mortals. No more is He the creator of the so-called material universe. God is the creator, then, of the true man, His spiritual and perfect offspring, and the spiritual universe.

> —*Albert F. Gilmore, Editor*
> *Christian Science Periodicals*

To me God is not a finite Being. Or perhaps I should say He is both finite and infinite. *(Is that possible?)* He has something very human in Him. He loves, and He can resent evil.

> —*E. Mullins, D.D., LL.D.*
> *(Baptist)*

[206]

God to me is that creative Force, behind and in the universe, who manifests Himself as energy, as life, as order, as beauty, as conscience, as love, and who is self-revealed supremely in the creative person of Jesus of Nazareth, and operative in all Jesus-like movements in the world today.

—Henry Sloane Coffin, D.D.
(Presbyterian)

To feel that God, the mighty spirit of humanity, needs me, is to feel stirred to the uttermost depths of my being. To feel that I am a part of and a contributor to the God, is to find myself lifted to the possibilities of purest and bravest life.

—John Dietrich
(Unitarian)

So far as we can judge from the divine handiwork, God is not infinite, certainly not omnipotent. All available facts would seem to prove the truth of the statement of William James, that "God is finite either in power or in knowledge, or in both at once." Such is God—not power but love; not the goal, but the road; not the victory, but the great adventure.

—John Haynes Holmes

When we speak of God we mean something which, while not a physical thing or human person, we take to be at least as real as any physical thing or human person.

—Douglas C. MacIntosh, Ph.D.
(Baptist)

Essential, that is how I still think of God. I think of Him as the Spirit whose energy produced the world with infinite variety of activities, and by whose will is directed the eternal procession of life.

—Rabbi H. G. Enelow

God is evidently Jehovah, the All-Fatherhood; by implication, the all-embracing love, purpose, or will side of His Being.

—Charles W. Harvey
(Swedenborgian)

Therefore my God must in the very beginning be possessed of two characteristics: He must be moral and He must be personal.

—Ralph Tyler Flewelling, Ph.D.
(Methodist)

For when we say "God", we mean that in which all that ever was or will exist eternally, ideally, potentially, perfectly. To think of it as "a magnified non-natural man" is no less absurd than thinking of it as a magnified lamb or lion.

—Horace James Bridges
(Ethical Culture)

MAN IN NATURE AND BEHAVIOR

Allah is God and Mahomet is His Prophet.

—El Koran

If the oxen had hands and the capacities of men, they would make gods in the shape of oxen.

—Xenophanes

My idea of God is the idea of the personified, idealized whole reality.

—Edward Scribner Ames, D.D.
(Disciples of Christ Church)

I think of God first of all as a Spirit, and of His relation to the world as that of spirit to body.

—Bishop Francis J. McConnell, D.D., LL.D.
(Methodist)

My All-God is within me. As I know that there is electricity in my study to give me light, so I know that God is in me. . . . I am the son of God, made in His image; Christ is the Son of God.

—Brown Landone, F.R.E.S.
Fellow, Royal Economic Society, London

Every concept of God is necessarily that of an idol.

—Fichte

When the astronomer Laplace was asked by Napoleon what part God had in his system he answered that God was not necessary in his system.

And Man created gods in his own image.

God is the shadow of man projected into the vast canvass of the cosmos.

The difference between the Theist and the Atheist is very small. The Theist affirms God with his lips and denies Him with his deeds. The Atheist merely denies Him with his lips.

God started as the alter-ego of man; later He became the scape-goat for his shortcomings and later yet, the repository of his lofty ideals and aspirations.

When someone speaks to me in the name of God I ask him for his credentials. So far nobody has been able to produce genuine and satisfactory credentials.

M ANY MORE PAGES could be filled with opinions and definitions of God no less contradictory, childish, irrational and absurd than these quoted above. God is spirit; God is personal and material. God is human, finite, impersonal and infinite. God is One but He is also three different persons.

God is incomprehensible and indivisible, yet He appears and speaks to men. God is Omnipotent and Just, yet His children have suffered injustice and other evils since the beginning of humanity. God reveals Himself to men, yet even within the same church there are many different definitions and images of Him. I could go on pointing out contradictions, but this should be enough to prove that nobody knows anything about God.

When Albert Einstein was asked: Do you believe in God? Einstein replied: "I believe in Spinoza's God who revealed himself in the orderly harmony of what exists; not in a God who concerns himself with the fate and actions of human beings." Many "divines" have grabbed this qualified declaration of belief in God and used the magic name of Einstein to fortify the shaky foundations of theism, made more shaky every day by the advances of science. Those people are not honest enough to admit that the God of Spinoza has nothing in common with theirs, that it is no God at all. God, says Spinoza, acts from the necessity of his own nature, and cannot act differently. The invocation of God as explanation, he says, is "the asylum of ignorance". There exists, he says, one Substance which we know only through its "modes and attributes". What kind of Substance is this? It is reasonable to infer that Spinoza did not know any more about that Substance or about God than we know today, and that is zero. Why don't philosophers and scientists have the courage and the honesty to admit their ignorance, and instead of confusing people, tell them the truth: we know nothing, absolutely nothing, about God. For, as Lord Kelvin has so aptly said: "Unless we weigh and measure a thing we know nothing about it." In the case of Spinoza and others who lived when denying the existence of God meant torture and fire, they must be forgiven, but in this age of freedom there is no excuse and no forgiveness.

To Sir James Jeans, God is a mathematician and the universe "a universe of thought". From this profound and startling definition of God it is easy to guess how Sir James earns his board and room: he is a mathematician, of course. As Xenophanes said long ago: "If the oxen had hands and the capacities of men, they would make gods in the shape of oxen." As for the universe being "thought", a scientist ought to be ashamed to make such an absurd statement. We have been unable to find thought outside of the human brain, and Sir James should be able to prove that the universe is "thought" or keep quiet. A scientist has responsibilities and duties toward Truth from which other men can be excused to some extent. It would be wrong to conclude that all scientists are so anthropomorphic in their thinking. Some years ago, Professor James Leuba conducted a poll among scientists and found that many are atheists; this is especially true of biologists and psychologists.

The lowest percentage of atheists was found among physicists and astronomers; these men deal with the cosmos, and with its parts, stars, galaxies, nebulae, planets, etc., and with their orderly movement. Naturally they are impressed by the order and vastness of the universe revealed by the telescope.

Biologists and psychologists deal with living matter, with animals and human beings and get a very different picture: a picture of ruthless struggle, conflict, confusion, failures, progress by trial and error, lack of intelligent planning, selfishness and cruelty. No real scientist can reconcile these facts with an Omnipotent and All-Knowing God. But few scientists have the moral stamina to come out openly and deny the existence of God and risk the economic reprisals that their confession of atheism is sure to bring upon their heads, so they evade the issue. Our boasted academic freedom is not much better today than it was when the immortal Shelley was expelled from Oxford for writing a pamphlet: *On the Necessity of Atheism.*

Now, why should the theist, who "has an Omnipotent God on his side" go into a fit of rage when his God is denied or "insulted", and try to silence the atheist with force and slander? Why does he not follow the wise advice of the Roman Emperor Tiberius who said: "If the gods are insulted, let them see to it themselves"? To a psychologist the reasons for such a contradictory behavior are clear. The Christian, for all his boasted believing and trusting in God, feels very insecure because no matter how blind he wants and tries to be to reality, it cannot be wished away. His God is like a statue on a very shaky pedestal that must be guarded and protected against the strong winds of criticism, so he hangs the *noli me tangere* sign around Him, and an attack upon his God is taken as an attack upon his person.

How did man and God get that way? To answer this question fully and intelligently we must go way back to the beginning of man. Just as the child is born without belief in God, thus was humanity born half a million or a million years ago. The first stage in the long quest for a good and reliable God is animism, which has been discussed already. By animism man spiritualized Nature. How long it took him to do that we do not know, nor do we know when, confused and bewildered by so many invisible spirits, man began to reverse that process and started to reduce their number. Instead of a separate spirit for every tree, he conceived one spirit for all the trees, a god of the forests, a god of the waters, a god of the winds, etc. By this economy of thought, man was able to get along with a relatively small number of gods, and religion entered in a new phase: polytheism.

The primary purpose of the god-myth is to "explain" Nature and all its phenomena. The *how* rather than the *why* is important. That is why among really primitive people we find no stories of the creation of the world which is taken for granted as having always existed. It is only with the growth of society and the development of imagination that the gods assume the role of creators and extend their power. At first the stories of creation are childishly crude, and animals play an important role in the ancestry of man and in the creation of the world. But man is still concerned with the *how* only; soon he will not be satisfied with the *how*—he will begin to ask *why* am I here, and many other *whys*.

Since man was the dominant figure in the clan or horde, the gods also were male. But later, with the development of agriculture, woman assumed a dominant position due to her fertility, and she was raised to the Olympus in the Goddess of Corn and the Goddess of Rice, in Isis and many other female gods. With the ascendency of patriarchy over matriarchy, the male gods won and practically dethroned the female ones.

There was a relative peace among the many gods dwelling in the mountains, in the seas, in the forests and in the temples, until Ikhnaton got the first visions of a strange God of love and mercy, superior to the other gods. This God Aton, he claimed, was the only true God and would not tolerate other gods; he was really the first intolerant god. This sublime vision of the epileptic Pharaoh was not welcome by the High Priests and when Ikhnaton tried to throw the old gods away from the temple, there was open revolt, bloodshed, cruelty and injustice. It is a rather tragic paradox that the first attempt to bring monotheism and establish one God of love and justice before Whom all men are equal, stirred the destructive emotions of men to such a fury that it ended in complete failure after a few years of strife and struggle, with the murder of the God-intoxicated Pharaoh.

But the failure of Ikhnaton did not discourage further attempts to destroy polytheism. We do not really know whether the Israelites were aware of the efforts and tragic failure of the Egyptian monarch, but if they were aware of it, they paid no heed to it and boldly picked up his cosmic struggle and went forth to make Yaveh the only God. It may have been the time, the place, the people, the methods or all these together—the fact is that the Prophets succeeded where Ikhnaton had failed, but their success has been so costly that it can be called a pyrrhic victory. It seems as if the gods would punish anyone who tried to dethrone them. Certainly the fate of millions of Jews has not been better than that of the Pharaoh and his followers, and to millions of human beings the Hebrew Ikhnatons have brought suffering, wars, misery, slavery and cruelty beyond the wildest nightmares, for soon after the enthronement of Jehovah as the only true God, his followers and believers were to unleash an orgy of persecution, intolerance, hatred, robbery and lust never seen before, and all in the name of a Merciful, Just and Loving God.

It is impossible to evaluate correctly all the factors and forces that pushed the Israelites toward monotheism with a fanatic zeal worthy of a better cause; perhaps it was their isolation in the desert where, like in the sea, the impact of the cosmic forces overwhelms man with all its might; perhaps their nomadic life that kept them awake at night watching their flocks, and the stars fired their imagination; or it may have been the fear of annihilation at the hands of their neighbors and of the hostile forces of Nature that turned their eyes away from the weak and tribal gods they had worshipped for centuries and toward a more powerful and mightier God with Whom they could change their sense of inferiority and weakness into one of superiority. Be it as it may, the tendency toward a unifying principle already adumbrated in the transition from animism to polytheism and inherent in the psychological development of man flourished in the minds of the Prophets. Isaiah, Jeremiah, Samuel and other god-hungry men speak to God and God speaks to them. Moses climbs Mount Sinai and receives from Jehovah the Ten Commandments, and with this culminating show of divine favor, the Israelites felt assured that they were the Elect of God—the Chosen People. But in spite of all this preference and constant communication with the Almighty who promised them help, the Israelites were defeated again and again by their enemies, driven from their homeland and scattered over the earth like leaves by a hurricane. However, the lucubrations of the Prophets were not lost and from them emerged the mightiest and noblest conception of God, so mighty, that before Him have crumbled into dust the majestic gods of the Egyptians, the beautiful and human gods of the Greeks, the martial gods of the Romans, the Sun-God of the Incas, the blood-thirsty gods of the Aztecs and the Mayas, and a host of other gods and spirits.

In one of the most strange, remarkable and incredible phenomena in the history of religion, Jehovah, who started as a mere tribal god, becomes the God of the Christians, and in no less incredible a manner—by incarnating in a Jewish woman—God becomes man, is crucified by the Romans and dies unrecognized as the Messiah and abandoned by his own people, who were anxiously awaiting Him. Here is the cosmic failure of a cosmic mission. How could a God make such a mess? How could He fail to convince even His own people? A mere mortal without foreknowledge, with no supernatural powers, could have done a much better job. The fact is that all these things—Virgin birth, Death and Resurrection, Trinity, Atonement, killing of the God, Holy Communion and a God-Man can be found in the religions and beliefs of non-Christian people, from whom they were unscrupulously taken and presented disguised with new names. The founders of the Christian religion can be accused of being the greatest plagiarists in the history of mankind. And behind all these myths is the Will to Live, the Law of Self-Preservation and nothing else.

What has God done to man and for man? Here again the answer is written in blood and tears; in every land and almost in every age the word God has been a fateful and tragic word that spelled sacrifices of human beings and animals. To appease the anger and satisfy the unquenchable thirst of the gods, man has poured rivers of blood upon their altars. Nobody will ever know how many beautiful maidens were offered to the Minotaurus. And who can tell us how many victims were immolated on the altars of Moloch? How many lives were claimed by Ammon? How many heretics were broken upon the rack and burned at the stake? How many lives were destroyed before the cold statues of Shiva? How many hearts were torn out of their breasts to please the Sun-God of Incas?

It is written that 70,000 human beings were sacrificed to celebrate the dedication of the temple to Huiziloch'ti, an Aztec God.

Everywhere man has toiled like a slave to feed the gods and their priestly parasites, and has felt their whip upon his back. Everywhere and in every age the gods have promised much and given nothing. Everywhere the priests have maintained the ignorance of the people and relied upon fear and mystery to preserve their power and to insure an abundant life at the expense of the faithful.

Man's attempts to picture and materialize his brainchildren have created works of art only in a few cases; in the majority, his efforts have produced ugly and repulsive monstrosities. Two-headed gods, many-armed gods, angry and wrathful gods, because the gods were representations and extensions of power of the king, and later of the father, not yet touched by the aesthetic emotion. With the Golden Age of Greece the mind became of age and the Greeks have been the only people who have created really beautiful and aesthetic gods. Who is not thrilled and uplifted by the beauty of the Venus de Milo, by the handsome and virile Apollo, and filled with an emotion of power by the mighty Zeus? The men who sculptured and painted these gods were not fear-ridden savages: they were artists for whom life was a glorious adventure. Here, for the first time in the history of mankind, we see gods not born of the unholy alliance of fear and ignorance, gods who do not demand sacrifices. It is for these reasons, and probably others, that those gods went down, temporarily at least, before the ruthless, sour-looking, frustrated and revengeful Old Man that is Jehovah, whose behavior has been that of a mean step-father and not of the Father he is supposed to be.

The Christian leaders became aware that Jehovah was lacking the appeal and attraction of the pagan gods, but they were stuck with Him; therefore, to compensate and mitigate his unfriendly appearance and his ill-tempered character, they gave Him a Virgin mother from whose womb the garrulous Old Man emerged as a sweet and beautiful child. The pagans had done the same trick before, and had let it go at that. But the Christian god-makers had been poisoned and perverted by asceticism and frustration so badly that they could not take life as a glorious adventure, as the Greeks did—to them life was a painful journey through a "valley of tears". Consequently, they were compelled by their neuroses to load this beautiful and lovely God-child with all their real and imaginary sins after submitting Him to a series of humiliations and tortures, which reflected their castration complex and their craving for punishment, they hung Him on the cross and made their God the perfect cosmic scape-goat. We do not know whether the Christian leaders were aware of the sexual meaning and symbolism of the Cross, used by the Egyptians as the symbol of the phallus and the testicles, and therefore as the symbol of life; but they must have been at least unconsciously aware of that fact, and in this light the crucifixion of their God upon the Cross gives a new meaning and reason for their fanatical hatred of sex and symbolize their sexual frustration and their defeat.

The expectation of a Messiah or Savior, another ingredient of the drama and tragedy of Redemption, had been born out of the suffering and injustice felt under the slave-master and was given a powerful shot in the arm by the Jews and capitalized by the Christian Fathers. These are the reasons why Jesus died and why Jesus had to die. Paraphrasing Voltaire, we can say that if there had been no Jesus, it would have been invented; perhaps he was invented out of not the whole cloth, but out of a little cloth. The pagan people invented many myths to appease their growing hunger for the *how* and for the *why* and to give meaning to a meaningless universe and a goal-less life. The fact is that we do not have a historical record of the "most important event since the creation of the world", an event of cosmic significance and from the knowledge of which depend the damnation or salvation of all the human beings born and unborn.

The Jesus of the Gospels is no more real than Don Quixote and his life and adventures; no more true than the fights and adventures of the mythical knight. Hyman Goldin, in his already cited book: *The Case of the Nazarene Reopened*, demonstrates that the events described in the Gospels could not have happened. The question is: Was there a real Jesus? Robert Eisler answers yes to this question in his scholarly and interesting book: *The Messiah Jesus*. But this Jesus has nothing in common with the God-Man of the Gospels. The Jesus myth is a hybrid product born of the union of the pagan conception of God and of the theological lucubrations of the Greek philosophers.

The pagan gods were one hundred per cent human, the abstraction of divinity as an attribute apart from and supernatural to the material was a result of mysticism and the growth of imagination, and appeared in India, in Greece and in Judea at the same time and prepared the soil for the greatest, the most unreal and the sorriest God ever conceived. There is nothing God-like in a man struggling painfully toward his death, carrying his own instrument of torture and jeered by the rabble; nothing divine in a man hung from the cross like a common thief and between thieves; nothing Omnipotent and courageous in dying with words of despair on his lips, and the body of a man hanging from a cross is the most macabre, the most grotesque, unnatural, ungodly and absurd picture of God ever imagined. It is repulsive to the aesthetic sense and insulting to the Will to Live, contrary to the craving for happiness and pleasure natural in man; that is why it had to be forced upon the people with threats of eternal hell and promises of everlasting bliss, with the sword and with fear. It is most unreasonable to suppose that without the help of the sword in the hands of a Roman Emperor who murdered members of his own family, Christianity would never have amounted to more than one of the numerous religious sects struggling for supremacy. What more eloquent proof of this do we want than the fact that after sixteen hundred years only about one seventh of the world's population has accepted the Christian God, and of these three hundred millions of so-called Christians only a very, very small part take Him seriously; the immense majority have remained and are pagans at heart, and show it with their deeds. Perhaps I should qualify this adjective in justice to the pagans by saying that the paganism of the Christians is not true paganism because it is tainted and distorted, perverted and suppressed, very often by that caricature of man and symbol of weakness and of defeat hanging from the Cross.

Up to practically the appearance of Christianity, the gods were not concerned with the problem of good and evil, for two reasons: one, because abstract thinking was still in a process of development and not mature as yet; the other, that human beings took good and evil in their stride, and had separate gods for good and evil. Monotheism confronted man with the problem of explaining evil in a God who was Good, Loving and Omnipotent.

The Persians found a rather logical and undramatic solution to the problem in their dualistic philosophy of Light and Darkness, personified in Ormuzd, the Good God, and Ahriman, the God of evil. Christians at first ignored this dualism, but soon found out that they could do without it even by sacrificing their God to atone for all the evil and sins of man. They solved the problem by taking Ahriman from the Persian mythology and introducing him into Christianity with a new name, new ancestry and new functions: Lucifer, the rebel angel who is cast into the fiery depths and from which he will carry on his fight against his own creator with considerable success. With this myth of the fallen angel, the Christian leaders served notice of what would happen to heretics and rebels against the authority of the Church.

Philosophers and theologians have wasted much time and precious mental energy seeking a solution to the problem of

Good and Evil, and trying to prove that God is responsible and must be praised for the Good, but must not be called to account nor blamed for the Evil. The strictures and difficulties of the divine propagandists arise from the false premises from which they start. The problem is very simple and may be stated in a few words. Good and Evil are only relative terms, not absolutes, as Aristotle believed, a belief that although enunciated by a pagan and heretic, was accepted and imposed by the Church and for a few hundred years nobody dared to criticize it openly without risking torture or roasting at the stake. There is nothing completely good nor completely bad, and both things must be viewed in relation to the individual and the community. In nature there is no good or evil as such; there are blind and impersonal forces—some good and favorable to man, and others bad and adverse to man; the same elements can be bad at one time and good at another. A rain at the proper time can be very beneficial, while at another time it may ruin a crop.

There is no good or evil in man, either. A human being isolated on an island cannot be good or bad; it is only while living with his fellow humans that his actions may be good or bad, partially or totally, for there are alternatives and stages between the two extremes, and what may be good for one may be bad for another. Behind good and evil in man stand the biological urges the satisfaction of which are the basis of both. It is clear then that the hypothesis God, instead of solving the problem of Good and Evil, complicates it beyond solution. Science has already achieved what the philosophers and theologians failed to do even with "divine help and inspiration".

Polytheists never had any trouble in finding a dwelling for their gods. Living in a limited part of the planet without the slightest idea of the shape and size of the earth and of the universe, they placed their gods in the mountains, the rivers, etc. The Greeks lodged their gods on Mount Olympus. The monotheist Jews had no trouble either in finding lodging for their Lord Jehovah, in the mountains and in the clouds—he was always within shouting distance. The Christians improved the "home" of the Lord Almighty, and gave Him a palace where, seated on a throne and surrounded by angels, he saw everything, heard everything (and did nothing about it) and ruled the stars and the earth with everything on it. With this set it was easy for divines to spin philosophical systems in which they were caught like the fly in the spider's net.

All went fairly well for a while for the believers in a personal God and a heaven right up in the sky, until the doubters and sceptics grew in number and boldness and upset the whole edifice so laboriously built. The believers were able, for some time, to silence anyone who contradicted the Holy (?) Scriptures, but finally they were overwhelmed and overpowered by an avalanche of facts coming from astronomy, biology, physics, and other sciences. Modern scientists have explored the sky and found no heaven, and geologists have sounded the depths of the earth and found no hell and no purgatory, leaving God, the angels and the souls homeless. The divines, who talk so surely about God as if they had a direct wire with Him, remain silent or give us the run around when asked where are heaven, hell and purgatory. Is it not strange that God should leave people in such ignorance about such important subjects? After all, the salvation of the soul is said to depend on believing that there are such places of reward and punishment. If we are to judge people by what they do instead of by what they claim to believe, very few Christians really take seriously heaven, hell and purgatory; even the priesthood, from the pope down, has indulged in the most un-Christian behavior— evidently they are not afraid of Satan and his devils and the burning fire.

Science is also playing havoc with the anthropomorphic conception of the Deity. Before the vastness and immensity of the cosmos with its innumerable suns, galaxies and nebulae, discovered by the telescope, the Lord Almighty, seated on a throne, becomes an absurdity unworthy of the slightest consideration. To escape this dilemma without giving up the cherished belief of some kind of God, many people believe in some kind of Supreme Power, Mind or Intelligence—one Spirit present everywhere. This pantheism is not new and it satisfies some people because they do not inquire critically into its meaning and nature; they are afraid to do that because were they to analyze those high sounding words in the light of science, they would find that the hypothesis represented by those words raises more problems than they solve. In spite of all these facts, religionists and some part-time scientists tell us that science does not disprove God, and some go as far as to assert that science proves the existence of God.

Let me state right here that this discussion of God is not an academic and philosophical pastime. Belief in God has played and still plays a major role and a vital part in the development of society and our "civilization". Even the Russian Communists have found out they cannot escape the enormous grip that God has upon the human mind. The sociological and psychological consequences of the belief in God can hardly be over-rated. It is more than proper then, it is imperative to grapple with this problem honestly and frankly. If there are proofs of the existence of God, let us have them now, and I will be the first to believe; but if there is no reliable evidence of God, let us admit it and stop being hypocrites and double-talkers. Science should really take up this subject boldly, but the majority of scientists are a frightened bunch of cowards afraid of losing their bread and butter if they attempt to knock down one of the stoutest pillars of the "status quo".

What are the proofs of the existence of an Omnipotent, Omniscient, Just, Merciful and Loving God? Let us hear what the divines have to say: 1—There must be a Creator and a First Cause; the world and all that is on it could not just happen or come into being by themselves. 2—There is "Law and Order" in the universe and this could not be without a God who rules and governs everything. 3—Life in general and the human body in particular are too wonderful, too purposive and too complicated to be the result of blind chance; they must have been created and be directed by a superior Mind or Intelligence we call God. 4—Without God life has no meaning; man would be an animal, and morality and goodness would have no reason for being practiced. 5—Man has believed in God since the beginning of time.

The answers to these questions are easy to find. Here they are: 1—Creation is not a sudden phenomenon that takes place once and stops; it is a continuous process going on in the universe all the time. New stars and new universes are in the process of creation and others are in the process of disintegration. Matter and energy are interchangeable, as the atomic bomb has proved so tragically for thousands of human beings; matter and energy are eternal and dynamic, ever changing and appearing under new forms. The first Cause reminds me of the Hindu story that the world is sustained by an elephant, the elephant by a turtle and the turtle? At this point the story-teller said—Let us change the story. Evidently he ran out of animals. Some Hindu philosophers with more wisdom have depicted creation by the serpent biting its tail to indicate there is no beginning and no end.

2—True, there is "law and order" in the cosmos, but these qualities are properties inherent in matter and the result of atomic and molecular attractions and repulsions. Have you ever seen a snow-flake under the microscope? It is beautiful and very orderly, a matter of chemistry and physics; man can duplicate those forms. Moreover, this picture of law and order is not as perfect as they want us to believe; it has many flaws. Chaos and disorder are also part and parcel of creation and are present in our earth which still shakes and trembles, often killing thousands of human beings.

3—Man and animals are very complex and complicated organisms, but they are too imperfect to be the work of a Supreme Intelligence. Evolution shows that they are the product of trial and error, and that many failures have occurred since the first organisms were formed by the aggroupment of cells.

4—Life has just as much meaning or more for the atheist than for the theist. And as for being good, the greatest criminals and sadists have been believers in God—Torquemada and company, Hitler, Franco, and so many others that many pages could be filled with their names. Everything a human being does, whether he believes or not in God, is done for selfish reasons; in other words, no act or deed is essentially unselfish.

5—This is not true; during the primitive stage of animism man did not believe in God. There are still some tribes that hardly have any conception of a supreme Being. To this answer I may add: (a) I cannot conceive of a God with the attributes and qualities of the Christian God who would tolerate the innumerable crimes and injustices committed in His name by His own ministers; (b) if there were such a God we should expect that He would reveal Himself to all human beings alike through the ages, and there would not be so many images, conceptions and definitions of Him; man would be born with a sense of his divinity, and belief in Him would come naturally, without having to be learned, and there would be no philosophical atheists and millions of plain atheists, like the Chinese, Hindus and Japanese.

What benefits has man received for all his faith and belief in God? With the exception of the priesthood and other parasites who live on the fat of the land, man has received much harm and suffering during his long quest for God. As Napoleon said: "God is always on the side of the best battalions"; that is, God is always on the side of the rich and the powerful. The fact is, for practical purposes, everyone from the pope down is an atheist; no one really trusts God. When the pope or the priests get sick, do they trust God and the "miraculous relics" they possess and just pray? Or do they call the best physician available and use the best medicines, like any other mortal? The answer is well known. The Christian Scientists are perhaps the only ones who are somewhat consistent in their beliefs, and prove that they trust God by refusing doctors and medicines when they are ill; but they suffer sickness and death just like an ordinary atheist, or worse; thus proving that God does not exist, or it is useless to pray to Him. Here is another example of the practical atheism of the believers in God. Let us take two farmers; one is very religious and prays to God every day, but he does not trust Him for the protection of his crops because if he did he would starve; he uses the same scientific methods employed by the atheist. Even the very houses of the Almighty God seek protection in science from lightning which, we are told, is controlled by God, and install lightning rods. What hypocrisy and shameless disregard for truth! It is obvious then that the words: *In God We Trust,* inscribed on that symbol of greed that is gold, are blasphemous and dishonest, and if men had any sense of decency, honor and sincerity, they would strike them out and inscribe in their stead: *In Gold We Trust.* This would be a truthful and honest expression of their sentiments.

Every invention and discovery is the product of long and arduous investigation and study; no scientist, even the most religious, has ever claimed that God has favored him with a revelation or help leading to a discovery or greater knowledge. The fact is that science has repudiated and proven false practically all the "divine revelations" found in the Bible and the "scientific" teachings of the Christian leaders, philosophers and theologians. God has told man that the earth is the center of the universe, that the sun moves around it, that the world was created in six days, that the sun stood still at the request of Joshua, and many other things which no self-respecting scientist can accept. Men have been tortured and burned at the stake for doubting God's "revelations" and scientists have been slandered and harassed by ignorant and bigoted divines who thought they had all the knowledge between the covers of their Holy (?) Book, and who today benefit from the discoveries of the very men they have fought with all their might. In spite of this record of God's ignorance of "His own world", there are scientists who still believe in God, such is the power of superstition when it is absorbed with mothers' milk. Unable

[224]

to refute or suppress the facts discovered by science, the religionists have adopted new tactics; now they say that the writer of the Genesis did not mean six ordinary days, but six long periods of time, and that though the scientist may be right about the origin and evolution of the body, the soul was created by God. Surely the human mind can skip on thin ice and rationalize the most obvious contradictions.

During the second world war somebody took what he thought was a clever crack at the atheists by saying: There are no atheists in the fox holes. This, of course, was intended as a disparagement of the atheists, but it boomerangs right in the author's face and it turns out to be a great compliment, for it shows that it is the Christians who go to war and murder their fellow men. Paraphrasing that aphorism, we can say: There are no atheists in jail.

I entertain no illusion about the power of my logic and of the facts marshalled in this book, to convince all my readers to discard their God as one discards a worn-out garment that no longer serves its purpose. Myths and images acquired in the formative years are too deeply rooted in the unconscious to be weeded out easily; it takes intellectual stamina, emotional maturity, purposive sincerity and a well integrated personality to get rid of them. On the other hand, I am encouraged by the growing dissatisfaction with God whose failure to live up to the hopes and expectations of man are tragically evident even to the average individual. More men and women are honestly and earnestly seeking a way out of the blind alley into which they have been led by false shepherds; but they feel trapped, confused, not knowing how to get out, afraid of breaking up with their ancestral traditions and beliefs, afraid to hurt and offend relatives and friends, afraid of the economic consequences, afraid of facing the unknown without that crutch that is God. Men who feel this way are still in their childhood; they have not grown up; they have not cut the silver cord to the Father-Mother complex. I hear them ask: What do I have to gain by giving up God? And I hear them answer, in an effort to rationalize their fear and their mental laziness: There is no harm in believing in God, after no positive proof of his non-existence has been presented. The tragic history of man's quest for a good and reliable God and his failure to find Him, briefly sketched here, answers both the question and the rationalization. Moreover, it would free man's mind from a ghost that has terrorized and haunted his life for thousands of years; it would break down a powerful barrier that separates people into innumerable sects and religions; it would make feasible and almost certain the much sought unity of man; it would put an end to divided loyalties and leave only one great loyalty— loyalty to humanity, which is also loyalty to oneself, for each one of us is a part of humanity; it would give man dignity and freedom from many parasites and leeches; it would remove the supernatural basis of authoritarianism; it would dissolve that fog which is the salvation complex and make it clear to man that he must save himself. "The brotherhood of men under the Fatherhood of God". Beautiful words uttered in some case by men of Good Will, sincere and overflowing with good intentions, in others, by sanctimonious hypocrites for the most selfish purpose. People of the first category are more naive than they have the right to be, in the face of the history of religion. Intolerance is part and parcel of religions and it is the essence of the Christian religion; this is frankly admitted by the Catholic Church with the explanation that error (other religions) does not have the same rights as Truth. The history of Christianity is the history of intolerance at its worst. The Treaty of Westphalia in 1648 put an end to the bloody Thirty Years religious war between Catholics and Protestants, but it did not put an end to religious intolerance and hatred which are gnawing at the vitals of Christianity under the *modus vivendi* and tolerance forced upon them by non-Christian forces and factors. Each sect and each church worships its own God and fears and hates the other. Each man has his own subjective experiences with God which he considers superior to the others and often tries to impose them by force.

Experience and communications with God can be most profitable. I ask myself why I don't get up one morning and shout to the world that I have talked with God and that for a consideration I will show others how they too can establish a direct wire with Him. It has been done, and it is being done right now. There is a Father (?) who has amassed a fortune by spouting the most incoherent and absurd discourses I have ever heard and in the name of God, for he has the effrontery to claim that he is God. The world can never be One World so long as people kneel at different altars, worship different gods and are not cleansed from their God-intoxication and its hangover. Only science at the service of humanity can accomplish this long desired and so much needed unity.

Man has gradually enlarged the power and attributes of his gods to meet new experiences and phenomena, but he can no longer keep up with the rapid progress of science; the God of Mount Sinai, even the God of the Middle Ages, cannot be the God of the atomic century. The pagan gods were amoral and unconcerned with ethics, but they also failed to satisfy the growing hunger for a better world. Out of this hunger emerged the Christian God who has become the repository of man's noblest and highest aspirations and ideals—a God idealized by man. But while admiring his creation he has neglected himself. Present man's relation with God can be compared to that of Pygmalion with the beautiful statue he had sculptured and with which he fell madly in love. So long as man gives life to his creation, he cannot capture for himself the good qualities he bestows upon his God and will walk in darkness with only a poorly reflected light to guide his steps.

If man wants to be the master of his fate, the captain of his soul, he must take the helm and acknowledge no other captain, no other power than himself; he must stand erect, with no supports, no crutches, his feet planted on solid earth and take the bad without flinching, without moaning and dropping to his knees, and the good without giving credit or praising anyone but himself; he must be fully aware that he is alone in the universe, aware of his limitations and his capacities, aware that he no longer needs God because he can do practically all the things he has been begging God to do. Only then will man fulfill his dream of being God.

Man, Health, Disease and Medicine

A specialist is one who knows more and more about less and less. Surgery is the cry of defeat of medicine.

—Dr. Martin H. Fischer

Health means the maintenance of the four basic equilibriums of the human body: Chemical, Physiological, Physical and Psychological.

Disease, in its acute form, is generally the effort of the organism to eliminate a disturbing element and therefore it is constructive and purposive.

In its chronic form, disease is a degenerative process and represents an effort of the organism toward adaptation to a disturbing environment or agents, internal or external that cannot be eliminated.

Old medicine was the art of guessing period. Modern medicine is still the art of guessing, but with the aid of two sciences, chemistry and physics, and with an ever-growing fund of experience.

Health is a corollary of the will to live; the healthy animal has greater chances of survival than the sick.

Health is the result of the harmonious relations of well nourished cells, all united in a single purpose: to keep on living.

Healing is a purposive effort of protoplasm to maintain and restore a disturbed chemical and/or physical equilibrium.

The best physician is he who interferes least with the healing power of the body.

Medicine should be, but rarely is, the art of removing the cause of disease, it is mainly concerned with the suppression of symptoms.

HEALTH can be compared to a good woman—it has no history, no past; only present. It is an intangible something that often vanishes like smoke and is appreciated only after it has been lost. Disease, on the other hand, is something very tangible, seldom disappears suddenly without leaving traces, and has a long and tragic history and a very dark past. To primitive man, disease meant evil spirits that must be fought and driven away, and at times appeased and propitiated, at first with words and gestures, later with ceremonies, offerings, sacrifices, tabus, amulets and prayers. Thus emerged the medicine man, the witch "endowed with supernatural powers" who protected the tribe from witchcraft and evil spirits.

As men became aware that this magic not always produced the desired results, new ceremonies, new words and new methods were used, but the faith in magic remained so strongly entrenched and rooted in the mind of man that even our scientific advances have failed to destroy it. But the complete failure of magic did dawn upon some men, the doubters, the skeptics, of whom fortunately there always have been a few, though not enough.

With the Egyptians and the Hindus medicine reached a higher level, but it still remained a function of religion performed by the witch, now raised to the rank of High Priest and oracle of the Gods. It seems that some of those High Priests were men of high intelligence and initiative, and it is possible that some of them got a glimpse of the truth, that is, that magic was pure and unadulterated humbug, but they were chained by myths and a superstitious people, and blocked in their search for truth by lack of instruments and knowledge of the human body.

We shall never know whether it was the food, the air or a shower of cosmic rays that produced some genetic mutation and a lucky combination of genes that so stimulated the brain of the Greeks and bestowed upon them the honor of being first in so many fields of knowledge, including medicine. The Greeks were the first people to see the relationship of food, ways of living and the natural forces to health and disease, and to take medicine out of the realm of magic and religious superstition and to put it on a rational basis. They were also the first to glorify health, beauty and the human body. Hippocrates can be called the father of medicine because with practically nothing to help him, he formulated his famous aphorisms among which shines: Only Nature Cures, shines like a sun, shows deep thinking and careful observation of the human body and its functions.

Unfortunately for humanity, the teachings of the father

of medicine—with them, the advanced culture of the Greek civilization—were partly destroyed, and those left were covered with the dust of ignorance and superstition. Even modern medicine, with all the biological and physiological facts at its command, has failed to grasp the enormous significance of Only Nature Cures, a truth enunciated by a man who lacked the instruments and knowledge of the human body we possess today.

To the long indictment of Christianity I have drawn in other chapters, several counts must be added in this one, to wit: the savage destruction of the bath houses of the Greeks and the Romans, the ruthless attacks against cleanliness, against the care of the body, against sun bathing and hygiene in general, against beauty everywhere and womanly beauty in particular, and the glorification of filth and dirt. The impartial student of history is both shocked and puzzled by the strange paradox offered by a religion that while claiming that God has created man in His own image, denounced the human body as evil, impure and oozing with sin and evil, and attempted to destroy it. Possessed by a satanic fury, maddened by frustration and groaning under the burden of sin, the Christian ascetics demanded and commanded, under severe penalties here and in the other world, that men and women—specially women— cover their bodies from head to foot at all times, as a dangerous and shameful object, usually with dirty garments. Bathing, washing and beautifying the body and other hygienic measures so common among the pagans and so beneficial to health besides enhancing its appearance, were anathematized as schemes and devices of Satan to tempt men and women and lead their souls into perdition and eternal fire. The cleanliness of the body was branded as the pollution of the soul and its biological necessities regarded as so many impediments and obstacles that had to be crushed in order to obtain salvation; since the body was only a transient and temporary home of the soul, while this was immortal and would be held responsible for what the body did, there was hardly any choice. Even so, many people were restrained in giving full rein to the pleasures of the body only by fear of punishment right here, and not in the other life.

The idea of sanctity is usually associated with virtuous deeds, such as charity, kindness, love for all human beings and sacrifices for the welfare of humanity. But very few of the Christian saints obtained sanctity on that score; the great majority of saints in the Christian calendar were fanatic, ignorant, narrow-minded, bigoted, extremely selfish, concerned only with their own salvation, cruel and even sadists, escapists, cowards afraid of life and its temptations, masochists craving humiliation and pain.

St. Mary of Egypt has no other claim to sanctity than to have done penance for past sins wandering through the desert without clothes, but not exactly naked, for she was covered by several layers of dirt, not having bathed or even washed her hands in forty-seven years. St. Euphraxia joined a convent of one hundred and thirty nuns who never washed their feet, and shuddered at the mention of a bath. It is said of Cardinal Bellarmine, one of the luminaries of the Church, that he used to allow vermin to bite him saying: "We shall have heaven to reward us for suffering, but these poor creatures have nothing but the enjoyment of the present life." So be kind to the poor louse and let it bite you; suffering is good for you and biting is good for the louse. St. Simeon Stylites became a saint by living on a pillar sixty feet high for thirty years, never coming down; other saints chose caves in the deserts, dark cells in high-walled convents, shirts with thorns or spikes or lived on grass like animals, and finally died covered with dirt. No wonder those saints died in "odor" of sanctity!

Since disease was a punishment from God and suffering was a kind of passport to heaven where it would be rewarded with eternal happiness, any attempt to cure disease by other means than prayers, relics and holy water was severely frowned upon by the Church as heresy and witchcraft whose punishment was as swift and cruel as possible. It is obvious that doctors and medicine could not survive, much less progress, under those adverse conditions. Dissection of cadavers was not allowed, therefore the knowledge of anatomy was practically zero.

In the eighth century the Arabs crossed the Strait of Gibraltar and conquered most of Spain where they established a sort of renewal of the Greek civilization. Art, literature, science, medicine and hygienic care of the body flourished in cities like Granada, Cordoba and Seville which boasted of having the greatest libraries and universities in the world. Bathing houses came again into use and cleanliness was observed. With Maimonides and Averroes, medicine was groping toward science, and philosophy was trying to break the chains of religion. Music and songs filled the gardens of Andalucia where Jews, Arabs and Christians lived in peace and tolerance. But far away, in the mountains and caves of Covadonga, the clouds of intolerance and bigotry were gathering and soon they would sweep down like a tornado, beating down and destroying another attempt of man to escape religious superstition and intolerance and enjoy life.

1492 is a memorable date in more ways than one, and can be remembered with pride and with shame because it is the year in which Columbus discovered the New World, but it is also the year in which Boadbill surrendered the keys of Granada and with them a way of life to the Catholic rulers, Ferdinand and Isabella. It is also the year in which the first religious persecution on a national scale was started and carried out with all the sadism and fury peculiar to religious fanaticism. Medicine was again chained and clamped into the dungeons of religious superstition. Why bother with investigation and science when all the answers about the structure of the universe, about life, about medicine and other subjects could be found within the covers of the Holy (?) Book every word of which was revealed by God? But for all its cruelty, terror and espionage, the "Holy" Inquisition could not completely exterminate all the heretics, the doubters and the sceptics, and though many heads were severed and many bodies roasted, the Reformation broke the back of the totalitarian Church, but Protestants took with them much of the intolerance and superstitions of Catholicism and burned Miguel Servetus, the real discoverer of the circulation of the blood, and hanged many other "heretics"; they also opposed, in some cases more sternly than the Church, any display of feminine charms, bathing and the hygienic care of the body. Such was the Protestants' fear of temptation, that they forced women to go about covered with somber and austere garments from head to foot; these poor women had to wear corsets to flatten their breasts and be extremely prude and modest to avoid offending the sensibilities of men. Not that men did not want to be offended and tempted, but they did not have the courage to admit it. Cleanliness, which now we are told is next to godliness, was tabu, not only to religious fanatics, but even to so-called scientific men. Semelweiss saw the ravages of dirty hands in women dying of puerperal fever and tried to introduce cleanliness among the doctors who went about touching women with their unwashed and filthy hands, but the poor fellow was driven insane by the violent opposition and slander of his fellow practitioners. Anesthesia was also violently opposed by the self-proclaimed oracles of God.

When finally people began to break the chains of a hypocritical morality and started to go bathing, they had to do it draped in long and cumbersome bathing clothes, so as not to display any offending part of the human anatomy. It is within our memory that men and women have thrown overboard all those silly, absurd and harmful "morals" and gone to the beach with a minimum of clothes. The Puritans revived some of the old asceticism that the Catholic priesthood already had more than forgotten, having gone to the other extreme. We can define a Puritan as a fellow who likes cake, eats it and enjoys eating it, but refuses to admit that and even puts on a sour face to hide his pleasure.

However, Protestants could no longer stop the tide of

freedom Luther had started, unwillingly of course, and were swept away by the forces of liberty. Thus, in spite of all the opposition to cleanliness, to asepsis and to people who saw farther than their noses, like Semelweiss and Florence Nightingale, science in general and medicine in particular entered a new era of activity against which bleeding and concoctions of doubtful value, if not useless, prayers and witchcraft fought a losing battle.

The real revolution of medicine was brought about by the invention of the microscope which was followed by the invention of other instruments without which neither medicine nor science could have progressed beyond empiricism. With the microscope medicine really became of age. No longer could the dark clouds of religious superstition cover with a fog that tiny and wonderful tube under which man could see the cells and real "evil spirits" that no longer could be exorcised with holy water and magic words. Aided by that powerful eye, medicine put on the Seven League Boots and marched forward from discovery to discovery, revealing both the wonders and the imperfections of the human body. From bleeding and witch brews to atomic medicine is a long way that has been spanned in almost a generation; but for all its scientific paraphernalia and boasting, medicine is not a science—it is still a glorified art of guessing where the best guesser is the best diagnostician and the best doctor.

These statements, I believe, need some clarification. Science means predictability; chemistry and physics are sciences because we know their laws and can predict what will happen when we mix certain substances and how steel or other things will react under certain conditions. But the human body is an individual with such a wide range of behavior and some possibilities of reactions that no accurate chart can be drawn to cover everyone. Moreover, the individual himself is an aggregation of individualized protoplasms also with a very wide range of behavior and possible reactions. That is why a drug may "cure" one person and kill another. No physician can predict with certainty how a patient will respond to an injection of penicillin or any other drug. Many patients show a wonderful response to penicillin while others are not helped at all and some are definitely injured. The same thing can be said of drugs taken orally. Herein lies the cause of the many failures and disappointments along the path of new drugs, usually hailed with hosannas as the "cure" of this or that disease, only to find out later that they do not cure every patient and that they have more or less injurious effects that restrict their use. Many of these failures, however, are unknown to the general public because of economic reasons; it will be well to bear in mind that medicine and the production of drugs represent powerful vested interests whose primary objective is profit. Who knows how many useless medicines are kept on the market through advertising? And who can tell us how many unnecessary surgical operations are performed every day for profit? I know of many cases where a person has submitted to an unnecessary operation. To the student of economics the reasons are simple. A physician may be honest at heart and try to stay that way, but let us suppose a situation that is very common. A doctor is hard-pressed for money; he may want a new car like the Joneses, his wife may want a new dress or a new coat, etc. Along comes a patient with an ailment that could be treated without an operation, but surgery may mean a profit of a few hundred dollars. The temptation is too great to be resisted, and it requires great moral courage and honesty to resist, especially when the success of a doctor is usually measured by his wealth. These conditions have been exposed by several magazines. Far be it from my mind to indict all the doctors; there are honest and idealistic persons in every profession whose honesty has not a price tag—men who cannot be bought nor will prostitute themselves for all the gold in Fort Knox, and for whom money is a necessary evil; but these exceptions do not alter the profit picture I have painted.

To prove that the public is not usually informed of the

failure of some drugs and that those drugs are used as if nothing had been proven against them, I offer the following. The
Journal of the American Medical Association (Sept. 24, 1949)
abstracts the following from an article published in *Scalpel* of
Brussels, Belgium, entitled: "Does Vaccination Reduce Diphtherial Mortality and Lethality?", by R. Rendu: "The mortality
rate from diphtheria has greatly decreased in certain countries
in which vaccination against diphtheria has not been practiced
at all or on a small scale. In others, such as the United States
and Canada, where vaccination against diphtheria is extensively employed, the number of deaths has likewise declined.
This reduction cannot be attributed to vaccination because the
decline had started earlier and it has continued even though
the proportion of vaccinated subjects in the child population
was too small to have influenced the mortality curve. In many
other cities and countries in which diphtherial vaccination has
been most extensive, the mortality and morbidity rates have
hardly changed. In some localities (Belgium, Copenhagen,
Geneva and Montreal) the morbidity has even increased since
the introduction of vaccination. In the cities and countries in
which a decrease of the mortality rate has more or less coin-
cided with a campaign for vaccination (the United States, Canada, England, Scotland and France), the downward curve has
been as noticeable in non-vaccinated adults as in vaccinated
children. Vaccination seems to have influenced neither the
mortality nor the morbidity rates of diphtheria. This would
seem to prove its inefficacy, since it would be better to refer to
mortality statistics than to those of morbidity in order to judge
the value of the vaccine." Professor Speransky, in his book:
A Theory for a New Basis of Medicine, has also pointed out
the injurious effects of some vaccines, but vaccination goes
merrily and tragically on.

It is reasonable to suppose that Dr. Rendu's case against
diphtherial vaccination applies as well to other immunization
practices. After sulfa drugs had been hailed as almost a magic
weapon against many infectious diseases and used extensively

on American soldiers during World War II, they had to be retired from circulation in the Army because their harmful reactions were too numerous and too severe, but this was done after millions of human beings had been used as guinea pigs and great profits had been made by some people, at the expense of the poor G. I.'s.

The fact is that the discovery of germs so fascinated and hypnotized doctors that they can hardly conceive a disease not being caused by some microbe or virus. This leads them to embark on a hunt for germs and for drugs with which to kill them; these drugs were found soon enough, but they had the annoying effect of also killing the patients or injuring the cells and the good germs. The great paradox of the germ theory of disease is its similarity with the evil spirit theory of disease. In both cases the cause of disease is an entity that stalks the body and attacks from the outside; the big difference of course is that the germs are real while the spirits are not.

It is only lately that some progressive doctors have come to realize that it is just as important to know which body has the germ or the disease as to which germ or disease has the body; in other words, that it is the body and not the microbe or foreign element that determines the character, the process and the prognosis of the disease, and since no two human beings are alike on all points, no two diseases are exactly alike, even if they are caused by the same microbe or virus. Hence, it is not so much the disease as entity that must be treated, but the patient as an individual.

This unpredictability of the behavior of the germ, the virus, drug and the patient is what gives gray hair to doctors and keeps medicine from becoming a science. The myopia of doctors has prevented them from seeing beyond the germs and has limited preventive medicine to immunizations and curative medicine to the administration of drugs, and also has deprived them from investigating and using other important and powerful weapons against disease, such as food, fasting, sun, light, air, water, exercises, heat and cold, use of the hands, colonic irrigations, electrotherapy and psychotherapy. In the last few years these "medicines" have come to the fore as physiotherapy or physical medicine, but are still relegated to secondary importance.

About twenty or thirty years ago hardly any medical doctor knew anything about diet and those natural forces already mentioned. Vegetarians, Naturopaths and Physical Culturists were the only ones using and propagating them, and they were smeared and slandered as quacks, crackpots and fanatics; today most of their "quackeries" have been accepted by the same doctors who so violently attacked them. These people are the same type who opposed and drove insane Semelweiss, who scorned and laughed at Florence Nightingale, who fought the use of the bath tub and who retarded the adoption of so many progressive methods.

About one hundred years ago a few pioneers revived the philosophy of Hippocrates and showed a different way to health; Rickli, Louis Kuhne, Father Kneipp, Priestnitz and others belonged to the category of Semelweiss and Florence Nightingale and suffered almost the same fate at the hands of narrow-minded, bigoted, ignorant, pedantic, jealous and selfish men masquerading as the very oracles of wisdom. And that type of men are also at work today blocking progress, more interested in their petty and selfish interests than in the general welfare of the public. Were the leaders of medicine really interested in the welfare of the people, they would have investigated with an open mind such movements as Naturopathy and Chiropractic which have restored to health millions of people when medicine had failed.

Since the importance of proper nutrition has been experimentally demonstrated by men like Colonel MacCarrison and others, and since good nutrition starts with the soil, medicine should devote more energies and time to insure good food with all the vitamins and minerals for everyone. And since psychiatrists are unable to cope with the growing number of neurotic and insane or almost insane people, medicine should launch a program of education of prospective parents—prevention is better than cure.

As I have said before—and I think it is worth repeating —the best physician is he who interferes least with the healing power of the body and helps it to carry on its marvelous work; when the healing power is weak or stops working, the best medicine and the best physician are useless and impotent to keep death away. If an ailment can be treated successfully without drugs and without surgery, so much the better for the patient—this is possible more often than doctors think. If drugs are necessary, they should be used sparingly and with discretion because practically all drugs have secondary effects more or less harmful and whose reactions, as I have pointed out, cannot be predicted with certainty. It is up to the physician well versed not only in the orthodox school of medicine, but in other schools as well, to evaluate all the factors and to choose not only the good and the best—for this is sometimes impossible—but the lesser evil for the patient.

Modern medicine has not given the human body the credit that it deserves for its enormous achievements and conquests in its long evolution; it has developed immunities and resistance to germs and other injurious elements or we would not be here: humanity would not have reached first base. It seems to me that the world is sick because so far medicine has studied disease and not health. Only lately have some scientists, not necessarily physicians, undertaken the important task of investigating health and to find out the factors and forces that enter into the making of healthy human beings. Finding the cause of disease does not necessarily mean that we have found what causes health; medicine has accentuated the negative instead of the positive. Another important reason is that medicine has been mainly concerned with symptoms instead of causes. In fact, most drugs are directed mainly toward the suppression of symptoms rather than toward the elimination of the causes. When a doctor prescribes a sedative for the nerves, or a drug for a headache or any other pain, he is just treating and suppressing the symptoms, not the cause of disease.

The emerging of the specialist is not a blessing, as some people are inclined to believe. As Dr. Martin H. Fischer, already quoted, says: "A specialist is one who knows more and more about less and less." The reason for this failure of the specialist is that he usually sees and treats only a limited part of the body. For instance, a specialist of the eyes will treat the eyes as organs by themselves; but the body is not an aggregation of independent organs, and although there is a certain amount of autonomy, all the organs are closely linked. Specialism has grown out of the mistaken theory that there are local diseases; what we have is local manifestations of a general condition. Therefore the wise and sensible thing to do is to treat not only the organ and the local manifestation of a disease, but to treat the whole body as well, and by this I also mean the psychological element. True, medical doctors are giving consideration to the mind, too much in many cases; the pendulum has swung to the other extreme and now, whenever the X-rays and other diagnostic aids fail to show a physical disturbance, they blame the mind and the nerves. They seem to forget that our diagnostic methods and instruments are still not sensitive enough to detect many changes and chemical processes going on in the human body.

The problem of the role of the mind in health and disease brings us to "miracles" and faith cures. It cannot be denied that "miracles" do take place in such shrines as Lourdes, Saint Anne the Beau Pre and other religious places by other virgins and saints, nor can it be denied that Christian Scientists and other faith healers perform amazing "cures". But to assume, as most people, even intelligent people, do that those cures are due to the supernatural powers of the virgin, the saint, the faith healer or that God takes part in restoring health is a most unwarranted, illogical and false conclusion. In the first place, humanity has been praying and begging to God, to the virgins and to the saints, for health for several centuries, yet during the Middle Ages when faith was greater and miraculous relics more abundant, mankind suffered the worse epidemics, plagues and diseases, and priests and popes died like most pagans and heretics.

Of the thousands of sick people who visit the shrines and faith healers, only a very small number get cured. Now is it logical to suppose that the virgin or saint, or even God, would cure a few people and refuse to cure others who beg and pray with just as much faith and fervor? Of course not. God and the saints would be unjust and most cruel. It is obvious then that those faith cures and "miracles" must be effected by forces other than supernatural; in fact, we have many cases in which a cure or "miracle" has taken place under influence of a sudden shock, like the cry of fire, lightning, etc. People who had been paralytic for many years have jumped to their feet and started walking after some sudden shock or excitement. This gives us a clue to those "miraculous virgins". It seems that the patient builds up an expectation, a state of tension and pitch and that when it reaches the site or comes under the close influence of the object of his faith and hope, something happens within the body and health is restored. What is the mechanism of those sudden changes? We do not know yet. Why do some people respond and get well while others remain just as sick as before? We have no answer for this question either. It seems that certain types of diseases and ailments, on the functional side, are most likely to respond to faith treatments.

Christian Scientists deny disease which they claim is an error of the mortal mind, and in many cases where the Christian Scientist Reader treats the patient, he recovers. But the fact remains that Mrs. Mary Baker Eddy herself was sick and ailing for a long time before she died; that Christian Scientists get sick and die just like any unbeliever. If they can cure a patient once by exorcising disease with their readings, why is it that they cannot perform the same trick again, and the patient dies? The answer lies in the fact that the healing power of the body acts in a most strange and puzzling manner, and it gets weak and stops working altogether, and then no virgin, no saint or Reader can stop death.

It would be unfair to deny that Christian Science has some good in it. By allaying fear, inspiring optimism, strengthening hope and invigorating faith, they seem to be able to mobilize the vitality and healing power of the organism; but these things can and often are carried too far by zeal and fanaticism. Wishful thinking has its limitations beyond which it can be very harmful, for it leads the individual to minimize and even ignore pains and symptoms of major impending disaster. For instance, some of the most fatal and dangerous diseases like cancer, diabetes, syphilis and kidney disorders start with minor discomforts which even non-Christian Scientists are likely to ignore and which properly treated at the right time most likely would be stopped in their destructive work before they do irreparable damage. Disease is a reality that no amount of magic and wishing can banish. Those who avoid a frontal meeting with facts usually are hit by them sidewise or in the back when they are not looking.

Since disease is rather rare in wild Nature and it is so common among "civilized" men and women, one of the immediate tasks of medicine ought to be the study of Nature which has been practically neglected by the pill pushers and syringe wielders, and from which they can learn very much; perhaps we could learn something important about the factors and conditions necessary for health. Health is indeed a priceless ingredient for the enjoyment of life and for the peace of the world, and it is high time science gives it the attention it deserves.

That the behavior of men and women is influenced by health and disease is obvious and logical. A person suffering from indigestion or from ulcers, or bad liver, for instance, reacts to things in a very different manner than a healthy one. It has been said that many wars have been due to the indigestion of a prime minister, or perhaps a king. Many quarrels between husband and wife and divorces could be traced to an irritable wife or husband who are ill. It should be interesting to see what would happen if we would retire and put to knitting all these garrulous, cranky, ailing old men who sit at the council table of government and of the United Nations, playing with the destiny of people, and put in their place healthy young men and women free from frustrations, ulcers, high blood pressure and other ailments. I am sure they would do a far better job—they could hardly do worse than it is being done now. Since youth is the first to pay the price of war, it is only logical and just that young people should be given the opportunity to decide if they really want to die on the battlefield before they have started to live. I believe that a healthy humanity would bring a healthy world. It is worth trying.

Man, the "Angel" and the "Devil"

There are thousands hacking at the branches of evil to one who is striking at the root.

—*Henry David Thoreau*

The evil that men do lives after them; the good is oft interred with their bones.

How far that little candle throws its beams—So shines a good deed in a naughty world. (*Does it?*)

—*Shakespeare*

The existence of evil, as Whateley well says, is the great theological difficulty; and the apparent want of success of good men in overcoming it, is but one branch of this difficulty.

—*Bristed*

We cannot do evil to others without doing it to ourselves.

—*Desmahis*

It is a proof of our natural bias to evil, that in all things good, gain is harder and slower than loss; but in all things bad or evil, getting is quicker and easier than getting rid of them.

—*Sir T. Browne*

To be good we must be good; and by doing good we take a sure means of being good, as the use of exercise of the muscles increases their power.

—*Tyron Edwards*

A good man doubles the length of his existence; to have lived so as to look back with pleasure on our past life is to live twice.

—*Martial*

Be not merely good; be good for something.

—*Thoreau*

Good nature is often a mere matter of health. With good digestion we are apt to be good natured; with bad digestion, morose.

—*H. W. Beecher*

When man stood erect and looked at the stars with interrogating eyes, good and evil were born.

To look for good and evil in Nature or in the cosmos is like looking for a needle in a haystack after having thrown it there.

Evil is a pathological condition of the biological urges of man.

[245]

An evil man is merely an animal without the limitations imposed by the structure of the animal and its lack of thought and imagination.

A good man is either a fool or very wise.

Why is it that man has been fighting a losing battle against evil despite all the enormous efforts, commands, threats of punishment and promises of reward by religionists, reformers and do-gooders? Because it is easier to clench the fist than to extend the hand open in token of friendship, and because it is so much easier to hate than to love.

There are many people who confuse goodness with the observance of current morality and with the absence of evil.

There are two main types of do-gooders: those who do good because they consider it a duty; these people usually expect gratitude and recompense and do good with much showing off; those who do good because they enjoy doing it; these people do good for its own sake and do not expect gratitude nor a reward, and they are never disappointed.

THE EARTH must have been a rather peaceful but dull place before man emerged from the tropical forests with a bigger and better brain that was no longer satisfied with seeing things, but was restless and capable of creating a new world and of populating it with spirits, gods, angels and devils who fought bloody battles to save souls from hell. With the appearance of man, the stage was set for the cosmic battle between the "Angel" and the "Devil", a battle in which strangely enough man has been fighting on both sides, being at the same time the "Angel" and the "Devil", the general planning strategic moves for both contenders and the victor and the vanquished.

The first skirmishes of the cosmic battle between Good and Evil were fought in the square of the embryonic village at the edge of the jungle; there, sometimes under the burning tropical sun and others by the light of the mysterious moon, man fought against invisible and intangible villains that made him sick, brought disease to his cattle and destroyed his crops. Since those villains moved in the world of imagination, his axe and his arrows were useless. We do not know man's first reaction to the new beings that his imagination had con-

jured up. Was he frightened and paralyzed for some time, not
knowing how to deal with his invisible enemies, or was he so
resourceful that he discovered his magic tricks as soon as he
was faced with the problem? Nor do we know how soon did
the witch make his appearance and take upon himself the responsibility of protecting the tribe against the "spiritual"
marauders. We do know, however, that those events took place
because they are still being repeated in their original form by
the savages and in a modified form under the very shadow of
great centers of learning, for what are the priests of all religious sects trying to do but to serve as intermediaries between
God and men and to protect their followers from evil, just as
the witch did and still does? True, the priest now is a graduate
from some college or university and no longer affects dress
and adornments or the manner of the witch to scare away
evil spirits, but the principle has not changed a bit and he still
relies on the magic of words, gestures, symbolic sacrifices and
other ceremonies believed to be effective in warding off evil
and attracting good.

The origins of this anthropomorphic conception of good
and evil and of the battles fought by these two abstractions
personified in the "Angel" and the "Devil" must be sought in
that tiny yet immensely vast labyrinth that is the fore brain of
man. There, in that narrow and thick walled fortress that is
the skull of man, protoplasm reached the highest state in
quality and organization, that made possible a kind of "nuclear
fission" and "atomic explosion", for when the first thought
flashed from neuron to neuron, its dark caverns were illumin-
ated with a magic light far more powerful and pregnant with
possibilities than the light that flashed across the Los Alamos
desert on that memorable day of the explosion of the first
atomic bomb, because under the magic light produced by the
sparks of his neurons, man saw a reflection of the external
world, yet he saw it so different that he thought he had discovered a completely new world the fantastic inhabitants of
which seemed to him more real and more important than the

very things he saw and touched. Moreover, it is all too obvious that without that "brain explosion" there would not have been an atomic bomb or anything else, for man would have continued living, or rather existing, in the darkness of the animal world. It seems to me that there is some analogy between uranium and grey matter. There are many minerals on this earth, but only uranium is a naturally radioactive element from which the spark of atomic energy can be struck; just as there are many protoplasms or cells, but only the brain cells of man are thought-active. I believe that if we had an adequate Geiger counter, it would tell us how active a determined grey matter is, because mental activity is a discharge of energy by the neurons. What kind of energy is this? I believe it was Freud who first suggested the existence of a "psychic energy". Dr. Wilhelm Reich, a student of Freud, commenting on his interesting *Orgone Energy Bulletin* (January, 1950), agrees with the Freudian hypothesis and goes on to say that ideas are "concentrations of energy quanta". None of these hypotheses are supported by biological facts.

There is evidence that the energy accumulated and discharged by the brain cells is not different from the energy used by the stomach, the muscles or any other organ and that there is only one source of energy—food. Deprive the brain cells of the energy brought to them by the blood and from oxygen to oxidize that energy and there is no "psychic energy", no "concentrations of quanta". Dr. Reich tries to explain thought and ideas by postulating a new energy, the *orgone,* for which he claims many things. I am not ready to pass judgment upon the existence of this energy, but I am ready to state that this hypothetical energy is not necessary to explain the processes of thought and imagination.

Ideas are not concentrations of energy or quanta. It seems to me that it is the other way around; ideas are the result, the product of concentrations of energy under special environment and structure For instance, we see a person or a sunset and suddenly an idea flashes in our brain. What has happened?

There has been an excitation of the neurons which has produced chemical activity and energy, and out of the relationship between innumerable neurons and images stored up comes the idea, an idea for which we may have been looking for a long time. Why did we not get it before? Because something had been lacking, either structurally, this means that new connections or pathways between neurons may have been established, chemically or engraphically, that is, some new image was necessary. Therefore the idea is not the "quanta" nor the energy but the result of the energy, the flash, the brilliance of the discharge and the new image formed with the combination of old materials.

So marvelous are the feats of energy in the brain that even men like Freud, who discarded the soul and other supernatural theories, had to invent some kind of special energy to account for them, and Dr. Wilhelm Reich, one of the most daring and revolutionary thinkers, falls into the same fallacy. The enormous difference between the manifestations and effects of energy in the brain, the stomach and in the muscles must not be sought in the existence of different types of energy, but in the special and peculiar structure and environment of protoplasm in which it is accumulated and discharged. The diverse feats and manifestations of electricity can give us an idea of this process. Electricity can heat an iron, give us light, and perform numerous and most diverse phenomena, depending upon the medium used for its discharge.

It took protoplasm millions of years to reach that special atomic structure and environment found in the brain of man, necessary to produce those flashes of thought and imagination that have blinded man with their brilliance, making it impossible for him to see their real origin, just as when seeing the power and brilliance of an atomic explosion no one would believe that it is produced by a very small amount of a lowly mineral element. As I see it, uranium is the most unstable element and has the highest "metabolism" in the inorganic world, while grey matter is the most unstable, and has the highest metabolism in the organic world. This high metabolism and exclusive molecular and atomic organization is what makes grey matter unique and capable of exhibiting such amazing and incredible phenomena as thought, imagination and ideas. When man discovers how this high metabolism of protoplasm that enables it to burn fuel like a fire and to assimilate and transform other forms of living and non-living matter into its own tissue came about, then he shall have the complete answer to the riddle and mystery of life; then perhaps he shall have found a unifying principle that unites the organic and the inorganic, for the basic patterns and methods of Nature seem to be few and simple. Biology needs and awaits the genius of an Einstein.

Primitive man had the inner light produced by the discharge of brain cells, but the light produced too many shadows and, lacking in experience, he mistook them for reality; therefore he approached the problem of good and evil in a pragmatic manner, the only one possible to his limited intelligence. Good and evil were phenomena and things either good or bad for the satisfaction of biological needs and those phenomena were the work of beings like himself, only invisible. Whether good and evil existed as absolutes in the universe beyond his immediate environment did not bother primitive man; he was only interested in surviving the struggle for life and not in higher abstractions of which he, of course, was still incapable. To obtain protection for himself and for his family and his food supply from all the evil spirits who were prowling around him ever ready to strike, was his most important task. This he attempted to accomplish with magic words and ceremonies that grew and changed with time. The primitive anthropomorphic solution of the conflict between good and evil more or less modified by knowledge and experience, lasted for many centuries, until the Jewish prophets, forerunners of Christianity, pulled Yaveh out of the obscurity of a tribal god and made

Him the one and only God and invested Him with all the attributes of Superman.

It was then that man began to find increasing difficulties in reconciling an omnipotent and all good God, creator of the world and man, with the abundance of evil. But while the Jews initiated this cosmic conflict between good and evil with their monotheistic doctrines, they seem to have lacked efficient theologians and philosophers, and early in the creation and shaping of Jehovah they gave up the idea of reconciling the irreconcilable and left that impossible task to the Christians who went to work on it with a zeal and vigor worthy of a better cause.

It is not necessary to review here the incredible absurdities, the childish fantasies and the monstrous myths invented by the fertile but distorted mind of Christian ascetics and theologians in order to absolve their God from all evil while upholding Him as the creator of everything and the Supreme Ruler and Director of every phenomena—cosmic, animal and human. Had these myth-makers and weavers of fantastic tales imitated the Greeks and contented themselves with creating their heaven and hell, their angels and devils and their God and presenting their creations to humanity for acceptance or rejection, they could be forgiven and even admired, just as we admire the Greeks for the beautiful gods and goddesses they gave to the world. But the ascetics were made of a different stuff, had different ideas and lived in a different environment; so they took their visions very seriously and set out to impose them upon every human being, first by the force of reason, and when that failed, by the reason of force. The sword, the fear of hell and of its imitation, the burning pyre of the *auto-de-fe* and of the instruments of torture, took over the task of "convincing" people where reason and persuasion were ineffective. Thus they tried to fight evil with more evil, by flooding the earth not with goodness, love, kindness and compassion, but with hate, intolerance and cruelty, with the obvious negative results of bringing more and worse evils than ever. For these crimes against humanity they must be indicted as the greatest evil-doers and as the "killers of the dream".

So powerful is the influence of those myth-makers and philosophers and so great is the hunger of man for cosmic importance, that even today, in this age of science, there are part-time scientists and self-styled philosophers who still attempt to solve the problem of good and evil with the use of discredited and unsupported theories and metaphysical symbols which no self-respecting scientist can handle without stepping out of character and damaging his prestige as a well integrated scientist. To be specific, I have in mind *Science and Cosmic Purpose,* by Kelvin Van Nuys. He makes a very brave attempt to flatten down the principal blocks to the belief in God, namely (1) the mechanistic concepts of the universe, and (2) the existence of evil, which contradicts the notion of good purpose in the cosmos. Like other philosophers before him, he fails completely; his failure is due to the mystical and metaphysical approach. "The dynamic idea of good does not prove God's existence, but only makes it permissible and plausible" (p. 118). To say that good as dynamic consists "in the transition from conditions of tension and disorder toward conditions of relative resolution and order; in which transition inhere feelings of dissatisfaction change to satisfaction" (p. 20), does not explain anything about good and evil. Since good and evil exist only in the relation of Nature to man and in the relations between human beings, these can be understood and dealt with properly by approaching them from the biological angle.

It is a well known axiom that the solution of a problem requires as an essential prerequisite a correct formulation. No mathematician can solve a problem if the symbols are incorrect and in the wrong place. The problem of good and evil is no exception; it has not been satisfactorily solved although man has been wrestling with it from the moment his creative imagination began working. It could hardly be otherwise because man did not possess the necessary facts and knowledge to establish correct evaluations and relations between himself and Nature. Consequently, the first step in the solution of the problem of good and evil is to clear the ground from all superfluous and misleading symbols and from all myths that have been blocking the way to a correct understanding.

First, let us take a critical look at the cosmos and see what is going on there, and whether man is right or wrong in projecting his ideas of good and evil into the universe. It is true that the stars, the nebulae, the galaxies, the sun and the planets move in an orderly procession, keeping their distances; however, it is not always so peaceful and orderly—there are cosmic collisions and an occasional disorder. Our own planetary system seems to have been born and existed in disorder for a long time, according to the Whipple theory. Man sees only order in the universe and pronounces it good because it spells security for our planetary system in general and for our tiny planet in particular. However, intrinsically, there is neither good nor evil in this cosmic order; it merely happens, being the result of the attraction and repulsion of atoms and molecules acting individually and collectively. The newer knowledge of matter shows that it is capable of doing remarkable things without the help of a Superman or any mythical force. It is clear then there is no room for good and evil in the cosmos.

If we come close to the earth and observe Nature, we find the same basic situation. Man speaks carelessly and ignorantly and says—Nature does this and that; Nature is wise and good; we must obey Nature's laws or be punished. This anthropomorphic conception of Nature has no place in the scientific world. Nature is not an entity. What is Nature then? What we designate with the noun Nature is an aggregation of forces, things and phenomena partly or wholly good, that is, favorable to life in general and to man in particular; or partly or wholly evil, that is, adverse to life and man. A hurricane, an earthquake, a drought, a flood, the tse-tse fly, the malarial mosquito, the insects that eat our crops and other harmful things are just as much a part of Nature as a beneficial rain, the fertile valleys, the refreshing springs, the fruit-bearing trees and the flowers. The forces of Nature are erratic, blind and impersonal, without an intelligent plan; otherwise why should there be a drought in some places while in others the crops are being ruined by too much water? Why should hurricanes and tornados come and go, leaving in their wake death and destruction? Why should the earth shake and tremble, killing thousands of people and leaving more homeless?

Primitive man was awed and frightened by those forces and tried to appease the "gods that produced them" with sacrifices of animals and human beings and with offerings. With the development of science, man began to fight Nature with more effective weapons that enabled him to control floods and droughts and pests, to some extent, and to increase the fertility of the soil. There is an interesting analogy between Nature and man; weeds and foodless plants grow abundantly without being planted and without any care or cultivation, while food-producing plants and trees must be planted, fertilized and defended against all kinds of enemies. In man, evil and anti-social impulses and deeds sprout very easily and grow abundantly, while virtues and goodness must be planted, fertilized and cultivated, and protected against such powerful and ever-present enemies as hate, cruelty, envy, greed, selfishness, etc. We can say that both Nature and man are biased toward evil. It is obvious that in Nature good and evil are accidental phenomena that emerge from the action and interaction of impersonal forces, being the result of the character-isics of matter and of the position of our planet in the solar system. In other planets the forces adverse to life seem to predominate, and good and evil have no meaning where there is no life. Whether those conditions are permanent or transitory we do not know, although since the position of the planets in regard to the sun seems to be fixed for as long as our solar system lasts, and that position seems to be essential to life, we can take it for granted that our earth is the "favorite and privileged child" of the sun. From these facts the only conclusion possible is that good and evil do not exist as moral principles or absolutes, either in the cosmos or in Nature.

We come now to the realm of life, where good and evil have meaning in terms of sorrow, pain, happiness and unhappiness, life and death. I have already pointed out elsewhere that in the animal world good is what satisfies the biological needs and gives security, and evil whatever deprives the animal of satisfying his needs and helping his survival. True, animals have not communicated to us their feelings, but we can be sure that this is a correct interpretation of their sentiments and attitude towards life. Primitive man and children behave very much like animals in this respect. Thus it is evident that good and evil are basically biological phenomena and have emerged out of the will to live or self-preservation. Moreover, since every function and activity, animal and human, is primarily subordinated to this supreme biological urge, it can be stated that all anti-social acts and evil doings of man are perversions or exaggerations of this will to live at the expense of other human beings.

In animals anti-social acts, if they can be called that, are limited by their own anatomical and psychological limitations and good and evil present no problem and no conflict. But in man it is another story. His capacity for evil seems to be infinite, while his capacity for good is rather meager and rare, like a beautiful and delicate flower among weeds—a flower that is easily damaged or destroyed by the elements or the pests. It is a common and bitter experience, both individual and collective, that anti-social acts and evil deeds come very easily and flow like water from a copious and inexhaustible spring, while kindness, love, compassion and other good qualities are scarce and apt to be abused by unscrupulous and selfish human beings. Expressed in different terms, it can be stated that it is easier to clench the fist than to extend the hand of friendship; easier to frown and to scowl than to smile. Theologians and philosophers burned the midnight oil and wrestled with these disagreeable facts and brought forth a mouse in the form of supernatural explanations that explained nothing; merely hide their ignorance behind pompous and empty words. Man is born evil because of his original sin, they say; he must be cleansed and washed of that sin, and since water washes away dirt, it seemed quite logical that it would also wash away sin; thus baptism was invented, and its failure is duly proven in the bloody pages of history. No one will pretend that baptized persons are good or even less evil than unbaptized ones.

It is the will of God that man suffers, for suffering is good for his soul, has been another stock argument to justify the abundance of evil. The fallacy of these rationalizations is too obvious to be even discussed. The answer is that most of those qualities we designate as good, like kindness, compassion, altruism and love had no survival value; only cooperation, and within the narrow circle of the family and the tribe, had survival value. On the other hand, aggressiveness, rapaciousness, selfishness and violence have had a great survival value. While man lived in hordes or tribes and hunted, his anti-social acts were very limited for the following reasons: (a) Hunting took much of his time and provided with an outlet for his aggressiveness. (b) He was satisfied with the essential necessities of life—food, shelter, mate and very little clothing, if any. (c) The sex urge was rather weak and periodic and he could always capture a mate. Therefore sex, which in our society is the source of much evil, was no problem in primitive life. (d) Money is another important source of evil in our "civilization" that was absent among savages.

With the growth of population, life became more complex —its necessities increased much faster than the resources, and the struggle for power became an abundant source of evil. The strongest and smartest and more aggressive person got to the top and monopolized the good things of life, while the majority suffered want and looked with envy toward them. Under these conditions evil was bound to increase, and it did, while good did not have much of a chance. From the struggle for power, first fought with the club or the stone axe, to our days in which it is fought with atomic bombs, evil has increased in quality and intensity at such an alarming rate that it threatens the foundations of our "civilization".

It should be clear by now that good and evil are not absolutes and have no existence outside man's mind; they are things and phenomena the goodness and badness of which are evaluated and measured according to the effects upon the welfare of the individual or the community. Culture and experience also influence the evaluation of good and evil. What was considered a good and ideal life by Christian Fathers has lost its glamor and goodness. Who wants to spend his life in prayer and contemplation, mortifying and depriving the body of some of its biological needs? Very few people. Who believes that pain and suffering are good things? Very few people, and even those who believe that would like to avoid them. The growing belief in the relativity of good and evil is very well expressed in the proverb: "There is not an ill wind that does not bring some good". Like most proverbs, this is a feeble approximation to truth and a rationalization of an inescapable fact. It must have been invented primarily to take away some of the sting from evil and to absolve God from sending us pure and unadulterated evil. Against this unfounded optimism that we live in the best of worlds possible and that everything happens for the best, Voltaire shot some of his sharpest arrows in that little but mighty book, *Candide,* in which he ridiculed the super-optimist in the person of Dr. Pangloss.

There is no doubt that there are some evils which bring benefits to some people; the last war, for instance, brought death and immense sorrow to millions of people, but for some people it was a bonanza, for they amassed much wealth without suffering. But there are also evils which bring little or no good at all. What good did the religious wars of the Middle Ages bring and the religious intolerance that strangled science and covered Europe with the darkness of ignorance? What good is there in the Black Plague, in the tse-tse fly and in the malarial mosquito? Or in a hurricane or an earthquake? The fact is that man lives in an environment in which hostile and friendly forces act blindly and erratically in varying degrees of intensity and kind, and man himself is under the compulsion of forces that have emerged from the qualities and character- istics of the material of which he is made and of the growing complex structure brought by organic evolution and culture.

I believe it is necessary to inquire more deeply into the nature of good, which seems to be less tangible than evil and harder to define.

It seems that the Greek philosopher Protagoras (born about 480 B.C.) was the first to approach the problem of good and evil in a scientific manner and to take away those two qualities from the gods, claiming that they emerged from the development of man and society. He had a few followers who were known as Sophists, a word that has degenerated with age. Socrates (born 469 B.C.) came out against the Sophists seeking more solid support for their morality. "Virtue", he taught, "is not revelation from the gods, but a rational innate knowledge of what is truly good, and of what makes man capable of liv- ing without oppressing others, but treating them justly; mak- ing him capable of serving society, and not himself alone".

In the light of modern science, we can say that Socrates was over-optimistic about man, for he is born without that innate knowledge of what is truly good, and as for serving society, his record is quite black—he rather serves himself. Epicurus, Democritus and other materialistic philosophers also contributed much toward a rational and scientific interpreta- tion of good and evil. But along came Plato with very differ- ent ideas and introduced into Ethics the idealistic and super- natural interpretation of morality, thus setting the clock back, for after all, his supernaturalism was a modified version of the primitive beliefs which some of his fellow-countrymen were trying to throw into the ash can, where they belong. It is inter- esting to note that this darling of the mystics and other purveyors of bunk who did so much to save superstitions from the onslaught of the materialistic philosophers, retained slavery and the death sentence for slaves for not reporting another's offense and for citizens in general when guilty of disrespect toward the established religion. These were some of the features of the model society he proposed in his *Statesman* and *Laws.* Plato thus called upon men to commit the very crimes that so strongly aroused his indignation when Socrates, his teacher, was executed by religious intolerance.

Pythagoras and Aristotle reinforced the supernaturalism of Plato and, together with the Stoics, did spade work and prepared the soil for the Christian ascetics and mystics, and an era in which men who did nothing else but run away from life into caves or cells and waste their time in prayers and mortifications and lived in filth, begging their sustenance, were held as paragons of goodness and virtue, while human beings who dared to refuse to swallow their dogmas were ipso facto heretics, evil and dangerous, to be exterminated from society. St. Thomas Aquinas taught that heretics have no right to live. Whether a heretic was an upright man, kind, honest and altruistic was irrelevant and immaterial—he still was evil and dangerous to society; was hunted by the religious gestapo and tortured and burned when caught. On the other hand, those who went to church and accepted all Christian doctrines without questioning were considered good members of society, even if they were cruel, selfish, lecherous, dishonest and worthless parasites. This absurd and disastrous degradation of good and evil is still with us to a great extent.

Like all other human qualities and emotions, good and evil have a biological basis and grow in the soil of human relations. A human being alone on an island cannot be good or bad. Kindness and sympathy toward other human beings are primarily an expression of kinship and spring from the maternal instinct, for it is here that a human being, the mother, identifies herself with another human being, and out of what begins as a mere physiological attachment, has emerged the most beautiful of all emotions—love. Cooperation also sees its light in the reduced confines of the family and has not gone much farther yet. But as I have stated, in the struggle for life, these desirable qualities appear rather late and have played a limited and secondary role in the survival of the individual.

Although environment plays a paramount role in molding the character of the individual and in determining whether he will contribute good or evil to society, or a mixture of both in varying proportions, there is no doubt that there is a chemistry of goodness and badness, about which we know little as yet. In the same environment some men, the majority, will grow to contribute mostly or completely evil, while others, the very few, will become kind and good natured individuals, overflowing with the milk of human kindness. It seems to depend on the chemistry of the glandular secretions, perhaps also in the quality and structural organization of the brain cells and in the direction and intensity of the biological drives that we must seek the answer why some men will open the door to a stranger with a gun in their hand, and others with a glass of water.

There is ample and irrefutable evidence that social reformers, mystics and religionists have failed and are completely incapable to cope with the growing monster that is evil, for it has increased in size under their mismanagement of society. Only the proper and extensive application of knowledge discovered by scientists in general and psychologists in particular can enable us to win the battle against evil. This battle must be fought with the weapons provided by science in the psychological, in the social and in the economic front. The first is concerned with the formation of a well-integrated personality, free from frustration and fears and fully conscious of man's place in society and of his kinship with all other human beings. It must give man the intellectual tools to direct and control his biological drives and to satisfy them without harming other human beings. The second and the third are concerned with the arduous task of removing as much as possible the sources of temptation to evil, such as great wealth on one side, and extreme poverty and hunger on the other, and by making possible for every human being to have a job that provides him with a high standard of living.

Preaching goodness in an adverse environment is like sowing wheat in the desert—most of the grains will be lost; two thousand years of this practice have amply proven its inefficiency. Yet man still persists in it as if he had learned nothing from history.

The age long battle between the "Angel" and the "Devil" is about to enter its most decisive phase in which men, armed with the flaming sword of knowledge, will burn with its fire the "Devil" and all the monsters that lurk in the dark caverns of his brain and guide out of the biological labyrinth his growing aspirations for a world free from evil.

Man and His Purpose

Life has one primary purpose: to live. To this man adds another purpose: to enjoy life.

Man has been reading his own purpose and his destiny in the stars instead of his actions and his own self. That is why he has suffered so many disappointments.

Gold has become the major purpose of life. No one has expressed this better than the immortal Shelley:

" . . . But in the temple of their hireling hearts
Gold is a living God and rules in scorn
all earthly things but virtue."

There are a great number of people who, with beautiful words, tell us about a high purpose, a spiritual purpose toward which man must direct all his energies. But in practice, most of those people crawl in the gutter of materialism.

A man with the wrong idea is far more dangerous than a man with the wrong purpose.

For me life has only one purpose: to obtain from life the maximum of happiness without harming others or myself. And one goal: to leave this world a better place than I found it.

WHAT is the meaning of man's existence? Has the universe as a whole and life in particular a purpose? Is there an intelligent integration in Nature, a goal to which all phenomena and things are linked and toward whose fulfillment every activity is directed? If so, what is this purpose, this cosmic goal? We can be sure that animals are never bothered by these sixty-four-dollar questions, and that primitive man did not lose any sleep over it. To live and to satisfy the biological needs is enough for animals, for the savage and for many millions of "civilized" people.

But with the growth of consciousness and the ever widening circle of experience, came the power of making higher abstractions and of interpreting experience in moral and purposive terms. It is then that those disturbing and challenging questions were flashed by the newly awakened exceptional brain cells of some exceptional men. We can observe this interesting process in the birth and development of the child which is a concentrated capsule of the birth and development of humanity. It takes quite a few years before the individual tries to justify his existence with moral and "spiritual" goals or purposes; to live and to enjoy life is enough for him.

Although the problem of purpose in the universe and in the life of man is intimately linked to religion, it is not found in all religions. In pre-Christian cultures the purpose of life is purely material; for the poor to work and eke out a miserable existence; for the rich to enjoy an abundant life crammed with the pleasures of sex and food. With the appearance of asceticism first and of Christianity afterwards, this materialistic interpretation of life was severely denounced and condemned, and life and the universe were invested with a "spiritual" purpose, the glorification of God and the salvation of the soul. The fact that this "spiritual" purpose had to be propagated with the sword and maintained with fear, does not speak very well of it; in fact it proves that it cannot be true.

Since science has refuted Christian cosmology and shown the fallacy of its "spiritual" hypotheses, purpose must also be denied. This leaves man again a purposeless creature in a purposeless universe—a pawn of blind and impersonal forces, a mere stage-hand in the cosmic drama. This is a large and most bitter pill for man to swallow. Consequently, philosophers and theologians undertook the task to distort the facts and to cover them with a mantle woven with beautiful but meaningless words in a pattern of wishful thinking. Look at the order and beauty of the universe, at the wonders of life, at the intelligence and achievements of man, at the beneficial relations between living creatures and the environment, at the integration of Nature into a harmonious whole and other phenomena; can these things be the product of mere chance, of the action and interaction of blind impersonal forces without a goal and a purpose? Of course not, they answer. But the real scientist remains adamant because the picture is not as pretty as they paint it and he fails to find that purpose in the movement of the stars and of the planets and in the attractions and repulsions of the atoms and the electrons. He can explain these movements without postulating a supernatural Being and a "spiritual" purpose.

True, living creatures show a behavior that is purposive and adaptive to the environment, but this purpose is material and it is explained as the effort of a dynamic substance, protoplasm, to maintain its physical and chemical equilibrium and stability, as I have shown elsewhere. Thus the only real purpose found in the animal world is the purpose to live. With the emergence of more and more complicated organisms the purpose to keep alive has also become more complex and manifests itself in the most varied and unrecognizable forms and disguises, even as the wish to die. What purpose can even a theologian find in the tse-tse fly and in the mosquito whose bites spread death and disease, in the glacial ages, in the earthquakes, hurricanes, floods and other disastrous elements of Nature? None, of course. These phenomena, like those beneficial to life, are the result of the action and interaction of blind and impersonal forces actuating in the microcosmos and in the macrocosmos, in the atom and in the stars and galaxies; death and life come and go in the wake of their incessant activity.

There is great beauty in the sunset, in the butterfly, in the flowers, in woman, in the plumage of birds, and still more, in the amazing and startling beauty in the depths of the sea where nobody can admire it, and where it serves no purpose at all. The average student of science knows that the beautiful colors of the sunset and the rainbow are the result of chemical and physical processes, and that given the material we find in the earth and the sun, it could not be otherwise. The same principle holds true for living creatures. Would anyone affirm that oysters create beautiful pearls with a purpose? That the molluscs inhabiting the gorgeous shells have an eye for beauty and build their colorful and symmetric homes? That the butterfly makes her beautiful wings to be admired, and that the peacock chooses the incomparable dress it displays, and that the sun paints the clouds with the most vivid harmony of colors to please our eyes? That a beautiful woman is made with a purpose? If he does, he is simply indulging in wishful thinking and blocking the door of reality with illusions that, although they seem harmless, are dangerous and already have caused more than enough trouble and suffering. There is beauty and ugliness in Nature, but whether they are found in the non-living or in the living world, they are always the result of atomic and molecular attractions and repulsions. This is clearly demonstrated in *On Growth and Form*, by Sir D'Arcy Wentworth Thompson.

Of course, most of the behavior, movements and functions of living organisms must be purposive or they could not survive. There are lethal genes that destroy the organism they are supposed to build, but since they die with it, they are stopped cold in their tracks and only those organisms with beneficial genes are left to live and pass on the torch of life. Animals are moved by instincts and tropisms usually favorable to life, but there are exceptions: the moth flies into the light that will destroy him because his organism is positively heliotropic and cannot resist the powerful attraction of light. The male risks death and sometimes dies in the process of possessing and fertilizing the female, both in the animal and the human worlds, because he is positively chemotropic and cannot resist the chemical attraction of the female.

Superficially examined, sex appears as one of the most, if not the most, purposive behavior of living creatures; yet when it is examined carefully and with the critical eye of science, its purpose to reproduce the species vanishes. The reproduction of life through the mechanism of sex is an incident emerging from the efforts of cellular colonies to maintain their chemical and physical equilibrium; the primary function of sex is one of elimination of disturbing cells from the organism. This explains the imperfections and contradictions and

enormous variations of the sexual mechanism and of the sex
life of animals and man. No purposive intelligence could have
produced such a poor and imperfect job.

There is what Henderson calls "the fitness of environment", which means that there has been a harmonious development and unfoldment of matter in different forms, yet so
intimately related that if we were to change the qualities or
the quantity of one single substance by the smallest fraction,
life would disappear from the planet. Let me illustrate the
meaning of this statement with just one substance. Water is
the inert constituent of the atmosphere, the inactive and universal solvent. The specific heat of water, greater than that of
any other substance except hydrogen and ammonia, is very important because it tends to maintain the seas, lakes and streams
at an approximately constant temperature. Water moderates
summer and winter temperatures and the ocean currents tend
to equalize the circulation of the planet and its temperature.
Another extremely important property of water is its latent
heat freezing point and evaporation; it has the highest latent
heat of freezing of anything known, except ammonia; this acts
as a thermostat for our planet.

The thermal conductivity of water is also much greater
than that of any other liquid; it stands absolutely alone in its
property of anomalous expansion when cooled to temperatures
near freezing. In other words, when water freezes it expands,
and this exhibits a behavior exclusive to itself. Were it not so,
ice would sink instead of floating and soon the oceans would
become a solid mass of ice and life would be impossible. It is
obvious that this "fitness of the environment" must have preceded life for a long time. Thus we can say that there is a
Universal Teleology, a kind of purpose running through the
universe, but this teleology is inherent in the structuration and
evolution of matter; it is material purposiveness, and it has
nothing in common with the teleology and finalism of religionists and vitalists. As Henderson so well says:

"Mechanism is enough for physical science which no less

than biological science appears to manifest teleology; it must therefore suffice for biology. Science has put the old teleology to death. Its disembodied spirit, freed from vitalism and all material ties, immortal, alone lives on, and from such a ghost science has nothing to fear. The man of science is not even obliged to have an opinion concerning its reality, for it dwells in another world, where he as a scientist can never enter."

The fact that we live in a mechanist world through which we pass as shadows upon the screen of time, should not be cause for despair and pessimism. Quite the contrary; the knowledge of this reality, instead of paralyzing our actions, should stir us to remedy this situation by a greater enjoyment of life, by using our energies in setting up a program of constructive purposes and devoting our minds and bodies to their realization. Too long has man followed a phantom purpose, never catching up with it because it is only a ghost—the creation of his own mind. Let us give it prompt and complete burial from which it can never arise again and remain loyal to life and its high and only purpose which is to attain the maximum of sensation and feeling and enjoy it to the limit of our capacity.

The Making of Man

The new born child is a complex and delicate machine, the most complex and important machine in the world. Yet it is left in the hands of good-intentioned but ignorant people who fail in the most vital job in life: that of making a man out of the child.

Most of the efforts and time used to change people after they have become adults is wasted. Few men change habits, mentality and beliefs acquired in childhood.

Man is not born good or bad; he is born with capacities for both, but his capacities for evil seem to be much greater than for good.

As the sculptor chisels away the rough stone and gives form and beauty to it, thus is man formed under the strokes of environment. And, like the statue of the sculptor, it may emerge a beautiful and inspiring work of art or an ugly monster.

Education alone is not the answer to the wish for a better world; it must be the right kind of education at the right time.

Clothes do not make the man. Wearing a shirt, tie and striped trousers do not make one a gentleman. Mental and emotional maturity are the real clothes of man.

THE BIRTH of a child has always been a mystery and a wonder for men and women, sometimes wanted and welcomed, and many times unwanted and unwelcomed—a burden thrown recklessly by the gods upon the meager resources of the parents. Here, in the birth of the child, we find more evidence that his gestation and birth cannot be the work of an intelligent Being concerned with his welfare. Why should a woman carry the child nine months in her womb and suffer more or less discomfort in pregnancy and in labor? Why should woman suffer so many handicaps, psychological and sociological, for bringing a child into the world? Women have been severely penalized and degraded for bringing men into the world, and more for bringing women. And why should man be born weak and helpless and remain so for such a long time? More questions could be asked, but these should suffice to show that any intelligent person could have planned things in a more rational and beneficial way for both—the parents and the children.

Moreover, for countless generations children have been reared and treated according to absurd and irrational tabus, traditions and religious beliefs, diverse and changing with time, place and culture, but on the whole the life of the child has been most unhappy and even cruel. Most parents have looked upon their children as objects to be exploited, as slaves without rights. All these facts, if faced squarely and realistically, lead to the conclusion that the gestation, birth and infancy—in fact, the whole life of man and man himself—is the product of blind impersonal forces which we are beginning to understand. This rather than diminishing, increases the wonders of life and man.

There is evidence that at the dawn of humanity the treatment received by the child was not much different from the treatment animals give to their offspring. Tender, conscious mother love had not yet emerged from animal instinct and physiological attachment; and since there was no physiological relationship or attachment between father and child and no awareness of the role played by man in the procreation of children, the bond between father and child was even less strong than among some animals. Under these conditions we should not be surprised that infanticide was often practiced to get rid of unwanted children (another argument against an intelligent plan) and education, as we understand it today, was completely unknown and non-existent.

The growth of religion brought the "spiritualization" of man and naturally it affected the treatment and education of the child, but it did not make his lot much better—in some cases it made it worse. The child was the property of the parents who could do with him as they pleased, with no interference from the state or the religious leaders. If the parents were poor, the child was put to work as soon as he was able, after a miserable infancy; no toys, very little or no paternal love and affection and usually hungry. If the child was fortunate enough to be born with a silver spoon in his mouth, his lot was much better, of course, but still no better than a slave subject to the whims and arbitrariness of his parents, at least until he was married.

Among the Greeks and the Romans education reached new heights and more children than ever before learned to read and write, but books and knowledge were still very scarce, so that only a limited and selected number of children got an education—the great mass of people remained as ignorant and untouched by learning as ever. Thus knowledge became the monopoly of a few, a class that ruled and exploited the people, keeping them in ignorance and bondage.

With Christianity man and child became essentially souls created by God, and the triumph of Christianity over paganism brought a revolution in the education of the child. Theoretically this revolution should have improved greatly the lot of the child and given him many rights, but like so many other things, in practice it made childhood worse than it was under paganism. Under this distorted view of life, the infant was considered as a little man who only needed to grow up; all education and instruction was imparted with only one objective in mind: the salvation of the soul. Therefore any knowledge or study that contradicted the dogmas and beliefs of the Church was ruthlessly suppressed.

The invention of printing alone was bound to break the monopoly of knowledge enjoyed for so many centuries by the priesthood and make censorship first difficult and later impossible; but, together with the Reformation, it worked faster and opened new and vast horizons to education. The rapid development of trade, commerce and industrialism of the Renaissance made necessary a greater knowledge of the earth, of the stars and of Nature in general, and as it has been said, necessity is the mother of invention. Curiosity which muzzled had strained at the leash held by the priesthood, broke loose after several attempts, and the crude printing machine of Guttenberg soon became the greatest weapon against ignorance ever wielded, and from the printing presses came out an avalanche of books against which neither the Inquisition nor the Index Expurgatorious could fight, they were swamped and practically drowned by the flood of written pages. But all the increasing knowledge, the education of the child did not really change— it remained authoritarian, dogmatic and "spiritual", the salvation of the soul still being the supreme goal and end of all knowledge and education. The child continued to be regarded as the possession of the parents, especially of the father, and was no better off than a chattel. Early in life the child was taught that he owed eternal gratitude to his parents for having brought him into the world; that he had not been consulted whether he really wanted to come into such a nasty world nor given the opportunity to choose his parents and that he may have refused to come into this world or chosen better parents, was completely ignored. The child must be thankful for having been given life, regardless whether he was born in a hovel or in a palace, or whether his parents were good and wise, or brutal and cruel. The parents had power of life and death over the child and were, as they still are, his first gods; the state and the church remained completely indifferent to the fate of the child, much more so than under paganism. The chances of a poor child of ever obtaining a good education and reaching the level of the privileged class were very, very slim; if he was born of serfs, he usually died in servitude, and if he was born in a palace, he lived in luxury and ruled over men. In either case the child was a slave—if poor, he was put to work as soon as he could earn some money, and if he was rich, his chains were gilded; that is all. His career, his work, his friends—even his wife—were chosen by his totalitarian parents and he, in a returning revenge, would do the same with his children, thus perpetuating a most vicious cycle.

With the development of the modern state, the authority of the Church and of parents was challenged, and the triumph of the theory of evolution reduced the soul to a useless ghost and presented man in his true nature—an animal whose ancestors lived in the trees and with the same basic biological needs. Laws for the protection of the child began to come out of legislative councils, and schools and universities grew by leaps and bounds. Christian leaders, Catholic and Protestant, fought tooth and nail against the state's encroachment upon their authority, but lost the battle. The state, in turn, has become in some cases a tyrant no better or perhaps worse than the Church. Thus the free educator has to fight against two enemies, both bent on dominating the child and cramming into his juvenile mind their deleterious dogmas and beliefs.

Organized religion opposes the loyalty demanded by the state with the spurious argument that God has entrusted the child to the parents and therefore they have complete authority over the child. The fact that the Church has been and is the worse offender against this principle, is conveniently ignored. Although science in general, and psychology in particular, have made obsolete the supernatural and spiritual theories and demonstrated how harmful to the child and to society are the methods of education based upon those fallacies and the education of the child is the most important and difficult task, it is still left in the hands of men and women who are ignorant of how to handle and direct the dynamic and explosive energies hidden in that small bundle of weak and helpless flesh that is the new born child. Nor are school teachers much better qualified—the immense majority of them just cram a few facts into the brain of the pupil; they impart instruction on schedule and in a hurry, very much like the workers on a conveyor who hastily put pieces into the machine that passes before them.

That the child has two sets of needs—physical and "spiritual" or psychological—has been known to philosophers and educators for a long time; but modern science has given us a clear understanding of the nature of these needs, and of the best and most efficient methods and ways to satisfy them.

Since intelligence and imagination give man almost unlimited power for good and evil, the basic problem of education resolves itself not merely in teaching to read and write and imparting knowledge about the world, but in establishing in the child correct evaluations of his body-mind and of the environment; in giving him a true perspective of his position in life and in society, and in equipping him with a goal and the necessary instrument or tools to reach his goal.

The biological needs of the child are rather easy to understand and to satisfy; any person with a normal intelligence can prepare food for the child and attend to his physiological care. The psychological care of the child is far more difficult and demands more skill, more knowledge and wisdom from the parents and educators. Let us look at it.

THE BIOLOGICAL CARE OF THE CHILD—I believe that the biological care of the child has been complicated and perverted by pompous specialists who pretend to know more than the human body. These medicine men do not seem to have heard of the wisdom of the body so well stated by Dr. Walter Cannon in his book: *The Wisdom of the Body.*

During its millions of years of existence, protoplasm has acquired and developed marvelous defensive and protective mechanisms and instincts without which animals and man could never have survived in a more or less hostile environment. Long before modern medicine man and the pediatrician emerged from the magician, the High Priest and the Alchemist, the human body was using a healing power that, if given a chance, can accomplish marvelous cures and keep the body fairly healthy.

Although in man the guiding instincts have become weak and even lost or perverted, to a certain extent, under the pressure of civilized life, the child, being somewhat free from "civilizing" influences, is nearer to the animal and possesses a good amount of biological wisdom. The infant knows when and what to eat better than most pediatricians. Hunger is a better guide to food than the clock, and experiments conducted with children have shown that if given a chance, they can select a good, nourishing and balanced diet.

The infant has a birthright to the breast, and the mother has the duty, both toward the child and to herself, to give it to him. Breast feeding is very good physiologically and psychologically for the child and for the mother. Unfortunately few mothers are able and willing to nurse their children, especially here in America. Many mothers complain that their little darlings refuse to eat, and become frantic with fear at the thought that they may starve to death. It is impossible to get those mothers to understand that no animal starves to death if food is within its reach. Biologically and physiologically, the child is an animal primarily concerned with living and with the satisfaction of hunger and other bodily needs. But the child soon learns that he can get attention by refusing to eat his meal. Moreover, refusing to eat is a weapon against his mother, and a protest against the many suppressions and inhibitions inflicted upon him; it is also a form of revenge and the best manner in which to assert his personality, his ego and his independence. The best thing to do is to leave the child alone with his food, and if he refuses to eat, to take it away until he asks for it. There is no need to worry that the child will go on a hunger strike or voluntary fasting: when hunger grips his little tummy he will eat anything. A well balanced diet, cleanliness, fresh air, sun, play, rest and the right amount of love are the most important things for the physical care of the child.

THE PSYCHOLOGICAL CARE OF THE CHILD—With the birth of the child, parents are entrusted with the most delicate and wonderful machine in the world and assume responsibilities that are too often beyond their awareness and their capacity. We would not think of leaving any of our machines in the hands of an unskilled and ignorant person; we demand skilled mechanics and engineers. Yet, very few parents possess even the most elementary knowledge of the human machine, of its mechanism and behavior. This, of course, was logical

and excusable in pre-scientific days, but not today, because
that knowledge is available to anyone who really wants it.
Consequently, parents still cling to antiquated notions, harmful habits, false conceptions and incorrect evaluations about
the child, his capacities and his needs. The result of this
global and enormous ignorance has been disastrous for the
child and for mankind. The wonder is that so many children
turn out so well despite the ignorance of their parents and
educators. Putting the problem in terms of mechanics and performance, we can state that in order to get the maximum efficiency and work from a machine, it is essential to know its
laws and internal mechanism. Since man is not logical nor a
rational human being, he fails to apply this truth to the human machine.

There is no doubt that the prompt and thorough application of the scientific knowledge we have today to the education of the child, from the moment he is born, would change
the world within two or three generations and would bring an
era of peace and good will between all the peoples, as only
dreamed by idealists. It would banish wars and most violence and hatred and make this earth a paradise. But the application of this knowledge would make obsolete and unnecessary churches and other institutions that are the pillars of society, and of the profit system. Not that I am against the
profit system because everything that a human being does is
done for profit; hence the enormous resistance that these
forces offer to the radical changes in education necessary to
make man capable to live up to the image of his super ego.

There are a few fundamental things that parents should
know and bear in mind when that tiny but important guest
makes his entrance in their home. The child is born without
mind, and the mind begins to be formed as soon as the child
takes his first breath and utters his first cry; his plastic brain
receives avidly and keeps a record of every sensation and
image that enters through the five doors that are his senses.

The child comes from a paradise where he had complete

quietness and where he was protected from changes of temperature and other things by a most ingenious mechanism. All of a sudden the child is torn from this paradise and catapulted through a narrow passage, where he almost chokes to death, into an unkown, strange, hostile and noisy world where it is either too hot or too cold, and where people sometimes handle him roughly, where he hears all kinds of loud noises, and where hunger and other biological necessities are a frequent source of discomfort and pain.

It is reasonable to suspect that the Christian myth-makers knew about the uterine paradise and had it in mind when they placed Adam and Eve in a garden where everything was perfect, and birth is symbolized in their expulsion by an angry God, and that sin is the sin of growing too large for the womb. If such a paradise had existed, it would have been known to other people; but even as myth it is of late vintage and appears when men have the necessary images to serve as a model. We must remember that the mind creates nothing—for every myth there is a counterpart in the real world, impressions and images that have entered by the senses. The mind merely weaves new robes for those images, just as we do in our dreams; that is why we do not recognize our images when presented out of their natural context and are greatly magnified and distorted. It is like seeing oneself in a concave mirror.

Freud was the first to point out that birth represents a trauma which he says is the cause of much anxiety and neurosis. Otto Rank and Dr. Karl A. Meninger follow Freud in this matter. There is no gainsaying that violent expulsion of the child from the uterus and his passage through the narrow gorge that is the vagina are an uncomfortable experience; but no positive evidence has been offered that its psychological effects are any more lasting than the physical. Animals and savages do not show evidence of any harmful effects from their violent and traumatic entrance into this world, and with proper care the child recovers quickly from his harrowing experience. The lesson from the above facts is that the child must have peace and quiet, be handled as little as possible and then with great care and very gently. As the child opens his eyes and his ears to the world, these should receive pleasant and harmonious sensations or impressions.

The child is afraid of only two things: a loud noise and lack of support; all other fears are acquired. It is the duty of the parents to see that the child grows free from unnecessary and irrational fears that, like a dark cloud, will shut away the sun and give him a feeling of insecurity and make his life unhappy, and perhaps evil, in relation to other lives. The first year of the child's life is dedicated mostly to the opening of pathways for the nerve-impulses to the organs and muscles and in getting control of the voluntary muscles.

We speak of sexual education in very broad and vague terms. It seems to me that there is a difference between sexual education and sexual knowledge. Education means behavior and to some extent, the meaning of knowledge. The child must first be given knowledge and later education. Sexuality appears in the child at an age when neither education nor knowledge can be given. The important thing, as we have learned from the development of psychoanalysis and the study of primitive people, is that sexuality must not be suppressed nor opposed; the child must be left completely free to satisfy his curiosity and the limited pleasure he derives from the emerging eroticism. If he is playing with his genitals, he must be ignored; sexual knowledge must be imparted as the curiosity of the child requires. There must be no attempt to brand any function of the body as bad or evil, nor any of its organs. The child must be allowed to go around naked as much as possible, and he should grow used to seeing his parents and brothers and sisters naked. This practice of nudism I consider a very important part in the sexual *education* of the child. By avoiding false prudery and seeing nude adults around him, the child will grow without that morbid and pathological curiosity and false modesty, or rather hypocrisy, that afflicts most adults. There is nothing shameful about the body, and the child must learn very early to respect and admire the human body as a wonderful work of art, and not something to be ashamed of.

Every home ought to have a few anatomical pictures of the human body so that the child gets familiar with himself. This knowledge must be given in a progressive manner and by the time the child reaches puberty he will be ready to receive sex education, and to understand the social and ethical responsibilities of sex. It is absolutely wrong to wait to give sexual knowledge and sex education in the school, because when the child reaches puberty, he usually has gathered a certain amount of sex knowledge, but contaminated with mud; then he cannot any longer receive sexual information without blushing and forming distorted or erotic images in his mind; in other words, at puberty the boy cannot be as objective and candid as he was in his childhood—sex has already acquired a different meaning for him, and no amount of preaching and threatening will change that meaning and his attitude.

There should be in every city abundant nurseries where children could play naked, when the weather permits, all by themselves, but under expert supervision, of course. This, together with the other measures already recommended, would be the best and most efficient remedy for sex delinquency and crime; no child who grows with a healthy and scientific attitude will ever become a sex delinquent or a problem, nor is he very likely to be afflicted with neurosis and anxiety.

There is more harm and future tragedy in bringing up the child isolated from other children in such an island that is the home, by himself; he not only grows selfish, self-centered and conceited, but he also acquires a kind of armor, a hard shell that will prevent him from establishing cordial and friendly relations with all human beings, and also from adjusting himself easily and harmoniously to people and conditions. This isolation blinds him to the vital fact that every human being is a link in a long chain that goes around the world, that he is a member of the community and that his welfare is closely related to the welfare of the other members. Here in the nursery is where the child must get his first practical lesson in democracy and self-government.

Children should be encouraged to solve their own problems and conflicts arising from their play and other group activities. Adults should assist in the capacity of supervisors. Any anti-social act should be called to the attention of the whole group and let them be the judges and the jury; thus children will grow with a sense of responsibility, self-importance and capacity for adjustment practically unknown now. Violence and authoritarianism can and must be defeated in the children's nursery, and here too, by mixing children of all races on an equal basis and by establishing a feeling of comradeship and security among them, can racial and religious prejudices and intolerance be prevented from taking root. We can see every day how costly those prejudices are, both in money and in suffering, and how difficult, if not impossible, it is to free human beings from them.

"Words, words, words" . . . Who has not been held spellbound by and has not laughed at the attempts of the child to form his first words? And what mother and father has not been thrilled beyond description by the word "papa" and "mama" so tenderly and laboriously uttered by their child? The child repeats the infancy of humanity, and with a little imagination we can see primitive man uttering sounds, shaping them into words, going around talking to himself, to the trees, to the animals, to rivers and the sea, to the spirits and to the gods. With speech man had conquered the best means of communication and the power to transmit his experiences to other human beings. The brain would no longer be a soundless receiving instrument; ideas and thoughts not only could be given form, but speech had provided the brain with a new and potent stimulant that would do wonders for its development. But like everything else in the world, speech is not an unmixed blessing. Before long, words became the tyrants of their own creator, a tyranny that has grown worse with the development of intelligence and culture. Words became things, sometimes as powerful as the thing or symbol they represented; words got man into awful situations from which he tried to extricate himself with more words, with little or no success, for strange as it may seem, words of hope, healing words do not have the power and influence of damaging and "evil" words. A person can be injured psychologically and socially, maybe for life, by just one word, while there is no one good word that will achieve the same results in a constructive manner. It takes many, many words to minimize or counteract very slightly the harm and damage caused by just one or two words.

The reason for this strange and unfortunate phenomenon lies in the fact that "evil" and destructive words elicit and provoke the same destructive emotions they represent and these emotions, ancestral and primeval, are developed in the struggle for life, while good words, words of hope and of love, are rather newcomers into the human vocabulary and they stand for and represent also emotions of more recent origin. Consequently, they lack the explosive charge of destructive and fighting words, and even when they produce a very strong reaction its effects are not lasting.

We shall never know when, nor exactly how and much less by whom that wonderful thing that is speech got degraded and prostituted, but it did. Used at first as a means of conveying thoughts, ideas and feelings, it became the means to hide those very things, to deceive and to give life to illusions and hallucinations. It seems to me that men got caught and entangled in their own lies and meaningless words, held by them just as prisoner and helpless as if they were steel chains. We can see this situation all around us. This process of the slavery of meaningless and empty words must have come gradually as men came to realize that many of the entities and symbols with which they populated the universe were not real, that there was nothing where they thought there was an entity. But they had so become influenced and conditioned, not only individually but collectively, that they could not very well drop that word or give it a completely different meaning without dislocating the whole fabric of their culture and economy. Once this process was started, the rest was easy; there was no end to it; it grew and grew until it is now crushing man with its weight. Modern man has made an art of lying, of saying what he does not mean and of hiding what he really thinks. Our printing presses pour out an enormous stream of words every second the object of which is only to hide the truth, to dope the people, to keep them from thinking, to frighten them into submission and to amuse them, to lead them to the slaughter, to make injustice palatable or to cover it with the mantle of justice and righteousness, to make slavery sweet and attractive, to get money painlessly, to satisfy his inordinate sex hunger by calling it love, to prostitute, abuse and misuse the very things he holds most holy and noble. The printed pages have become Augean stables awaiting a Hercules who will turn the river of Truth upon them and sweep away the accumulated dirt of many centuries.

It is obvious then that there is more than meets the eye to the art of teaching speech to the child. Like primitive man, the child speaks the truth as he sees it; he says what he means and means what he says, and it must be a painful disappoint-ment to him to learn that he has to lie, to hide his real feelings, to censor and suppress truth. But society soon makes a consummated liar of the child with most tragic consequences for himself and for society. The task of the true and honest educator is to introduce the child to the new world of words in such a manner that he will form correct evaluations of the words and of things they represent; to teach him to use words without becoming their slave; to accentuate those positive and constructive words and to strip destructive and damaging words of their fuse and of their TNT, so that they become harmless, unable to produce hatred, terror, fear and violence.

THE RELIGIOUS AND MORAL EDUCATION OF THE CHILD—
The failure of religious education has been amply discussed

elsewhere in this book, therefore there is no need for repetition; moreover, the futility of religious teachings in childhood is evident to anyone who has even an elementary knowledge of the mentality of the child. To speak to the child about God is like speaking to a savage about the cyclotron; to the child his father is his God because he provides for his necessities. Prayers have as much meaning for the child as a mathematical equation has for an illiterate person. It has been the function of religion, to a great extent, to give man a picture of the universe and to answer his questions as to *how* and *why*. But since science has clearly shown that religion has been misleading man by giving him wrong answers to his questions and has taken away from religion the function of imparting knowledge and information about the world, there is no need for it. This does not mean we must ignore and neglect the sense of wonder in the child; it would be grievously wrong to do so. The child must be introduced to the wonders of life and Nature, trained into the contemplation of beauty; his curiosity must be stirred and his senses sharpened, and his emotions fed not with the coarse and hard bread of cynicism and scepticism, neither with the metaphysical broth made of hallucinations and wishful thinking, but rather with the solid food of reality. The wonders of Nature and life are no less wonderful because there is no master magician behind them; they are more wonderful and worthy of admiration because they are an unfoldment of matter and the result of blind and impersonal forces in an endless struggle of trial and error, in an ever dynamic effort of change and creation. Here then is room for a natural, for a scientific religion which will provide an outlet for emotions and religious feeling of the child. In this natural religion there must be no parasites, no temples; Nature must be its temple and its phenomena its ceremonies.

The unity of the human race must be inculcated and illustrated by all available means and the advantages of cooperation must be demonstrated and practiced with other children. The child must be shown that without cooperation his own body would not be possible, and that struggle and competition must work hand in hand and be subordinate to cooperation.

There is plenty of ugliness and "evil" things in Nature and in the world of man and these must not be gilded or ignored; they must be presented as an integral part of life and reality and as a challenge to his imagination. As the mind of the child grows, he must be given goals and purposes in this purposeless world. To make this planet a better place to live, to establish permanent peace and friendly cooperation between all the peoples, to be healthy and to enjoy life without harming anyone—these are the purposes and goals worthy of the creative and dynamic mind of the boy.

Practically all children indulge in day-dreaming and fantasies and populate the world with mythical beings just as primitive man did. There is nothing harmful and wrong in this if he is taught to distinguish between fact and illusion, between dream and reality; there is a technique of escapism that makes it harmless and even beneficial, as we shall see later. Imagination must not be frozen by the winds of reality nor its wings crippled by hallucinations. If the child day-dreams and talks about his visions, he should be encouraged to write them down and their true origin and mechanism explained to him. All questions asked by the child must be answered truthfully, according to the scientific knowledge available; if the parents do not have the answer ready, they would do better to admit their ignorance than to try to cover it up; the child is very sensitive and soon will find out if his parents deceive him. Deceiving and lying to the child is the best way to lose his respect, admiration and confidence; it is also a sure way to plant the seeds of mistrust and maladjustment in adult life.

If a man is a soul, as the religionists assure us, and the salvation of the soul depends upon leading a moral life, we should expect the child to be born with an innate morality and the knowledge of right and wrong. The fact is that the child is born without morals, and good and bad for him are very relative terms concerned only with his welfare. Thus the child acquires the morals, tabus and customs of the group or nation in which he is born, even if those morals and tabus are in open contradiction, as they usually are, with the morals and tabus of other groups and countries.

Religious leaders and professional moralists have poured upon mankind an avalanche of moral codes and commandments covering every human activity and which provide the text for Sunday sermons; that those commandments are violated and ignored by the moralists is a well known fact. The reason, as repeatedly pointed out, is that those moral codes are unnatural and anti-biological. The Ten Commandments were given to Moses on Mount Sinai with much thunder and pomp, so they say, and Moses descended from that rendezvous with Jehovah and with Destiny to find his people having a gay time and breaking all commandments, so he broke the stone tablets upon which God had inscribed his moral code, in a fit of anger. This should have been a lesson to God and to Moses and a hint of what was going to happen to those commandments—practically everyone was going to break them. Who loves his neighbor as himself? Who does not covet his neighbor's wife, if she is very pretty? Who does not commit adultery if he has the chance and can get away with it? Only a small minority. Therefore, either the whole thing is a colossal hoax invented by the Israelites, or God did not know anything about man, the creature he had created in His own image, for He must have known that man could not, even if he wanted, keep those commandments, having the biological urges He had given him.

Since the Ten Commandments and other moral codes are treated like an antique piece of furniture which nobody uses but makes good decoration, the child must be given a morality that is based upon humanism and is consistent with his biological nature, and this morality must be theoretical and practical, for it will do little or no good at all to tell the child "be good, don't do this or that" and then do those very things. A person who smokes has no moral authority to tell another to stop smoking because it is very bad.

On the theoretical level the child must be shown that the moral imperative to treat others as if he were the others, is practical, feasible and to his own advantage. We must take into consideration the fact that the child is naturally and essentially selfish, and that all the preaching, bribing and threatening is not going to change his nature. To know whether a thing is bad or good, right or wrong, he needs only to ask himself how he would feel if it were done to him. I am sure that this lesson learned very early in childhood is the best check, the most practical moral law, stronger than the fear of hell, stronger than all the Commandments of God and his self-appointed oracles, and more effective than all the laws and cruel punishments devised by ignorant and frustrated men. Any other morality is disguised immorality and will breed cynicism and hypocrisy, as we can easily observe.

To spank or not to spank presents the parents with a difficult choice. There has been much debate on this subject. Psychiatrists and psychologists have denounced spanking as a brutal and revengeful act unbecoming to civilized parents, which may bring all kinds of evil consequences and warp the personality of the spanked child. However, there are a few souls who cling to the past and refuse to be convinced of the failure of the rod, and it is possible that their faith in it is not altogether misplaced. The truth, it seems to me, is not found in either extreme. There ar children who at times need a spanking and would benefit by it, while other children never need even that mild show of violence, and probably would be harmed by spanking. The reasoning capacity of the child emerges at different rates of speed in different children and for a period of time the child is at the animal level, unable to understand reasonable advice and arguments. When spanking is necessary, it should be administered with a minimum of anger, in small quantity and at the precise psychological moment.

The authority of the parents, especially the father, is necessary for the normal development of the personality of the child; in fact, the child expects and looks for that authority, and he is terribly disappointed when he does not find it or finds it unjust, arbitrary, too weak or too severe. The parents are, for a while, the super-ego of the child and must function as such until he forms his own super-ego. Authority and discipline must have as a goal the development of self-discipline and a healthy super-ego without which the adult is dangerous to society. I have found the following illustration very helpful in making boys understand the necessity of discipline and of accepting the decisions of the father without bitterness or resentment. The home can be compared to a ship and the family to the crew. Without the direction and authority of the captain, the chances are that the crew would be negligent in the performance of their duties and that the ship would go off course and hit the rocks. The father is the captain and the final authority, and his decision must be final, like a decision from the Supreme Court, for he, together with the mother, is the supreme court of the home. Both father and mother must act as a team and there must be no split decisions.

The boy must be shown that starting in life is like sailing unknown seas and that he must use the charts made by those who have sailed before him or run greater risks to be battered and shipwrecked by the storms and rocks. But the father must be fair and remember that he too was once a boy, and must temper with kindness and understanding his tendency to be harsh and impatient, too much like a dictator. Freedom is like walking—one learns by using it and by making mistakes. As early as possible the boy must be given responsibility and treated like an important member of the crew; he must learn to make decisions and to contribute, with his mind and actions, to the welfare and good running of the ship that is the home.

There are no bad children, but there are exceptional children for whom the usual and normal rules and behavior do not fit; these children have stronger and more powerful biological urges and an enormous amount of energy that, like lightning, hits blindly and powerfully. No rules can be given for these exceptional children; they must be treated individually by competent psychologists and physicians because very often behind an anti-social behavior there are physiological and chemical causes, rather than moral issues and an evil personality. The trouble with our congested "civilization" is that children do not have enough space to play and give free rein to their endless energy without annoying parents or grownups. To ask a child to stay quiet is like putting a bird in a cage and asking it to stop flying. We need more parks where children can play in the sun and spend a happy childhood, for this is very important and is the foundation of a healthy adulthood.

School marks a very important event in the life of the boy because with his entrance in the classroom he begins the serious and necessary task of receiving organized and official knowledge about the world and the people living in it. There is much in our education that deserves harsh criticism; its deficiency and shortcomings are appalling; it has no relation to the real needs of the child in society. The present purpose of education is to cram the brain of the boy with a maximum of information or knowledge in the minimum amount of time. Much of this information is forgotten more rapidly than it was learned, but that does not seem to disturb our educators who go merrily on, leaving a trail of failures behind them.

The main objective of the school seems to be the elimination of illiteracy, and this is very necessary; but there is another kind of illiteracy that the school ignores—intellectual illiteracy, which is just as dangerous as the first and which our teachers do not seem to know even exists. The ability to read carries with it a great responsibility of which the boy hardly ever hears. Therefore he comes out of the school fair prey for all kinds of propaganda. Unfortunately the newspapers accept with equal favor the ravings of a Hitler, the vapid nonsense of the metaphysicians and the truth of the scientists; herein lies the greatest danger to freedom and to democracy, for people who cannot distinguish between truth and unreality, between facts and propaganda, are easily caught in the net of the demagogue and the unscrupulous politician hungry for power. We have seen this happen in Germany and it almost happened in our country. We were saved from dictatorship not by the intelligence of the people, but by circumstances alien to them.

The real function of the school and its most important task is to promote and develop clear and scientific thinking and to equip the pupil with tools with which he can form correct evaluations of things and phenomena and to establish rational and ethical relations with other human beings. The primacy and superiority of reason and intelligence over brute force must be inculcated with images and sounds until it is well absorbed and stored in the brain cells. Therefore the school must open wide its doors to criticism and to controversial subjects, which are now tabu, by frightened, incompetent, sanctimonious, reactionary old fogies who have no place in modern education. Criticism is the life blood of democracy, the wheels upon which progress marches on to new conquests and greater perfection. Where criticism is suppressed there is stagnation and intellectual death.

If the child is not taught and trained to give and take criticism in every field of knowledge, he will not be able to take it later and will grow into an intolerant and narrow-minded bigot, dangerous to freedom and to the community. We see plenty of this type of people around. The boy must learn that ideas and opinions are not sacred nor tabu; they must be investigated and criticised if they deserve criticism, that nobody is infallible and everyone can be wrong, sometimes. Moreover, controversy and criticism, when conducted in an intellectual and scientific level, sharpen the mind, bring out whatever ignorance of the subject there is, and act as a stimulant to greater study. Doubt is the beginning of wisdom —when it does not lead to cynicism, and to know that one does not know, is important knowledge.

It is good to study history and learn about past events, but if that learning is limited to memorizing dates and events, it is a perfect waste of time and energy on the part of the teacher and the pupil and waste of money for the taxpayer. The events of the past must be linked and related to the present, which they have begotten, and to the future which is in process of formation. Far more important than remembering the date of a battle or the name of a king or conqueror is to grasp their social meaning and to understand the forces and factors which wrote them in the pages of history. Thus history becomes a living thing and we can learn from it how to cope with many problems of the present. Let the teacher challenge the imagination of the pupil with living issues and with problems of real life as they affect human beings individually and collectively and invite the criticism and comments of the students; the development of the critical and analytical faculties in the student is one of the most important labors of the teacher, and these faculties can only be developed by training and exercise, just as we develop the muscles by using them. Religions and philosophy must be studied as any other subject, with the same scientific attitude that we apply to other matters. Any religion or faith that cannot stand the acid test of criticism and scientific analysis is a hindrance to humanity, not worth having, much less fighting and dying for.

As the onset of puberty approaches, it is time to give the child sexual education and a broader knowledge of his organs and sexual functions, and since the matter is already very familiar to him now, he can take it without blushing and as a matter of fact. Sexual education must be concerned with the ethics of the sexual act, already discussed in another chapter. The psychology, physiology and anatomy of woman should be given much attention, for it is far more important for the happiness of man to know these things than to know who won the battle of Hastings or even who signed our Declaration of Independence. Under our present educational system the boy comes out of school in blissful ignorance of the human beings with whom he has to live intimately practically all his life and with whom he will form a family—no wonder he is such a horrible failure as a husband and as a father. Although nothing can take the place of sexual relations, there is no doubt a certain amount of sublimation that can and should take place in the boy; this can be achieved by directing his attention and his mental energy toward things he likes and in which he can use some of the aggressiveness of sex and the craving for conquest and dominance. Since boys respond differently, it is up to the teacher to treat each boy individually and to guide him through the shoals of sex life.

We have failed to make our schools the unifying centers they should be; in the sacred hall of science that is the school, there are not, or there must not be, Catholics, Protestants, Jews, etc., nor Negroes or Whites, nor Americans and foreigners—only human beings united in forming and creating a peaceful and abundant world. Labels divide and separate, science unites because it shows the kinship of all races and human beings. If the brotherhood of man is possible and feasible, it will be only under the fatherhood of science and wisdom, not under the fatherhood of a mythical, garrulous old man whom nobody really trusts.

The printed word is one of the greatest conquests of man because it has made man what Korzibski calls a time-space binding animal. Without the printed word progress would be impossible because we would not be able to transmit knowledge and experience to our descendants. But the printed word, as I have shown, can be very harmful and it has already become a giant octopus whose enormous tentacles emerge from the pages of books, newspapers and magazines and strangle the mind. It is the task of freedom loving educators, writers and other liberals, of whom fortunately we do have a few, though not enough, to battle this octopus before it destroys our liberties and our chances for the pursuit of happiness. This can only be done by uniting all those intellectual and progressive men and women in an aggressive campaign against the forces of reaction and for a complete overhauling and modernization of our educational system, which is as outdated and useless as the ox-cart is for transportation. With the right kind of education, in the right amount and given at the proper time, we can change the world. There is no other way nor any other method; but we are really unprepared for this most vital task. We must begin by educating the parents and by creating teachers who will continue the work started in the cradle— teachers who understand the forces operating in the human body and who can contribute their full share to the creation of the greatest and noblest piece of work that is man.

Man and His Future

Into the Universe, and Why not knowing
Nor Whence, like Water willy-nilly flowing
And out of it, as Wind along the Waste
I know not Whither, willy-nilly blowing.
Yesterday This Day's Madness did prepare;
To-Morrow's Silence, Triumph, or Despair;
Drink for you know not whence you came, nor why:
Drink for you know not why you go nor where.

—Omar Khayyam

Time is like the screen of the movies; the shadows move and pass over it, but the screen remains . . . unaffected by the things it reflects.

The future is not begotten nor molded by prayers and wishful thinking, but by deeds and actions.

How much of the future still belongs to us? There is no answer to this question, but there is no doubt that some of the future is already cast and that we are molding the rest every day and every moment. Yet, we must act as if the whole future were putty in our hands.

It is wiser and more profitable to plan for the future than to worry over the past.

Animals have no future because they have no past, and they haven't either because they have no thought and no imagination.

An armed peace is an interval between two wars.

Those who prepare for war will have war and die by war.

Cynicism is like a sharp knife; you can cut bread with it but you can also cut your finger if you do not handle it properly. There is a difference, however: cynicism will cut your "soul".

Capitalism, in the animal world, is the art of accumulating food for all the cells or all the members of the group. In our "civilization" capitalism is the art of accumulating money and food for the few.

Communism is the just and equitative method of distributing that food.

The most reactionary capitalist and the most rabid Communist are living examples that Capitalism and Communism can work together, or they would not be alive.

[293]

MAN IN NATURE AND BEHAVIOR

There was a time when time was of relative importance. But now that man has let loose in the world the Genii of the Atomic Power, time is of the utmost importance, because each second brings mankind nearer destruction or salvation; it all depends how we use that second.

Determinism can be, for the first time, a tool to shape the future.

NOT BEING a clairvoyant, I cannot read the future in a crystal ball; nor do I claim to be a prophet to whom God reveals His plans, or even a simple medium who can establish communication with the spirits. All I have are my limited senses, my reason and my imagination. But since we live in a deterministic world in which today was gestated by yesterday, and tomorrow is being molded by yesterday and today, and since the nature and behavior of man have not shown essential changes since the beginning of humanity and he is still moved to action by the same biological forces, namely, the will to live or self-preservation, hunger, fear or the search for security, sex, already discussed—we can get a peep into the future by studying and taking into consideration all those factors.

It has been rightly said that history repeats itself, for the above reasons, but each time in a new setting, with new personages who play their roles better or worse, in a vaster and more modern stage and against a growing background of experience. There are people who misunderstand the real nature and meaning of determinism, both in the religious and intellectual levels. In the religious level, they speak of predestination and the will of God; in the intellectual level they have Destiny and Fate, cause and effect; but in either case there is a tendency toward resignation to the evils of the present and indifference and inaction toward the future. The immense majority of human beings, however, live only in the present, without having a clear idea of how the past and the present determine the future. We need not despair because we live in a deterministic world, for if it were not so science would not exist and no progress would be possible. Moreover, wisely used, determinism is a powerful weapon for good, because by knowing how it works, its laws and mechanism we can take a conscious and intelligent part in determining the future.

It is obvious then that if we want to obtain a clear understanding of the present world situation and the forces stirring man's passions and shaking the very foundations of our society, we must analyze the past and take a good look at the beginning of our so-called civilization, when Christianity appeared on the world's stage and was flexing its muscles and arranging the material and "dramatis personae" for the greatest drama and tragedy ever enacted, and the scenes of which we are still playing.

This is the story briefly told. Christianity found the world in a chaotic state, with gods, religions and empires tottering and crumbling to dust. Although born as a spiritual power which despised and condemned material things, the Christian leaders soon found out that without financial and political power, spirituality was like finding a lot of money in a dream and the pockets empty upon awakening. Thus they took over the mantle of the Pagan emperors; the Pontifex Maximus became the Pope and the chair of St. Peter (?) substituted the chair of Caesar. The dreams of the Roman emperors to dominate and rule the world were revived under a new name—it was to be a spiritual empire, with one ruler, one church and one religion for the whole world. Does this sound familiar? Remember Hitler's dreams of one Fuehrer and one world?

With the cross and the sword, more with the latter than with the first, the Christian leaders began to materialize their dream, transforming it into a most horrible nightmare. Every method and every weapon their imagination could devise, no matter how cruel, how painful and how destructive, was used to bring about the unification of the world under one God and under one ruler—the Pope. As it was to be expected, the Christian leaders did succeed for a while in bringing Europe and part of the New World under one Fuehrer, with the aid of promises of heavenly joys and hell-fire terrors and of such persuading arguments, such as the burning pyre, the torture instruments and the filthy dungeons of the Holy Inquisition. (I cannot imagine a worse desecration of the word Holy.) But either God was not interested in their petty, and at the same time, grandiose schemes to make Him the ruler of the world, or He simply was not there, because Christianity failed completely and tragically in its attempt to accomplish the unity of the world under one spiritual ruler and his satellites, the temporal rulers, kings and feudal lords.

With the Reformation the shaky and violent unity of Christian Europe was shattered and the world became more divided than ever. Christian sects fought and killed with a zeal and fervor worthy of a better cause, and all in the name of one God. Here, as usual, God remained neutral and silent, not showing favor to any one; the side with the most of everything always won, whether Protestant, Catholic or infidel. With the treaty of Westphalia, concluded in 1648, the fratricidal religious wars came to an end, much against the wishes of the Papacy which refused to accept defeat and wanted the carnage and destruction of heretics to go on; but the people who did the fighting had had enough blood letting and suffering.

Napoleon made another serious attempt to bring the world under one ruler, but on the political level only, and after a series of brilliant strategic moves and many victorious battles, was defeated. Then, as if the world were never to be free from mad conquerors, came Adolf Hitler and Mussolini in the West, and Hirohito in the East, who took over where the Popes and other power-hungry war-makers had left off. These three modern and somewhat abbreviated versions of the Four Horsemen of the Apocalypse came very near success because science had put in their hands new and more powerful physical and psychological weapons. But for all their boasting and new jargon with which they dressed their ambitions, there is nothing essentially new in Nazi-Fascism; it is the same "philosophy" of force and might used by the strong man of the tribe and his successors. Since humanity has worshipped at the altar of Mars and believed that might makes right for such a long time, the three dictators spoke a language that was understood by everyone; therefore, when they cracked the whip, millions of human beings surged forward, eager to risk their lives in a mighty attempt to change the map of the earth and deter mine the future of humanity for at least "a thousand years",— the Third Reich was going to last no less, according to Hitler.

There is no doubt that those three architects of the future made their plans very well and came very close to their goal. Hitler and Mussolini, especially the former, showed considerable skill and insight for they obtained valuable help from the very people they had marked for extermination or slavery. This they accomplished by using one against the other and making promises they did not intend to keep, and by striking terror into their enemies. Into their followers they inspired the fervor of the Crusaders, more with the promise of looting the world than with any ideal. But despite their greed and the prospects of unequalled destruction and bloodshed, their banners were blessed by both Catholic and Protestant churches. The religious undertones of World War II may escape the attention of many people, but they were there very strong, again battling for the supremacy of the world. Since Hitler and Mussolini were Catholics and were fighting the greatest enemy of the Catholic church, it was to be expected that the Papacy would favor them and pray for their victory. But the Catholic church is very old and wise and has learned never to put all the eggs in one basket because the unexpected can always happen. Moreover, by seeking refuge in the inaccessible peaks of spirituality and fatherhood to all mankind, the Papacy was able to keep the appearance of neutrality, even when committing its most unneutral actions.

To believe that the Western democracies went to war with Hitler to save freedom and democracy would be worse than foolish, for they had armed and encouraged him, knowing full well of his plans and intentions. But Hitler double-crossed them and forced them into being reluctant enemies when he refused to march eastward against the Soviet Union only. It was only when the capitalists saw that Hitler wanted all that they decided to fight, even if that meant to save Communist Russia from destruction. Thus Hitler made very strange bed-fellows, for a short time, because that partnership did not last very long.

Those who expected that the defeat of Hitler, Mussolini and Hirohito would leave the world free from greedy conquerors have suffered a rude awakening, for we still have three aspirants to rule the world: Communism, Catholicism and Capitalism. To the superficial observer these three ideologies appear unrelated and extremely opposed to each other, each claiming to be the only way to salvation. Consequently, they generate much fear, suspicion and hatred which may lead us to another war. It would not be an exaggeration to say that war has already started, because this cold war seems to be the conditioning period during which we are physically and psychologically being prepared for the shooting war. The biologist smiles sadly as he looks around and sees all the wrangling, quarreling and bitterness between Capitalists, Communists and Christians, for he well knows that the ideas for which they fight and are ready to bathe the earth in blood, spring from the same biological sources: the will to live and the search for security, and pursue the same basic ends. Only on the surface do they appear opposed and only their manifestations and methods are new.

What is Capitalism? Webster's dictionary defines it as "an economic system in which capital or capitalism plays the principal part; the concentration of capital; the power or influence of capital as when in the hands of a few." The dictionary's definition of capital is no more enlightening than that of capitalism. Marx, for all his noise, did not give us much more basic knowledge, either. Capitalism is the accumulation of capital; but what is capital in the last analysis? Food, civilization has added shelter and other things. The single cell swimming in the primeval seas already accumulates food around its nucleus. As the cells formed colonies, "capitalism" grew but still remained a function of the organism. Millions of years ago, the ants, the bees and other insects learned to store food outside of the organism and thus became the first capitalists, while other animals continued living from meal to meal, depending only on the food stored as fat in the tissues to tide them over until hunger could be appeased.

Primitive man must have learned soon the necessity of hoarding and storing food, and to barter it along with other things. Later shells, copper and gold became symbols for food, and they could be exchanged for it, provided some one had a surplus or was willing to share it. Man has developed many other needs, but food still remains the basic necessity and the basic capital, for without it nothing can be produced, not even gold. The best way to give a practical lesson on the value of food and gold would be to place an avaricious person on a barren island with plenty of gold bars and coins and let him get so hungry until he would give all his gold for a single morsel of hard bread.

It is obvious then that capitalism is very old and that intrinsically there is nothing wrong with it; it is only the new meaning given by man, and the methods used to accumulate and to withhold capital from circulation and just distribution that makes it evil and dangerous, as cancer is dangerous to the body. In fact, cancer cells are the capitalists of the organism and they must be destroyed or they will destroy the organism. When will man learn this important lesson in sociology given us by the body? Man has changed and perverted a useful and necessary biological function into a curse for humanity, and it seems that capitalism ceased long ago being the beneficial social function that it is among the insects; with the growth and development of industrialism, capitalism, or rather, capitalists have become more greedy and dangerous to society. I would propose a new definition of capitalism which would really define its present meaning and methods, namely: capitalism is the art of getting as much as possible from each individual and giving as little as possible to the individual and to society.

Communism is, to a certain degree, younger than capitalism, though we must take into consideration that there is a form of universal symbiosis, a kind of cosmic "communism", as shown by the harmonious relations existing between different forces and things on this planet, without which life would not have appeared nor survived. Biologically speaking, Communism is an equitative method of food and energy distribution established a long time ago and without which higher organisms, including man, could not have evolved. The human body, then, is the result, among other things, of capitalism and Communism, acting harmoniously to maintain its life and health, which depend greatly upon the proper accumulation and distribution of food. As the biologist sees it, there is no basic conflict and incompatibility between Communism and Capitalism; only selfish, greedy and ignorant men on this and on the other side of the "Iron Curtain" mislead people into believing those two ideologies cannot work and live side by side, and that one must destroy the other in a bloody war.

The present struggle between Communism and Capitalism is merely symptomatic of the inner struggle and conflict that is taking place in man; for whereas in animals individualization did not go beyond group individualization and was terminated long ago, human beings are still undergoing a process of individualization, of development and assertion of their personalities, and these processes are characterized and even require aggressiveness and selfishness. On the other hand, man has felt the necessity of a greater social integration and of establishing closer ties with other members of the community, and even of the world. The yearnings and aspirations for brotherhood among all men preached by some religious leaders were the crystallization of the feeling of kinship experienced by exceptional men, but which could not penetrate into the consciousness of the masses. Science by building a network of "nerves" that already links the most remote places of the planet into one central point and by shortening the distances, is speeding and pressing this process of social integration and making possible One World. But this process of real social integration and closer interdependence demands and requires the elimination of some of the characteristics and qualities needed for individualization, like selfishness, that is, unwise selfishness and aggressiveness. Thus man is torn between the growing necessity for uniting humanity into an organic whole similar to the human body, and the craving for asserting his personality and his independence above others. With yearnings for friendly cooperation and brotherhood, man soars to the stars, while his supreme egotism and the isolationism absorbed with the milk, drag him into the gutter. In his ignorance man acts like a blindfolded person beating his arms against an unseen enemy. The leaders of both Communism and Capitalism have no better understanding of this problem than the average man who does not see beyond his nose; besides, they are not interested in enlightening the people for fear of losing their privileged positions.

The biologist also smiles sadly seeing the fervor and zeal with which many people defend traditional tabus and superstitions and oppose the wave of the future, which is a form of Communism. They may retard it, but cannot stop it, no more than they can stop the tide with a broom. Just as morphologic evolution brought biological Communism, social evolution is already bringing human Communism—one is as inevitable as the other. The fact that many attempts to establish and impose Communism have failed means nothing. Who knows how many failures, how many trials and errors took place before some cellular colonies succeeded in establishing a well integrated cooperative community? The road of evolution is strewn with many of those failures. Moreover, man is a newcomer on this planet, and group co-operation is still young. True, it has been practiced by the clan, by the horde and finally by the family, but in a rather sporadic and rudimentary form. All human institutions, including the family, have broken down or are in a process of disintegration, because none of them respond to the biological and psychological needs of man. The vitality and time resisting qualities shown by some religious institutions are not derived from any supernatural or divine source, as their leaders claim. These institutions, besides satisfying a psychological need, demand very little from the individual in the way of co-operative living. Perhaps I should say they demand much, but are satisfied with very little or nothing, so long as the member pays lip service to religion and contributes financially to its support.

The failure of Communism in the early days of Christianity and now in the U.S.S.R., is due to the facts already discussed; in other words, man is not yet ready to accept it, much less if it is imposed by violence; Communism must come in the form of progressive changes of our present economic system, resulting from an ever growing awareness of the individual of his kinship with all other human beings and of community interests with all the people of the world, and of the greater benefits that can be obtained by close cooperation. It must also bring a minimum of regimentation and loss of independence and must assist the development of the human personality to its fullest expression. Mental superiority must not be used and abused to exploit and enslave others less gifted; it must be considered a privilege to have a greater share in the service of the community.

Another very grave error, very prevalent that must be dispelled, is that Capitalism must be destroyed in order to bring about some form of Communism or Socialism. We have already seen that Capitalism plays an important function in the body economy and it cannot really be destroyed; what needs to be done is to submit Capitalism to the biological laws that govern it in the human body, that is, to place it at the service of the community instead of the few. At the present time Capitalism thrives on artificial scarcity, while Communism is cursed with and handicapped by real scarcity. The exorbitant and unnatural power of money must be curbed and brought to the service of the people, not the people to the service of money.

Catholicism, which is political Christianity, is not essential for the survival of man as Communism and Capitalism are. Christianity appears very late in the life of humanity and it touches only a very small part, fortunately, because it is anti-biological and unnatural. I have already shown that Christianity started with asceticism, which is the negation of life. Proof? Had all men and women followed the counsel and obeyed the commands of the Christian ascetics and practiced virginity and chastity, humanity would have committed mass suicide and left the world to the animals several centuries ago. Moreover, Christianity, like every other idea and organization, has very earthly origins and springs from two biological urges: the will to live and the search for security.

Although political Christianity and political Communism are at sword's point, preparing for mortal combat, they have very much in common in their beginnings, in their development and in their methods. I believe that an analysis of their similarities may help to take off some of the hateful wind that blows their sails. Christianity was a rebellion against the abuses of paganism, and appealed mainly to the poor and the oppressed, to whom it promised the Kingdom of God, but in the other life. It even adopted Communism as a way of life, and the monasteries remain witness to that effect.

Communism is also a revolt of the oppressed and the exploited, the result of the abuses of feudalism and capitalism, and like Christianity, promised heaven . . . on earth. The millennium is at hand—just around the corner—called revolution; but this heaven is just as elusive as the prosperity promised by Herbert Hoover; the Russians are still looking for it. The Communist leaders are behaving like the Papacy and are committing the same tragic and costly blunders in attempting to bring the world under one faith, via the revolution. The Communists do not believe in God, but they believe in Karl Marx who, with Lenin and Stalin, form the Holy, or should I say, the un-holy Trinity; they have their "sacred scriptures" which nobody inside the "Iron Curtain" dares to doubt or criticize, openly at least, without suffering the fate of the heretics in the golden days of the Church. Of course they do not burn heretics at the stake, but they silence them just as effectively.

The Catholic Church has one international which consists of all the priests and bishops who give first allegiance and loyalty to the Pope who is also a temporal ruler, the head of the Vatican State. That the interests of the Pope are very often at variance and even decidedly inimical to the democratic principles of our country, is well known. A case in point is the recent speech of the Pope against divorce in which in a round about way told the Catholic American Judges that they cannot dissolve a marriage. Naturally the Pope does not dare command the Catholics to revolt against the authority of our government and to disobey our laws, nor do the judges dare to do so for fear of losing their positions; but the judges are on the spot and cannot very well be completely loyal to the laws of the country and to the Pope or their Catholic conscience.

The Communists also have their international, with parties almost in every country that, like the Hierarchy, give allegiance and loyalty to a foreign dictator. That the interests of Stalin and the Politburo often are inimical to American principles and methods is also too well known. It is clear then that the Communists cannot give undivided loyalty to our country or to any country except the U.S.S.R. Thus they are as alien as the bishops.

But the Catholic leaders have hundreds of years of experience and a greater knowledge of human nature, therefore they know how to pull the chestnuts out of the fire without getting burnt and with a minimum of offense to the people and governments. Moreover, religion and the name of God cover a multitude of sins, and both are the stoutest pillars of the "status quo"; while Communists have not yet learned the art of making friends and influencing people and go about doing the opposite, irritating and offending everybody.

Communism, like Christianity, has been forced by its impact with human nature and established patterns of behavior, to modify its dogmas and theories, and today there is as much Communism in Russia as there is Christianity in the world. If you think that I exaggerate, just look around and see how many real Christians you find; slap someone and see if he turns the other cheek; ask him to give everything to the poor; inquire if he loves his neighbor as himself.

In spite of the recent blasts against Capitalism, the Catholic Church is solidly behind the capitalist system because the Church is probably the wealthiest and largest capitalist organization in the world, with property holdings of every kind everywhere; therefore Catholicism and Capitalism march hand in hand against Communism, and that leaves for the moment two contenders for the supremacy of the world. But do we really quarrel with Communism because it is a tyranny and are ready to go to war to "save democracy" again? Pure and unadulterated humbug. Governments, like politicians, have always two reasons: the real one, which they keep and the false one which they shout to the people. If our quarrel were really against Communism because it is a tyranny, we would not embrace Tito and lend him millions of dollars, for he is just as communistic as Stalin, and makes no bones about it, nor does he promise to reform and give up Communism. Nor would we embrace dictators like Trujillo, Peron, Salazar, Franco (almost) and Chiang Kai-shek. The real quarrel is with competition, the fear of losing markets, oil fields and investments. Freedom, democracy and justice are magic words like God, love, heaven and hell with which men cover or attempt to cover their selfishness, avarice and cruelty.

Shall it be war or peace? Nobody can predict with certainty what will happen because the future is still in a fluid state, and subject to change—war has not yet become inevitable, but we can put in the balance the things that make for war and the things that work for peace and see which will tip the scales. Let us gather first those things that work for war:

1—Men have become so used to violence and force as a means of "settling" their disputes and "solving" their problems that almost automatically they draw the gun or use their fists. Thus we move toward war, as if driven by an inner compulsion. Every psychologist knows it is difficult, if not impossible, to change this mental attitude overnight.

2—Communism has become the scapegoat for practically all our ills, troubles and shortcomings, and the majority of Americans feel that war with Russia is inevitable, and even necessary to destroy them before they destroy us.

3—Our economy is geared for war. Strange as it may seem, we are afraid of peace because disarmament would throw a few million workers out of their jobs, and probably would bring a depression, besides leaving stranded and useless a large number of brass hats who will fight to the last soldier to keep their ranks and privileges. Our economy is also geared to continuous expansion to new markets, to more oil fields, etc., and our feudal lords, although Christians, will not follow the example of St. Martin who, when a beggar asked for his cape, cut it in half with his sword and gave one half to the poor.

4—The remnants of Nazism and Fascism, in Germany and throughout the world are trying to stage a comeback and are working for war with all their energies.

5—Religious leaders, Catholic and Protestant, have been using their forces for war. True, some leaders, especially Protestant, have spoken for peace and against war with the U.S.S.R., with all their might, but religion as a whole has preached war against "atheist Communism". The Catholic Church has at times demanded a holy war against Communism, not because it is atheist but because it is her greatest competitor in the field of salvation and because the loss of "souls" means the loss of money, wealth and privileges.

6—Communism teaches that Capitalism must be overthrown by force if it cannot be done peacefully; "truth must triumph over error". Do you remember this argument? It has been used by Christianity for many centuries.

7—The Communist leaders crave for more power and fear losing what they have. That is why they keep their people from establishing contacts and friendly relations with foreigners. The cold war is very useful in keeping people frightened by the bogey man of Capitalism, just as the Catholic Church has frightened people with the wrath of God and the tortures of hell; fear brings submission, here and on the other side of the "Iron Curtain".

8—Military leaders are itching for a chance to drop a few more atomic bombs, of the new kind, and see what they can do.

PEACE: 1—The United Nations is the greatest force for peace, but all members are there with reservations. This organism could and should be strengthened by giving it more power and making it a form of world government, as many people advocate. This would mean that the member nations would surrender some of their sovereignty, and this they will not do easily. It took our country a civil war to prove that the states must obey a central government. Nations, like the individuals of which they are formed, are still in the process of development and of asserting their personality, and are torn between the necessity for a greater integration and surrendering some of their liberties and rights for the common good, and blowing their horn and strutting around like roosters. All this makes the United Nations more like a debating team where people blow off steam, than a real force for peace; but we must work to strengthen and to give more power to the United Nations.

2—Religion is, theoretically, a force for peace, as I have shown; but in practice has been, and still is, a force for war—for division instead of unity; for discord instead of harmony.

3—The schism started by Tito is, in my opinion, a strong force for peace; it can be likened to the rebellion of Luther against the supremacy of the Pope. Of course, it could bring on a civil war with the U.S.S.R., but I doubt it because such a war would spread easily. To be really effective, this schism must spread to other satellites. There is also the possibility of a division within the Politburo that would split the U.S.S.R. wide open and bring a civil war. Such divisions happen in most organizations; however, this possibility is too remote because the key figures who hold power watch very closely for the slightest sign of deviation and rebellion, and crush it before it has had time to do any harm. Those who are on top realize that they must stick together or hang separately.

4—Fear of atomic bombs and other modern weapons does not weigh heavily in the scales because history shows that fear has never acted as an effective deterrent to crime or violence, neither individually nor collectively. Already some scientists are reversing their earlier estimates and telling us that the atomic bomb is not so dangerous as they thought; and together with the military leaders, they are feverishly seeking ways to counter-act atomic explosions, perhaps by living underground like moles, or going back to the times of the caveman. Is this civilization? The only secure and effective defense against atomic bombs is peace and friendly cooperation between all the people, and we can get that if we try hard enough.

5—The people as a whole want peace; this is especially true of Europeans who have suffered the ravages of war and have seen their homes and families blasted into nothingness. The American people are not as keen and sanguine for peace because our country has not been trampled by Mars and many people have made large and small profits from war. There are peace organizations in our country, but they have little power and are struggling against great odds. The peace makers are handicapped by the hypocritical and deceitful language of the war makers who give lip service to peace while sharpening their swords and priming their guns. We are arming for defense only, they say, while the Russians sing the same sing song. The result is heavier and heavier taxes and an enormous waste of money and effort.

6—Universal disarmament is the most positive and effective force for peace, but neither the U.S.A. nor the U.S.S.R. are in the mood to beat their guns into ploughshares. Without universal disarmament there cannot be a real and lasting peace; the beautiful dove with the olive branch cannot roost comfortably on the points of bayonets or in the muzzle of guns—she is allergic to that kind of steel. The official flim flam about loving peace, here and on the other side of the "Iron Curtain" is worse than a macabre farce; it is a tragic mockery of the noblest and highest aspirations of man.

7—The second world war left only two major powers capable of waging a global war: the U.S.A. and the U.S.S.R.; this, of course, works for peace, because it narrows the margin of war to two nations, and if these two nations succeed in getting along and establishing a friendly cooperation, peace will have a big chance. Global war has become a luxury, too costly for small countries.

I do not believe that the leaders of the U.S.S.R. want war, a nation that has been devastated and ravaged by war twice in twenty-five years, cannot be keen about another conflict that would dwarf all others; but for psychological and political reasons they seem to enjoy the cold war and behave as if they really wanted to fight again, against their former ally. Both sides ought to realize that playing with fire is dangerous; it may get out of control and burn the players and the spectators. It is clear then that the things that make for war tip the scales, and it would not help to place in the balance the light and dainty dove with only the olive branch in her beak and the heavy and clumsy Mars with all his armor and weapons.

MAN IN NATURE AND BEHAVIOR

The men who created the symbols of war and peace must have been very far-sighted and intelligent or they were very lucky in the choice of those symbols; the dove, with its fragile and restless body, and with its wings ready to fly away at the slightest noise or fear, truly represents peace which is so easily disturbed and lost among individuals and among nations; while the solid and stolid Mars does not seem to be in a hurry to go, nor can he move away very fast. He gives the impression of permanence and of saying—do not worry, I'll be here for a long time; I am not easily frightened and scared away like my competitor, the beautiful dove. I am afraid that he is right and it will take a great deal of effort and time to get rid of this expensive and troublesome guest and to build a solid and comfortable nest for the dove.

The next five or ten years will be the most crucial and fateful for mankind, because if war can be avoided that long, I believe it can be written off, for it will show that men have learned to settle their political problems and economic crises with peaceful methods, and humanity will at last have entered the most creative, the most abundant and happy of all ages. Devoted to constructive purposes, science can transform the earth into the mythical garden of Eden and fulfill the dreams of man. But if war breaks, then humanity and civilization will receive a serious setback, the duration and gravity of which no one can foresee. Freedom and democracy will be among the first victims, and the American people will be crushed under a mountain of taxes that will come in its wake. Nobody knows how many millions of human beings will be killed or crippled, nor whether Communism will spread all over the world. It seems to me that whoever wins will have a pyrrhic victory on his hands, for there will be no victors—only vanquished. Then humanity will have to dig itself out of the ruins and start to build again its cities and factories, to plant its ruined fields and to awaken from a most horrible nightmare. It is to be expected that the survivors will have had enough of wars and war-makers and that they will devote all their energies and time to peaceful pursuits. But why must humanity pay such an enormous price for peace? The answer is that it does not have to pay such a bloody price, but it probably will, for man seems to be incapable of learning the easy way. The Spaniard who said: "La letra con sangre entra"—letters or learning enter with spanking—knew what he was talking about.

All the other problems and troubles that beset man will be solved automatically, if we solve successfully the problem of war and peace. New sources of food will be found, the atom will be put to work for the benefit of mankind, the machine will serve man and not the other way around, sex education and birth control will form part of every child's learning, religion will be purged and cleansed of all its superstitions and dogmas, the United Nations will become a World Government and Capitalism and Communism will work together for the benefit of the social organism as they work together in the body for the benefit of all the organs and cells.

History has been repeating itself, and one war succeeds another in increasing proportions because man has been moved by the same forces as the master puppeteer moves his puppets. But history's mistakes, trials and errors need not go on forever with interminable repetition, because for the first time in his long and turbulent life man is aware of those forces, knows their laws and can manipulate the strings. Therefore man need no longer be the robot and puppet; he can and must be the master puppeteer. It is only now that man can give meaning and realization to the words of the poet: "I am the master of my fate—I am the captain of my soul".

time to peaceful pursuits, but why must humanity pay such
an enormous price for peace? the answer is that it does not
have to pay such a bloody price; it probably will not pay it if
it ceases to be romantic, if studying the price is, the prophet
earlier said. "The land consumes us"—a matter of laughter
enter with thinking, knew what he was talking about.

All the other problems and troubles that beset us will
be solved automatically, if we solve successfully the problem
of war and peace. New sources of food will be opened, the
nation will be freer, and not the giver ... around, sex, education and ... will crowd from part of every child's education will ... right and should ahead ... grow ... and
... religion, the liberal ... will become a ... cove-
ment and ... and ... will ... the ...
the benefit of any social organization is to the weight ... and of the
body and the benefit of all the organization ...

Today ... has been triumphant still, and one who succeeds,
another ... has been ... has been ... behind him has been imitated
by his race, but is as the master puppeteer moves his puppets
but ... inevitable repetition ... for the first time in
his long and ... history ... is in use of these forces. Their
fruit, lives and can manufacture the things. Therefore human
no longer be the robot and puppet; he can and must be the
master puppeteer. It is only now that man can give meaning
and realization to the words of the poet: I am the master of
my fate, I am the captain of my soul.

Index

[313]

INDEX

INDEX

Epicurus—15
Erasmus—168
Eros—48
Ethics—118, 258
Eucharist—121
Eve—117
Evil—251, 252, 253, 260, 261; definition of—245, 246; origin of—254, 255, 257
Exodus—133
Exogamy—104, 105

Faith—242
Fasting—54, 238
Fate—294
Fathers of the Church—22
Fear—56, 59, 60, 112, 134, 141, 154, 164, 171, 176, 185, 187, 243, 251, 281; origin of—57, 58; of menstrual woman—119; of punishment —232
Ferdinand, King—123, 223
Fichte—208
Fielding, H.—15, 79, 101
Fischer, Dr. Martin H.—229, 241
Ford, Father George B.—124
Fox, J. D.—197
Franco, F.—305
Frazer, Sir James George—118
Freedom — 108, 147, 149, 150, 151, 153, 155, 166, 167, 286; of speech —157, 158; from want—158, 159; from fear—159; of worship—160
Free will—149, 160, 161, 162
Freud — 48, 49, 129, 144, 169, 248, 249, 276
Friendship—174, 175, 255
Frigidity—112
Future of man—293, 294, 295

Geiger counter—248
Genesis—31, 101, 120, 225
George, Henry—31
Germany—26
Gilmore, Albert F.—206
God—101, 103, 106, 109, 115, 116, 117, 121, 122, 123, 125, 126, 127, 128, 131, 137, 147, 151, 152, 153, 154, 161, 165, 169, 170, 175, 180, 191, 196, 198, 201, 204, 206, 207, 231, 233, 234, 241, 242, 247, 250, 251, 252, 270, 276, 277, 282, 284, 294, 296, 303, 304, 305, 307; evo-

lution of — 211, 212, 213; sun — 214, 216; Christian — 217, 218; arguments for and against — 221, 222, 226, 227; of Mount Sinai — 228
Gold—262
Golden age—215
Goldin, Hyman—217
Goldsmith, A.—179
Good—245, 246, 253; definition of —254, 257; degradation of—259
Gospels, the—166, 217
Gould, Beatrice—186
Granada—233
Greed—254
Greeks — 106, 120, 157, 214, 216, 219, 230, 251, 270
Gutenberg—270

Hades—193
Hagdon, C.—105
Haldane, J. B.—101
Hamerton—179
Happiness—101, 108, 112, 146, 168, 177, 183, 184; definition of—179, 180, 181, 182; statistics of—186
Harvey, Charles W.—206
Hate—61, 141, 161, 168, 171, 176, 177, 213, 254
Hawthorne—31
Healing, definition of—229; by faith —241, 242, 243
Health, definition of—229; by faith —241, 242, 243
Heaven—194, 220
Hebrews—120
Heisenberg—163
Hell—107, 122, 194, 220, 298
Helmholtz—99
Henderson, Lawrence—266
Henry, Patrick—149, 153
Heraclitus—201
Hercules—281
Heretics—152, 218, 234, 242, 259
Herodotus—106
Heredity—80
Hetaira—106, 107
High Priests—194, 230
Hightower, Professor—125
Hindu Philosophers—202
Hindus—120, 132, 223, 230
Hippocrates—230, 239
Hirohito—296, 298

[315]

INDEX

INDEX

INDEX

INDEX